Towards an Authentic Adventist Theology

Towards an Authentic Adventist Theology

Updating "Present Truth"

Reinder Bruinsma

FOREWORD BY
Jean-Claude Verrecchia

WIPF & STOCK · Eugene, Oregon

TOWARDS AN AUTHENTIC ADVENTIST THEOLOGY
Updating "Present Truth"

Copyright © 2026 Reinder Bruinsma. All rights reserved. Except for brief quotations in critical publications or reviews, no part of this book may be reproduced in any manner without prior written permission from the publisher. Write: Permissions, Wipf and Stock Publishers, 199 W. 8th Ave., Suite 3, Eugene, OR 97401.

Wipf & Stock
An Imprint of Wipf and Stock Publishers
199 W. 8th Ave., Suite 3
Eugene, OR 97401

www.wipfandstock.com

PAPERBACK ISBN: 979-8-3852-7447-5
HARDCOVER ISBN: 979-8-3852-7448-2
EBOOK ISBN: 979-8-3852-7449-9

VERSION NUMBER 03/17/26

Unless otherwise indicated, all Scripture quotations are taken from the The Holy Bible, New International Version® (NIV®). Copyright © 1973, 1978, 1984, 2011 by Biblica, Inc.™ Used by permission. All rights reserved worldwide.

Other Bible translations quoted:

- The Holy Bible, King James Version (KJV). Public domain.
- The Message (MSG), copyright © 1993, 2002, 2018 by Eugene H. Peterson. Used by permission of NavPress. All rights reserved. Represented by Tyndale House Publishers, Inc.
- The Holy Bible, New King James Version® (NKJV®). Copyright © 1982 by Thomas Nelson. Used by permission. All rights reserved.
- The Holy Bible, New Living Translation (NLT). Copyright © 1996, 2004, 2015 by Tyndale House Foundation. Used by permission of Tyndale House Publishers, Inc., Carol Stream, Illinois 60188. All rights reserved.
- The Holy Bible, New Revised Standard Version (NRSV). Copyright © 1989 the Division of Christian Education of the National Council of the Churches of Christ in the United States of America. Used by permission. All rights reserved.
- The Living Bible (TLB). Copyright © 1971 by Tyndale House Foundation. Used by permission of Tyndale House Publishers, Inc., Carol Stream, Illinois 60188. All rights reserved.

Contents

Foreword

Writing the preface to a book is a difficult and risky task. Difficult because you have to be sure you have understood what is written. Risky because you must meet both the expectations of potential readers and the hopes of the author. However, Reinder Bruinsma greatly assisted in the writing of this preface: *its title says it all.*

Towards

This book could have been a kind of testament, written at the end of a rich pastoral and academic career. This is not the case. This work does not contain definitive analyses. It does not settle once and for all what one should think or believe. From its beginning to its end, it tries to open up a path, an invitation to research, never completed, which is rather rare for a work that aims to present a theology.

This impulse at the heart of this book must be placed in the following context: Bruinsma regrets the lack of dialogue within Adventism, the near impossibility of having calm discussions on fundamental beliefs. Some of these beliefs are no longer the "present truth," he claims. The risk for Adventism is that it will become a museum of the past, a situation that Bruinsma cannot accept.

Authentic

Bruinsma's roots go deep, well below the level of the Dutch polders. As we know, the Dutch people, who had to fight against adverse natural elements and, among other things, against the Nazi invasion, developed a strong capacity for resistance and a refusal to compromise. The theology proposed by Bruinsma is not contorted; it is transparent, in the manner proposed by the Gospel: *yes* means *yes*, *no* means *no*. He never resorts to half measures or circumstantial remarks to please any ecclesiastical or theological guild. Bruinsma has paid a significant price in his career for remaining upright and honest, faithful to his beliefs. Unsurprisingly, he maintains the same course here.

Adventist

Time and again, in various places and circumstances, I had the privilege of talking with Bruinsma about the Adventist Church, its current situation, its challenges, its strengths and weaknesses. Each time, he expressed his concerns. At times, his discouragement almost got the better of him to the point of considering leaving. These were moments of uncertainty, but they were quickly overcome: "If I leave, many others will leave too." This explains why he decided to stay, against all odds, despite the dark clouds; and it is why this book was born. Its goal: to resurrect the "present truth." To rediscover the spirit of the pioneers of Adventism, who were capable of sometimes heated discussions about the doctrines and beliefs of the nascent church. To give significance and meaning to the Adventist gospel in the twenty-first century.

Theology

In an earlier phase, the work was presented as a systematic theology. Even if this formulation has not been entirely retained here, it is indeed a theological elaboration; in substance, but fortunately not in form. Bruinsma's definition of the word *theology* is simple: "I am a believer and a theologian." The "and" can be understood here as explanatory: "I am a believer; that is, a theologian."

Great systematic theologies—the rather rare ones written by Adventist authors are no exception to this observation—are often off-putting, complicated, aggressive, and pretentious. This book is far removed from these shortcomings. It is accessible to the widest possible audience. It is honest: the summaries of the various doctrinal options are balanced. It is direct and precise, far removed from the Adventist chatter that claims to be exhaustive and aims to prove everything once and for all, sometimes at the price of distorting the Bible.

A few probing topics:

Regarding the Interpretation of the Bible

Bruinsma rejects the plain literal reading of the Bible. An average Adventist reader will discover the names of philosophers, theologians, and hermeneutists such as Schleiermacher, Dilthey, Gadamer, Ricoeur, and Derrida, who are largely ignored by Adventist authors, if not considered to be dangerous miscreants.

He forcefully asserts that "insisting that we must—and can—do away with our personal lens, or must all look through an identical lens, which is provided by a particular theological current or a corpus of denominational leaders, carries the danger that a faith community is transformed into a cult, rather than functioning as a living organism" (p. 47).

Regarding the Spirit of Prophecy

Bruinsma warns, "There are many questions that cannot be ignored and need honest answers. If those answers are not given, the confidence of many church members in the continuing relevance of Ellen White's writings will be seriously undermined, and many may even decide that they no longer want to be part of a denomination that is unwilling to be transparent about such an important aspect of its identity" (p. 51).

Regarding the Triune God

Bruinsma humbly acknowledges, "At the very moment when we think we have defined an aspect of the triune God, we must in all humility step back and remember that our human words remain totally inadequate to describe who and what God is. However, while taking that step back, we must be deeply grateful that we can have a loving relationship with this indescribable God and can worship him and serve him with all that we have and are" (p. 78)

Regarding Christ's Two Natures

Bruinsma wisely refers to Ellen White's suggestion, in 1898:

> When we approach this subject, we would do well to heed the words spoken by Christ to Moses at the burning bush, "Put off thy shoes from off thy feet, for the place whereon thou standest is holy ground." We should come to this study with the humility of a learner, with a contrite heart. And the study of the incarnation of Christ is a fruitful field, which will repay the searcher who digs deep for hidden truth.[1]

Regarding the Sanctuary

Unsurprisingly, this topic is addressed in an excursus, emphasizing that it is the "most *controversial* Adventist teaching" (p. 161). Bruinsma's analysis clearly highlights all the points on which the Adventist interpretation is virtually indefensible. It also emphasizes that as it now stands, it is difficult to understand and of little interest to twenty-first-century believers.

Regarding the Sabbath Rest

This long, well-argued chapter ends with the story of a journalist who decided to observe all the laws of the Bible for a whole year, including the most obscure ones, and to write a book about his attempt. At the end of his experiment, he was joined by his wife in acknowledging that they would "no longer pay attention to these, mostly cumbersome, biblical rules. But there was one thing he (and his wife) did not want to give up. He said he had fallen in love with the Sabbath. It had become an essential part of his life."

Bruinsma's commentary following this testimony is significant: "Millions still need to make the same discovery" (p. 190). Here is Reinder Bruinsma, a great lover of the good news, a great lover of Adventism, who does not want to become a disappointed lover under any circumstances.

In concluding this preface, I cannot help but think of Bruinsma's motivation. Said Jesus, "I have not lost any of those you gave me" (John 18:9).

1. White, "Search the Scriptures," para. 6; quoted on p. 105.

Not to lose any of his brothers and sisters in faith. To gain others. Such is the theological faith and the mission of Reinder Bruinsma, expressed in this work.

Dr. Jean-Claude Verrecchia

Coordinator of the revision of the
French Ecumenical Translation of the Bible (TOB)
Alliance Biblique Française

Preface

Truth is eternal, because God, the source of all truth, is eternal. Our comprehension of God's truth is always limited and temporally conditioned by our humanness. What we understand of divine truth always depends, to a significant degree, on how our interpretation of what God has revealed as truth resonates with the time in which we live and with the culture we have imbibed. The founders of the Seventh-day Adventist Church adopted the term *present truth* from 2 Pet 1:2 (KJV) to designate the close relationship they saw between the era in which they lived and the discoveries they made as they studied their Bible.

In the nearly two centuries that have expired since the pioneers of Adventism laid the foundation for the global denomination that currently has some twenty-five million members, there have been momentous changes in our world—politically, socially, and economically, and especially in the way people think. The religious landscape in the Western world has altered dramatically and will continue to do so. As the world around us has changed, so has the Adventist Church, not only in how it *does* things, but also in what it *believes*. In fact, the teachings of the church have, over time, undergone a constant development and have been modified to a much larger degree than many (perhaps most?) church members realize. Numerous aspects of what was present truth in the nineteenth and early twentieth centuries are no longer regarded as such.

Many church members—theologians as well as people outside the world of theological academia—realize it is time to revisit our Adventist teachings so that they will remain present truth in the second quarter of the twenty-first century. There needs to be a willingness to take a critical look at some of our doctrines and to discover how traditional Adventist theology can be restated in such a way that it responds more clearly to the questions people of all generations are asking today. It is, I believe, even more essential that the church creates the space and atmosphere in which such rethinking is not just tolerated but actually encouraged. One of the greatest tragedies in current Adventism is that many of its thought leaders, as well as members in the pew, do not dare to openly express their questions and doubts, for fear of being ostracized, or worse. As a result many, sooner or later, leave the church.

This book is not the work of an official committee or some self-appointed group, but it is my personal project. If you do not agree with some of its content, do not blame anyone but me. If you feel some of the things I say have been helpful, share that with others. Of course, I have been influenced by people in my network, by conferences I have attended, and books I have read. I have asked a few persons to read the manuscript and have benefited from their comments and advice. I have, however, not asked them for any endorsements, as a public recommendation of this work may have a negative impact on their role in the church.

Towards an Authentic Adventist Theology is the result of my own journey in the Christian faith and in Adventism. I am sure it will not be applauded by many of my fellow Adventists. I fear it will probably be largely ignored by the church's top leadership and condemned as a betrayal of "God's remnant church" by some independent organizations and conservative institutions that are part of the "right" wing of the denomination. My deep-felt hope is, however, that it will be a blessing for many who are seeking for ways to, once again, experience their Adventist faith as "present truth."

Zeewolde, the Netherlands
Spring 2026

Acknowledgments

Single paragraphs and, in some cases, a few consecutive paragraphs, have been adapted from books and articles I have authored in the past. They are listed below, in chronological order. For page references, see the information in footnotes.

The Day God Created. Grantham, UK: Stanborough Press, 1992.

Our Awesome God. Nampa, ID: Pacific Press Publishing Association, 1999.

Seventh-day Adventism and Fundamentalism: The Beach Lectures for 2000. Occasional papers, no. 4. Bracknell, UK: Centre for the Study of Religious and Cultural Diversity, 2006.

Keywords of the Christian Faith. Hagerstown, MD: Review and Herald Publishing Association, 2008.

The Body of Christ: A Biblical Understanding of the Church. Hagerstown, MD: Review and Herald Publishing Association, 2009.

Present Truth Revisited: An Adventist Perspective on Postmodernism. Self-published, 2014. Kindle.

Facing Doubt: A Book for Adventist Believers "on the Margins." London, UK: Flankó Press, 2016.

In All Humility: Saying No to Last Generation Theology. Westlake Village, CA: Oak & Acorn, 2018.

I Have a Future: Christ's Resurrection and Mine. Grantham, UK: Stanborough Press, 2019.

"Is the Adventist Hermeneutical Approach to Daniel and Revelation Changing?" *Spes Christiana* 31, no. 2 (2020) 5–24.

He Comes: Why, When and How Jesus Will Return. Grantham, UK: Stanborough Press, 2021.

"Who Controls Our Theological Narrative?" *Adventist Today*, January 15, 2025. https://atoday.org/who-controls-our-theological-narrative/.

Introduction

I HAVE WRITTEN BEFORE about my Adventist beliefs. Those who have read at least some of my earlier writings will note that there has been a substantial continuity, but also a development in my thoughts about Adventism's doctrinal teachings. Early in my many years of church employment I served as the manager of the small publishing house of the Adventist Church in the Netherlands. I combined this managerial task with the role of general editor of our denominational publications. One of my first books written in this busy period was a compact survey of Adventist-Christian doctrine. It was published in the context of a special "missionary campaign." With an initial printing of eighteen thousand, it was later reprinted in the original Dutch language and also published in a few other languages. Its title was *It Does Make a Difference What You Believe*. From time to time I meet church members who ask me whether I still stand behind what I wrote in 1978, when the book first appeared. My answer is that for the most part I do, but that today I might phrase some things somewhat differently. It has often amazed me that through the years the book has remained quite popular, and that there has not been more criticism about the fact that in several instances I remained rather indistinct, and that various core Adventist teachings were not explicitly mentioned. Perhaps the fact that the book especially targeted non-Adventist readers gave me an alibi for not presenting the "full" truth.

Twenty years later, the Pacific Press Publishing Association published a small book with such a long title that I often had to look at its cover to remember it: *It's Time to Stop Rehearsing What We Believe and Start Looking at What Difference It Makes*. It is still available as an e-book. I have from time to time considered going back to this book and to work on a serious update. Over time I probably had more positive reactions from readers of this small book than I have had about anything else that I wrote. It dealt with all fundamental beliefs (at that time there were twenty-seven) of the Adventist Church. The readers must have noticed that, even though I took a close look at all official doctrines, I did not deal with all aspects in the same depth and left many questions unanswered. I approached each of the twenty-seven fundamental beliefs from the perspective of one single question: What difference does it make that I believe in this particular doctrine? Does believing this make me a better, more pleasant, and more balanced human being? Does it make me a more sincere follower of Jesus Christ? In other words, what practical implications do these beliefs have for me? For many readers it was a meaningful approach but, in all honesty, it is perhaps not so difficult to discover some "liberal" traces in this book.

Almost another twenty years later (in 2006) I wrote a book that was simultaneously published in Dutch and English by the Stanborough Press (the Adventist publisher in the United Kingdom): *Faith—Step by Step: Finding God and Yourself*. It was, once again, a book that provided a summary of the main Christian teachings and of the more specifically Adventist doctrinal insights. I wrote it when the Trans-European Division (the office that has the oversight of the Adventist Church in a few dozen countries, mostly in Europe) tried to find new ways of reaching the increasingly secular public in its territory. I had become very interested in the subject of postmodernism[1] and decided to write a survey of the Adventist message, but to do so from a postmodern angle. I do not know to what extent I succeeded. Unfortunately, neither the Dutch nor the English language edition was very effectively promoted. Writing the book, however, gave me great satisfaction. I felt I had, at least to some extent, succeeded in providing a coherent narrative that could make sense to a postmodern person. But if people were to complain that I was selective in what I wrote and that many traditional Adventist terms and themes were missing, I would have to plead guilty as charged.

In 2009 followed a book titled *Keywords of the Christian Faith* as a companion book for the adult Sabbath School lesson quarterly for the worldwide Adventist Church that I had been asked to write. It dealt with thirteen different key concepts of the Christian faith, with a few chapters

1. See my e-book *Present Truth Revisited*.

dedicated to subjects of special importance for Adventists, as for instance the chapter on the Sabbath. The structure of the book allowed me to be selective with regard to the topics I would treat and to skip those that I felt less comfortable dealing with.

This present book is in some ways a sequel to the previous four, but it is less reticent in asking questions about some long-held Adventist positions and in attempting to bring the doctrinal narrative of Adventism into the present. I will argue that some aspects of the "present truth," as they are defended in the conservative segments of the church, are no longer *present* truth for me and for many others, and that we must do all we can to ensure that the church does not become a museum that is dedicated to ideas of the past but no longer provides us with a guide for our journey into the future.

Theology

This book is about theology. For me this means it is about faith. For many people these two aspects are indeed insolubly connected: *theologians speak about their faith*. But others are not so sure and point to theologians who admit that they do not (or no longer) have any real faith—at least not faith as an unwavering personal commitment to an almighty and loving God, with whom one can enter into a meaningful relationship. For them, theology has drifted into the realm of religious knowledge. For me, having faith and "doing theology" cannot be separated. I am a *believer and a theologian.*

All of us—irrespective of whether we are religious academics, paid clergy, or laity—who are seriously interested in theology and are searching for greater depth and meaning in what we believe may regard ourselves as theologians. I may not have written a multivolume systematic theology or a series of learned monographs, but I think I do have a good general view of the domain of theology and of how theology developed over time to what it is in our day and age. This gives me the confidence that I have enough background knowledge to contribute to the theological debate in current Adventism. Besides, I am often told that people appreciate my ability to explain things in a clear and systematic way. I do not know whether that is objectively true, but it did encourage me to pursue this particular project. It will be for others to judge whether I succeed in giving a convincing and coherent explanation of what an authentic Adventist theology, for someone who writes in 2025, might look like.

The word *theology*, like so many terms, is derived from the Greek language. It is a combination of the word *theos*, which means "god," and the word *logia*, which stands for "study" or "discourse."[2] Thus, theology is the discipline that studies God. It is the umbrella term for the domain that has developed into various subdisciplines. Some of the best known of these branches are historical theology (how did the Christian doctrines develop?), biblical theology (what does the Bible say about the basics of our faith and doctrines?), and systematic theology (how do the doctrines form a coherent whole?). Furthermore, scholars differentiate not only between Old Testament theology and New Testament theology but also between the theological study of specific themes: Christology (teachings about Christ), soteriology (teachings about salvation), eschatology (teachings about the "last things"), anthropology (teachings about the nature of man), and so on.

This book will be a modest (but, hopefully, not superficial) *introduction* to systematic theology. (This explains the word *Towards* in the title.) That is, it will attempt to give a bird's-eye view of the teachings of the Christian church, in a systematic fashion, and from an Adventist perspective. But at the very beginning of this exercise I need to make one point absolutely clear: *theology is always a human undertaking*. I believe it is essential that, when "doing" theology, we have the right understanding of the concept of truth. Many believers assert they have found the truth. This claim is only valid if they mean that they have found faith in Jesus Christ—who is the Truth (John 14:6)—and that this faith is the center of their lives. It does not mean they are able to produce the final and perfect systematic theology because they know everything about God—who he is and what he does.

In our postmodern world it is argued far and wide that there is no absolute truth, but that we all have our own private truths. This mode of thinking has led to a wave of relativism: *You have your truth, and I have mine*, and we should leave it at that! There are solid arguments to refute this kind of total relativism. But postmoderns are not completely wrong in their views of truth, for absolute truth, indeed, is not to be found in the world of which we are part. No theory or philosophy can claim to

2. McGrath, *Historical Theology*, 1–8.

encompass the full, absolute truth. No church or religious movement can claim to "have" the full truth. Even the Bible is not truth in the absolute sense. Absolute truth is something exclusively divine and thereby beyond our reach.

Theology is a human endeavor to describe aspects of the divine truth, as they are revealed in the written word (the Bible) and through the living Word (Jesus Christ). Theologians do their utmost to find human words to express what is, in fact, inexpressible. As theologians we have no other words at our disposal than the words that have a particular meaning in our own lives and in our descriptions of events and phenomena in the world in which we live. The problem is that we must use these human words when we speak of the things that belong to a totally different realm. There is, however, no other option. So, we must always remember, in our employment of these words, that they can never totally and accurately describe divine reality. To take this one example, when theologians say that God is a "person," they try to say that God is more than an impersonal "something." But we must realize that in this case the word *person* does not have quite the same meaning as when we say that our neighbor is a person. God is infinitely more than a human person. But we have no other term at our disposal to describe him.

Theology is always conditioned by the constraints of human language. But there are also other considerations. Theologians can never embark on their study of the Bible without any bias or preconceived ideas. They are always children of their own time and are influenced by the philosophies that are current in the age in which they live. To blame the church fathers for having been influenced by Greek philosophy is unfair, just as it is unfair to blame eighteenth- and nineteenth-century theologians for having been influenced by the philosophical currents that were trending in their time. William Miller and Adventist authors of the nineteenth century built their interpretations of apocalyptic prophecies on the writings of people who went before them and on the thoughts of contemporaries. And the Adventist theologians of the early twentieth century were influenced by the powerful trend of fundamentalism that soon had many denominations in and beyond the United States solidly in its grip. Theology always takes place in a distinct philosophical and cultural milieu. It is impacted by societal trends in the region of the world where a theologian happens to live and, of course, by his denominational affiliation.

"Doing theology" never happens in a vacuum. A theologian, of whatever professional or nonprofessional stature, is always influenced by other theologians. The place where one has studied and the professors one listened to during one's theological formation, as well as the books that one has read, all have their profound influence. As a result, theologians work with different perspectives and will have a distinct approach to various theological (and other) issues. This brings a wonderful enrichment to the study of theology. More often than not these various approaches complement and enrich rather than flatly contradict each other.

Sakae Kubo (1926–2025) held a special place among the Adventist theologians who profoundly influenced me.[3] He helped me to leave the fundamentalist trajectory on which I had begun my theological pilgrimage. Among other theologians I am especially indebted to are Alvin Plantinga (especially through his book *Warranted Christian Belief*), Hans Küng, and N. T. Wright. I also benefited a great deal from my cooperation with Cornelis van der Kooi and Gijsbert van den Brink, who both taught systematic theology at the Free University of Amsterdam. I translated their handbook of systematic theology into English. It was published in 2017 by Eerdmans Publishing Company under the title *Christian Dogmatics: An Introduction*. During a period of about three years this project took a great deal of my time and kept me focused on the field of systematic theology. It proved to be a great learning experience.

For the reasons mentioned above theology is never static. It is always a work in progress. To simply keep repeating a particular expression of the theology of the past is not a sign of commitment to "keeping the faith" but rather a denial of the essence of the task of theology. The challenge for Christian believers, as individuals and as a community, is to "grow in the grace and the knowledge of our Lord and Savior Jesus Christ" (2 Pet 3:18). Our theology must therefore reflect a process of spiritual growth. This applies to Christian theology in general but also to *Adventist* theology—and certainly also to our own theological journey.

Authentic

When I was thinking of a good title for this book I initially settled on *Towards a Liberal Adventist Theology*. Several friends with whom I shared

3. This was especially true during the academic year 1965–1966 when I was privileged to take some of his classes at Andrews University (Berrien Springs, Michigan).

the manuscript, or parts of it, advised me against using this title. Why would I, they argued, choose a title that would straightaway cause a lot of animosity? Do I deliberately want to escalate the doctrinal hostilities that plague a substantial segment of Adventism? Do I not realize that the very word *liberal* evokes all kinds of negative associations, since for many it is equivalent to a negation of the biblical gospel and of the miracle-working authority of an all-powerful God? And am I deaf to the many voices of fellow Adventists who tell me that a liberal Adventist is, in fact, an oxymoron, since a genuine Adventist cannot be a liberal?

I intended to use the term *liberal* because I want to underline that this book is not just one more publication in a long range of reviews of the main Adventist teachings. Just looking at my own library I see a few dozen of such books: Adventist theologies, written by Adventist theologians and other church leaders. They differ from each other, and their emphases vary, but they all claim to be true to traditional Adventism. The books from Adventist authors that focus on particular doctrines or dogmatic themes show more diversity in what they stress and in aspects they downplay or ignore. However, in general, Adventist books on doctrine profess to be in line with official Adventist teachings. This is certainly true for publications that are issued by the denominational publishing houses. I have not seen any Adventist book that intentionally and candidly claims (or admits) to be liberal. In choosing to include the word *liberal* in the title I wanted it to be clear that I take the *liberty* to question some aspects of our Adventist theology. Eventually, I opted for the term *authentic* in characterizing my understanding of Adventist theology. However, let me explain why I am not as averse to the term *liberal* as most of my fellow Adventists tend to be.

Liberal originates from the Latin word *liber*, which means "free" or "unrestricted."[4] It was originally used to signify persons who were not enslaved and were free, both in a physical and social sense. Later, especially in the seventeenth and eighteenth centuries, the term was increasingly attached to political and social philosophies, and this is still the case. Being a liberal was being an advocate for civil liberties, equality, and democratic government. These elements seem in many ways akin to the biblical concept of a church in which all members have the same status. Leaving that aside, *liberal* still carries the sense of freedom and openness to new ideas; it suggests the possibility of a reinterpretation of

4. *Oxford English Dictionary* (3rd ed.), s.v. "liberalism."

former conclusions and of a reorientation when external circumstances change. I believe that Christian freedom, of which the apostle Paul was such a vociferous advocate, includes the liberty to take a new look at traditional views, to reinterpret particular historical conclusions, and to seek connections between our doctrines and actual life in the twenty-first century. I take some ideas a step further than many other Adventist authors. I refuse to be a doctrinal contortionist, who twists himself in unnatural theological positions just to safeguard traditional ideas. I want to be free from such constraints as I try to describe what I, as a Seventh-day Adventist, have come to believe.

I realize that in many Adventist circles being liberal is akin to committing the unpardonable sin. In nominating committees in the Adventist world a single statement about the perceived liberalism of a candidate for a leadership role is often sufficient for having his name eliminated from any further consideration. Critics of liberalism effortlessly cite a range of objections against liberal theology. First of all, they warn that liberals do not take the Bible seriously and are selective in what parts of Scripture they are willing to accept. Furthermore, they tend to water down essential doctrines and to place an overemphasis on human reason, thereby diluting the supernatural. Liberals are inclined to accommodate secular world views. Furthermore, in debates about moral issues, liberals are often prepared to endorse a moral relativism, especially with regard to sexual ethics, gender roles, and the sanctity of life.

Liberal theologians reject these accusations and argue that their main objective is to make the Christian faith more meaningful in a rapidly changing world. They want to bridge the gap between faith and reason and are adamant that critical thinking, scientific enquiry, and intellectual honesty do not necessarily threaten Christian belief but will give it credibility and will enrich it. Liberal theology does not necessarily undervalue the Bible but stresses its human context. It wants to encourage a spiritual engagement with the Scriptures to discover its meaning for the present. Liberal theologians demand the freedom to explore questions, express doubts, and develop new ideas without being subject to hostility and a constant allegation of heresy. Moreover, liberal theology wants to actively engage in issues of social justice, human rights, and environmental stewardship as essential aspects of obedience to the gospel of Christ.

In his book *Theology for Liberal Protestants*, Douglas Ottati, a prominent Reformed theologian (b. 1950), affirms that liberal Protestants "have always tried to contribute faithful ways to restate, rethink and revise Christian believing in the face of contemporary knowledge and realities."[5] This author maintains that liberal theology must be based on the Bible and also on how the Christian tradition has expressed the biblical faith in various ways through the ages. At the same time, liberal theology must consider the developments in other disciplines (both in the humanities and the natural sciences) and attempt to translate the Christian faith in such a way that it will resonate with a twenty-first century public. I believe this is a fair presentation of what Professor Ottati says. I can only say, "I want to be a liberal Protestant, more specifically a liberal Adventist, in the way Ottati describes!"

A similar sentiment is echoed by Michael Baumann (1950–2019), an American specialist in medieval and renaissance theology. He opines theology ought to be "both a statement of present belief and an explorer's compass for further intellectual navigation."[6] What Baumann says of Christian theologians in general also applies to Adventist thought leaders: they are called to be "seekers after truth, not merely its custodians."[7] Of course, there is the risk that this search will not always deliver the answers we are looking for, but Baumann reminds us that "it is better to travel hopefully and never to arrive than to settle prematurely."[8]

As a reader of this book you will have to determine how liberal its content is. Just note that we are dealing with a very imprecise term. In the eyes of many in other denominations even the most progressive or liberal Seventh-day Adventist is still very conservative. Yes, I will question some elements of traditional Adventism, but the reader will (hopefully) discover that the book is not as liberal (in the negative sense this word often has in Adventist circles) as he/she might fear! And thus characterizing what follows in this book as *authentic* rather than *liberal* is, after all, the wiser way to go. I will do my best to be honest and open about what I believe but also about the things I am not so sure about. I will not try to be "politically correct" or skip the questions for which I have no answers. In other words, I will do my very best to be authentic.

5. Ottati, *Theology for Liberal Protestants*, 2.
6. Baumann, *Pilgrim Theology*, 10.
7. Baumann, *Pilgrim Theology*, 11.
8. Baumann, *Pilgrim Theology*, 20.

Adventist Theology

Readers of this book may expect, from what I have thus far said in this introduction, some *discontinuity* with how Adventist theologians have traditionally defined and interpreted the content of the Adventist faith. However, they will find more *continuity* than *discontinuity*. This book is definitely still *Adventist*.

Fritz Guy (1930–2023) began his seminal book *Thinking Theologically* with this statement: "This is a book about thinking theologically as an Adventist—that is, about the process of developing and articulating an Adventist interpretation of faith—and doing it as well as possible for one's personal growth and satisfaction, for the good of the community of faith and the world it is called to witness, and for the glory of God."[9]

I could have begun my introduction with these very same words (without implying, however, that I will come in all respects to the same conclusions as Professor Guy). Of course, the ultimate motive of all theology should be to glorify God. Theology must always be an exercise in the service of God and for the spiritual benefit of the community of believers. Guy underlines that "doing theology" is not a static repetition of traditional statements of belief but must be a process of further developing and articulating—to the best of our human ability—what the faith (and *in casu*, the Adventist expression of the Christian faith) means for our own spiritual benefit and for the spiritual growth of the church.

I believe there is probably no better definition of the core value of theology than is found in the words of Anselm of Canterbury (d. 1109). He described theology as *fides quaerens intellectum*, or "faith seeking understanding."[10] For him, this captured the basic principle of doing theology. It must be the result of a deep desire to comprehend and reflect upon the things one believes. Faith, Anselm says, comes first. But we need our brain to explore what this faith means. This is expressed in his famous statement *Non quaero intelligere ut credam, sed credo ut intelligam*—"I do not seek to understand that I may believe, but I believe in order to understand."[11] Anselm does not primarily address nonbelievers in an attempt to lead them to faith, but he speaks to those who already believe and invites them to embark on an intellectual and spiritual

9. Guy, *Thinking Theologically*, 3.
10. Wikipedia, "Credo ut intelligam."
11. Wikipedia, "Credo ut intelligam."

journey. Thinking about their faith will not remove all mystery, but this exploratory process will bring them closer to God.

This is how I also embark in this book on my exploration of Adventist theology. I have faith—even though I readily admit that uncertainties and doubt are never far away. I must constantly repeat the prayer of the man who came to Jesus for the healing of his epileptic son: "I do believe; help me overcome my unbelief!" (Mark 9:24). Since being a teenager I have, with various degrees of intensity, tried to do what Anselm suggested: seek to understand my Christian faith. And later on, with ever more urgency, I have applied Anselm's words to my understanding of the core teachings of the denomination to which I have chosen to belong.

Baumann, whom I cited earlier, pointed out that most theologians have a particular confessional background. Some are Roman Catholic, others are Anglican, Lutheran or Reformed, Baptist or Methodist, and so on. This means that they must in some way relate to formal statements, such as creeds and confessions of faith, which their denomination has adopted. This can prove to be a major challenge in their theological endeavors. Baumann made a very pertinent comment: "The problem is not that theologians are confessional, but that they treat their confessions as if they were impregnable and unassailable truth rather than well-established but still provisional working hypotheses for further theologizing."[12] Unfortunately, in Adventist circles the twenty-eight fundamental beliefs, though not formally defined as a creed, are also more and more regarded and protected by church leadership as an "impregnable and unassailable truth" and not as "provisional working hypotheses."

The Seventh-day Adventist Church has consistently maintained that its statement of fundamental beliefs is not a creed. In reality, however, it very much functions in that way. Remarkably enough, in its early history the church was very reluctant to accept any form of organization, but 150 years later the Adventist Church is one of the most highly structured religious organizations in the world. For a long time the denomination also showed great hesitancy in producing anything that could be interpreted as a creed. However, with the acceptance of a statement of twenty-seven fundamental beliefs in 1980 (with later revisions in 2005 and 2015), the church created a summary of its doctrines that was no longer merely a *description* of what Adventists commonly believe but rather a detailed

12. Baumann, *Pilgrim Theology*, 41.

list that *prescribes* what members are expected to believe in order to be counted as "true" Adventists.

This, of course, raises the question of how much freedom there is for an Adventist in the "Anselmian" pursuit of a deeper understanding of his faith. I believe that, in actual practice, there is more freedom than we can at times conclude from statements that come from denominational top leadership. Officially, the (now) twenty-eight fundamental beliefs are not poured into solid theological and canonical concrete. When this statement was first voted at a world congress of the church in Dallas in 1980, a preamble was added, which, though sometimes ignored, has never been revoked. It reads,

> Seventh-day Adventists accept the Bible as their only creed and hold certain fundamental beliefs to be the teaching of the Holy Scriptures. These beliefs, as set forth here, constitute the church's understanding and expression of the teaching of Scripture. Revision of these statements may be expected at a quinquennial General Conference Session whenever the church is led by the Holy Spirit to a fuller understanding of Bible truth, or if better language is found, to express these teachings of God's Holy Word.[13]

Admittedly, the preamble does not mention the possibility of deletions or major alterations, but it does refer to a possible "fuller understanding" and to finding "better language" to express the church's teachings. That possibility was utilized in 2005 and 2015.

There is another pivotal principle in the Adventist organizational structure that ensures a degree of freedom. Theologians must respect that a formal change in the church's teachings can only be made at the church quinquennial global meeting. In the meantime, the top organizational echelon can put pressure on lower ecclesial bodies to discipline or dismiss salaried employees who are theologically suspect, but the actual hiring and firing is mostly in the hands of the respective employing bodies. Men and women who are employed by the church may face serious consequences when their theological convictions do not align with the official interpretation of the fundamental beliefs. But to determine whether one remains a "real" Adventist in "good and regular standing" is the exclusive right of the local congregation where an individual holds

13. General Conference, "What Do Adventists Believe?"

his[14] membership. It is quite seldom that a theologian who has ideas that deviate from official teachings loses his membership through a decision of a local congregation.

In addition, there is a development within the Seventh-day Adventist Church that leads one to ask, Who, in fact, controls at present the theological narrative of the church?[15] As the Adventist Church went through the twentieth century, the theological professionals, in the educational system in the US and elsewhere, played a major role in the further development of Adventist theology and in communicating its official version to the church and to the outside world. Theological conferences, especially targeting pastors and teachers, were held to stimulate doctrinal unity, especially at times when this unity was threatened by serious dissent. Denomination-wide procedures for screening theology professors were devised to ensure that the church would retain a firm grip on the formation of future ministers. Book committees in the official publishing houses functioned as an important check on the orthodoxy of the manuscripts that were submitted.

Today, in most denominations, the institutional control of their theology is no longer as solid as it once was. In the past, theologians were privileged in their access to theological materials in specialized libraries. Today a vast number of sources are accessible online, which has made it quite easy for many more people, including lay members, to directly engage with these materials. More importantly, we see how social media, podcasts, and a wide variety of online platforms result in a plurality of voices that participate in the theological discourse. Theologians must increasingly compete with pastors, bloggers, and other influencers for attention, thus reducing the impact of prominent academics, and also limiting the level of effective denominational control. This development is most definitely also a reality in Adventism.

A further complication is that the Adventist Church has probably, more than most other Christian denominations, an unknown (but very substantial) number of "independent ministries." These vary from one-person enterprises with a laptop and a copying machine in the basement

14. Whenever I use the pronouns *he*, *him*, or *his* to refer to a person in general, these words should be understood to include both genders—that is, *he/she*, *him/her*, and *his/her*.

15. In the following few paragraphs I rely on an article I wrote for *Adventist Today*, "Who Controls Our Theological Narrative?"

of a private home to organizations with hundreds of paid employees, large facilities, and multi-million budgets. Independent organizations/ministries are first and foremost an American phenomenon, although they have also made their entry into the church in other lands. They fit with the American pragmatic approach to things. There is no doubt that these independent organizations have a strong influence and that many of them tend to push a doctrinal agenda that is rather fundamentalist. In these circles we find widespread doubt regarding the doctrine of the Trinity, significant enthusiasm for Last Generation Theology,[16] a strong resistance to the idea of full equality between men and women in ministry, a total unwillingness to fully accept people with a nonheterosexual orientation, and a naive and uncritical attitude towards the ministry of Ellen G. White.[17] I am glad to note that the theological narrative of Adventism is not completely dominated by the conservative administrative centers of our church organization, with the support of a range of independent voices that mostly echo sentiments and views of the past. In recent years independent progressive communication channels like *Spectrum* and *Adventist Today* have matured and are having an increasing impact on the church—a fact that is applauded by many, but also feared by those who do not want to lose control of the Adventist narrative. In the world of the print media significant developments have taken place. The print-on-demand technology and the ease of self-publishing has ended the near monopoly of denominationally controlled publishing houses. And we should not underestimate the influence of individual Adventists in the digital world who, through blogs and posts on social media, question some traditional views and want to delve deeper into what present truth could mean in the second quarter of the twenty-first century.

To summarize, the Adventist theological world is not as uniform and as solidly under official control as it was in the past, and in the future it may not be so easy to safeguard the contours of Adventist theology as it once was. But whatever else Adventist theology may be, it

16. Last Generation Theology (LGT) is a theological current within Seventh-day Adventism that emphasizes the idea that the final generation of Christians, living just before Christ's second coming, must attain a state of moral perfection. Proponents believe this generation will fully reflect Christ's character and vindicate God's law before the universe.

17. Ellen G. White (1827–1915) was one of the founders of the Seventh-day Adventist Church and is regarded by most Adventists as a prophetic voice. She authored dozens of books and thousands of articles and letters, focusing on health, education, theology, and spiritual growth.

"must be contemporary because the challenges it faces are new in every age. The problems confronting the church today are not the same as the ones it met before. Theology must speak to these problems, if the Christian message is to be heard."[18]

Who Is a Genuine Adventist?[19]

If someone wants to be referred to as a Christian he must, I believe, affirm a number of basic Christian principles. It seems to me that a person loses the right to call himself a Christian if he no longer believes in a personal God and in Jesus Christ as someone who plays a decisive role in the relationship between God and humankind. Likewise, I believe that I must share some *essential* Adventist convictions with my fellow Adventist believers if I claim to be a Seventh-day Adventist. At this point it is important to have a clear idea of what is "essential" and "less essential" in our Adventist teachings.

Whether I am a *true* Adventist is, in the final analysis, something I decide myself. I must ask myself whether I affirm the basics of the Christian faith and whether I have sufficient affinity with the Adventist interpretation of the Christian faith, and with the Adventist faith community, to refer to myself as a genuine Adventist. On this basis I have no hesitation whatsoever in calling myself a real Seventh-day Adventist.

I agree wholeheartedly with Fritz Guy—the theologian I referred to earlier—when he listed key aspects of authentic Adventism.[20] He tops his short list with "having a spirit of openness to present truth." This means that a genuine Adventist never believes he has all "the truth." Like the earliest Adventist thought leaders, a real Adventist in our day and age must be willing to change his mind when needed, to continue learning, and to grow in his understanding of what it means to be an Adventist Christian in today's world (and not only what it meant in the nineteenth century).

We are genuine Adventists, Guy affirms, when we are Christians who have "God's comprehensive and universal love at the center of our personal existence." To be worthy of the name Seventh-day Adventist we must appreciate the "contemporary importance of the Sabbath" and have

18. Rice, *Reign of God*, 9.

19. The next few paragraphs are adapted from my book *Facing Doubt*, 151–72.

20. Guy, *Thinking Theologically*, 92.

"the hopeful anticipation of the reappearance of God in the person of Jesus the Messiah." Two other important elements that are cited by Guy, are "the idea of multidimensional human wholeness" and "the choice of the Adventist community as a spiritual home, with the adoption of the Adventist past as part of one's spiritual identity."[21]

Prolegomena

My attempt to sketch the outlines of an authentic Adventist theology will proceed from the points of departure I have described in the previous section. It will, definitely, be Adventist theology. I am a member of the Adventist faith community and realize that this will color my approach as I pursue this project. I intend to be loyal to my spiritual heritage, and I want this book to be meaningful for my fellow believers. I hope I can help at least a few readers to shake off some of the shackles that have obstructed their spiritual progress, so that they can continue their Adventist journey in greater freedom and with an increased sense that their faith really matters in their everyday life, in the context of the twenty-first century.

Most systematic theologies, even such modest undertakings as this book, begin with a section commonly referred to as *prolegomena*. This word, that (as so many other words) is derived from the Greeks, literally means "things spoken beforehand."[22] In a way, this introductory chapter functions as such, as it lays the foundation for the chapters that follow. In major systematic theologies these prolegomena may fill hundreds of pages as they provide a detailed exposition of the nature, the methods, and the sources of theology, while also dealing with such issues as the relationship between faith and reason and the roles of Scripture, tradition, and philosophy. In contemporary theology there is much less attention for these "things that must be said beforehand" than there was in the past. In our postmodern age there is, in general, less trust in universal rules and foundational concepts on which we all must agree, and this also pertains to the discipline of theology. However, the stress on coherence in our theological narrative, which has always been a key element in these prolegomena, remains an important prerequisite for a credible systematic

21. Guy, *Thinking Theologically*, 228–50.

22 Van der Kooi and Van den Brink, *Christian Dogmatics*, 35.

approach to what we believe and want to express in our theology. This is certainly something I will keep in mind as I embark on this project.

Logical Order and Coherence

In order to succeed in creating a coherent theological narrative, the *order* in which the important elements are presented demands careful thought. Different theologians have made different choices. Often the first topic to be addressed is that of *general* revelation. I will follow that approach. But, right from the start, I will emphasize how the *specific* revelation in the Bible, as the word of God, not only complements but supersedes general revelation. In many systematic treatments of the distinct theological themes, the doctrines related to the Godhead (God the Father and the Creator, God the Son, God the Spirit, and the questions about the Trinity) precede a discussion of the Bible as the channel of the revelation from the triune God. I believe, however, that it makes sense to begin with a discussion of the different aspects of revelation and not by only focusing on general revelation. In what follows—about the Christian concept of the Godhead as the Trinity and other key doctrines of the Christian faith and its Adventist interpretation—we will constantly refer to the Bible. So, we first need to determine how we should read the Bible. Do we go to the Bible for information and insights from a fundamentalist perspective, or do we read the Bible less literally and with a distinct openness for the historical and cultural context in which the words in this unique book are embedded? It will soon be clear that I follow that latter option.

For Seventh-day Adventists another aspect of revelation inevitably comes into play. Among the spiritual gifts that are promised to the followers of Christ is the gift of prophecy (1 Cor 12:10; 14:1–5; Eph 4:11, 12; Rom 12:6). Adventists have recognized Ellen G. White (1827–1915), one of the founders of their church, as a prophetic voice in their movement and have regarded her vast collection of books and other writings as "inspired." Many questions have emerged, and these have become more urgent as time has gone on. Does the divine revelation to mankind in our day and age include the products of this modern prophet? If so, how do they relate to the Scriptures?

We believe in God. But what can we say about One we have never seen? How can we find words to describe him—his nature, his character, his relationship with his creatures? What can we possibly mean when we say that he embodies incomparable love after we have seen on the six-o'clock news how brutal wars continue, and when we realize that small children die of cancer? What can it possibly mean when we call God a *person* and confirm the ancient doctrine of the Trinity with its enigmatic Three-ness in One-ness? How can we make sure that the God we claim to worship is not our own invention but the ultimate reality, who is our Creator and Sustainer?

Many questions, naturally, also emerge when we think about Jesus Christ. What does it mean when we say that he is God's Son? And that he is our Savior? Can we still agree with the leaders of the church in the early centuries, who concluded after long debates that Jesus is fully God and fully man? Was his death more than a tragic miscarriage of justice, and can we with confidence say that Jesus rose from death? Or must we admit that with these issues we move into the realm of myth? And what about the story of his ascension and Christ's subsequent role as the heavenly high priest? This latter aspect has been a hotly debated issue in Adventism. Did Jesus indeed begin a special phase of his high-priestly ministry in heaven in the mid-nineteenth century, as official church teachings claim? Or must Adventists concede (and perhaps apologize for it) that they have allowed their theology to be infected by a classic case of cognitive dissonance, after the disillusionment in 1844, when Christ did not return as the followers of William Miller had predicted?[23]

The next logical step is to pay attention to the Holy Spirit, who is sent by Jesus as his representative and as the spiritual guide for his followers. This topic prompts us to focus on the personhood of the Spirit and the specific role of the Spirit in the plan of salvation. How does the Spirit assist us in making our choices between good and evil and in our pursuit of a deeper understanding of spiritual things? What are the gifts with which he endows the followers of Christ, and how can believers avail themselves of these charismatic gifts?

With this basis of having some insights in our Christian belief in a triune God—Father, Son, and Spirit—our next focus is on how this God has dealt with the sin problem and has bridged the gap that spoiled the relationship between him and his creation. We will look at key issues concerning sin and salvation. What is the essence of individual

23. *Cognitive dissonance* is the tension that arises when a person has acquired knowledge that contradicts his religious beliefs but nonetheless wants to retain these beliefs and therefore attempts to find the justification for doing so.

and corporate sin? What went wrong with our planet? How will the sin problem be finally solved, and how can human beings be "saved"? How did the death of Jesus produce this gift of salvation? How does, according to the Scriptures, salvation or atonement "work"? Could God not have chosen another way to fix the dilemma of evil? Our conclusions—however tentative they may have to remain—are important for a better understanding of the concept of grace and for how we look at other aspects of God's plan of salvation, in particular the justification of the believer and the lifelong process of sanctification.

An important element in our sanctification is the *rest* God provides to us in his gift of the Sabbath. In this connection we will not only look at why it is important to stay loyal to the original timing of the seventh-day Sabbath, but also to grasp the God-given meaning of the Sabbath and to understand why Sabbath observance remains relevant in the twenty-first century.

All this must then be placed in a broader perspective. What does the daily life (and the lifestyle) of the Christian believer look like? At this point the issue of law and grace must be probed. If salvation is for the full 100 percent outcome of grace, is there nothing the believer must *do* to earn or, at least, to be worthy of that grace? What role does obedience to the laws and regulations that we find in the Bible play? And which of the precepts, once given to the people of Israel, are still valid for Christians today? How do we use the Bible in finding answers to the new moral questions of our times?

I will argue that stewardship is an essential—and perhaps the overarching—component of Christian living. Adventists have traditionally specified a number of lifestyle elements that give concrete content to what it means to be a steward of one's own body, of one's finances, and of the natural environment in which we live. When dealing with this, we will need to ask whether these principles should be seen as prescriptive and/or should be made a condition for church membership. The phenomenon of legalism is an ever-present danger that can easily destroy Christian grace-based freedom.

From Christian living in the *present* we will move on to the *future*, as we study an area of theology that is commonly referred to as *eschatology*—in other words, teachings about the last things. Christians believe that at some point human history will end. Christ will return from his heavenly abode and a new era will be inaugurated. For Adventists, the second coming of the Lord is so important that it is even enshrined in the name of their denomination. We will look at the *how*, *why*, and *when* of this event. How does the Bible, including its apocalyptic portions (mainly Daniel and Revelation), inform us about the "signs of the times," the end-time events, and the final judgment? Is historicism[24] the only valid approach to apocalyptic prophecy? Can we expect specific religious and political powers to dominate the last days of earth's history?

Then, what is next? What about the millennium that is referred to in Rev 20 and has been such a controversial topic, in particular in evangelical Protestantism? And what can we know about the new, eternal existence that has been promised to the people who have chosen to follow the Lord of life? What can we know about heaven and the new earth?

Do human beings have an immaterial, eternal soul, which leaves the body when they breathe their last breath, and does this soul immediately move into the presence of God? Or do we "sleep" until the moment of our resurrection? What prospect is there for those who are not among the "saved" who will enjoy eternal life?

As long as we are still in this world we are not on our own but are part of a community. We are members of the church. At this point some important issues must be explored. What is the nature of the church of God? Can a specific denomination claim a special status, as the Seventh-day Adventist Church has traditionally done? What kind of self-understanding has a sound biblical basis?

Contrary to Christ's intentions, his church has fragmented into numerous denominational entities, which often compete with one another rather than cooperate in their common mission. It raises the question what true Christian unity means. In this section of the book we will address such topics as baptism as the entry into the community of believers, the meaning of the rite of the communion service for the spiritual wellbeing of the church, and the importance of participating in worship. But intertwined with all these things is the fundamental equality of all members of the Body of Christ, since the Lord, rather than any human being, is the Head.

24. In theology, *historicism* refers to a method of biblical interpretation that sees prophecy as unfolding progressively through historical events, particularly in apocalyptic literature like Daniel and Revelation.

Finally, what is our mission as Christ-believers as we live, conscious of our own mortality, in expectation of the end of this present world? Christians must witness of their faith, and they must do so by what they say, write, broadcast, and share via their social media. But they must also sound a prophetic voice in this world through their protest against hate, violence, injustice, and inequality. And by being loving, honest, and forgiving (that is, Christ-like) in their interaction with the people around them.

This is the outline of my attempt to give a coherent description of what an authentic Adventist theology might look like. I know I will not be able to answer all questions. But I hope the book will provide direction and will also encourage the readers to continue their own authentic search for answers and, in many cases, to cheerfully live with their unanswered questions. Together we can succeed in updating the present truth that has been transmitted to us, as we try to seek ways to ensure that what we believe remains relevant for our everyday life.

I have concluded that, when all is said and done, we are called to *worship* God and should not expect to ever fully *understand* him.

Chapter 1

Revelation

The Dutch theologian Harry M. Kuitert (1924–2017) owed at least part of his fame to his frequently repeated statement that everything that supposedly comes from above actually comes from below.[1] With this oft-quoted assertion Professor Kuitert expressed his belief that the religious truths, and the doctrines which people attribute to divine inspiration, are in fact human constructs. This means that the God of the Christians is the product of their own thinking and imagination. In all honesty we must admit that many things we say about God are indeed the result of our own human speculation. Nonetheless, Kuitert's view runs contrary to what Christians through the centuries have professed—namely, that we do actually know certain things about God, because he has let himself be known and that, therefore, there are things that do indeed come from above to us, who are here below!

Is There a Foundation for Our Beliefs?

Most Christians believe that God has provided a revelation of himself, his nature, and his works to us humans. This, of course, only makes sense if one believes that there is an "above." *Theology must begin with faith in God's existence.* The Bible nowhere attempts to prove that there is a God. It proceeds on the basis that he exists as our Creator and as

1. He further developed this in his book *I Have My Doubts*, 21–49.

the One to whom we, as his created beings, owe our total allegiance. I will also proceed in this chapter and in what follows on that same basis. It makes more sense to me that there is a God than to accept the idea that there is no God. I choose to believe in God, even though I have no ultimate proof that he exists. One might ask, Is it reasonable to build on such an uncertain foundation? And, Is there in fact any solid *foundation* for our faith in God as the ultimate reality?

Foundationalism is the name for the attempts to discover absolute principles—beliefs that do not depend on other beliefs for their justification but are basic or immediate. There are several versions of foundationalism. *Strong* foundationalism builds on the conviction that our entire edifice of knowledge can, indeed, be grounded in some absolute and invincible principles.[2] According to this theory, those basic beliefs are self-evidently true. In other words, when you encounter them, they have such force that you cannot but accept that they are valid. Today, there are few philosophers and theologians who defend such a strong foundationalism. No one, it is argued by most thinkers, can approach these matters that supposedly are basic without preconceived ideas. And even if several of these principles that seem to be basic support each other, this concurrence does not constitute a watertight proof of their truth.

It has been suggested by many Christian theologians and philosophers that the foundationalist quest for absolute truth is seriously impeded by our human sinfulness, and the idea that it might succeed is, in fact, a token of our arrogance.[3] But if strong foundationalism is a bridge too far, does that mean that there is nothing solid to build upon? Many think that we can opt for what is usually referred to as *modest* foundationalism. According to this approach we must do with less than *absolute* certainty. But this is acceptable, for there is *enough* certainty on which we can ground our faith.

Modest foundationalists say that their core beliefs are not totally immune to some conceivable doubts, but they "are perfectly acceptable unless one has good reason to think that they have been undermined. They are innocent unless proven guilty."[4] In their description of modest foundationalism scholars often point to two distinct supporting theories: *reliabilism* and *coherentism*. The first theory maintains that

2. Wood, *Epistemology*, 83.

3. Wood, *Epistemology*, 98.

4. Wood, *Epistemology*, 99.

something may be considered reliable if a reliable method has been followed to arrive at it.[5] *Coherentist* theories of truth emphasize consistency. If a range of ideas are consistent with one another and form a coherent whole, there is strong reason to accept them as true. These beliefs must not just fit together in the sense that they do not contradict each other, they must form an integrated whole.[6] Following this line of thought, there is no assumption that a justified set of beliefs comes in the form of a complete *building*. Such a metaphor would make the truth claim too strong. But beliefs, so the coherentists say, are interdependent, each belief being supported by its connection to its neighbors and ultimately to the whole.[7] I am happy to count myself among the supporters of modest foundationalism and, as I already promised in the introduction, I will try to show myself a coherentist!

Individual beliefs may not seem sufficiently immediate, but taken as part of a set of coherent beliefs, we have a strong enough basis on which to proceed. Some philosophers refer to this set of basic beliefs with the metaphor of a *nest*, or a *network*. The American philosopher W. V. Quine (1908–2000) prefers the metaphor of a *web*, as the title of a book that he coauthored with a fellow philosopher indicates.[8] The image of a web suggests that individual threads may be fragile and vulnerable, but that all threads together can form a firm structure. Thus, individual beliefs may have weaknesses and may be subject to doubt, but a set of coherent beliefs is a strong enough basis from which to carry on.

Alvin Plantinga (b. 1932), a philosopher of Reformed vintage, who taught for many years at the prestigious Notre Dame University in South Bend, Indiana, introduced the notion of "warranted beliefs."[9] He argues that there may not be the absolute certainty for our beliefs that the strong foundationalist requires, but there is sufficient warrant for holding the beliefs that are at the basis of Christianity.

There is nothing inherently illogical in believing that the conviction that Gods exists arises in us when we have certain kinds of experiences. The French Reformer John Calvin (1509–1564) spoke of a *sensus divinitatis* (Latin for "sense of divinity") to describe the innate awareness

5. Dancy, *Introduction to Contemporary Epistemology*, 31–32.
6. Grenz and Franke, *Beyond Foundationalism*, 39.
7. Murphey, *Beyond Liberalism*, 94.
8. Quine and Ulian, *Web of Belief.*
9. See his book *Warranted Christian Belief.*

of God that, he believed, is common to all human beings. "A sense of deity is indelibly engraved on the human heart. And that this belief is naturally engendered in all and thoroughly fixed as it were in our very bones, is strikingly attested by the contumacy of the wicked, who, though they struggle furiously, are unable to extricate themselves from the fear of God."[10]

Calvin was convinced that atheism is not a natural state but a suppression of this inherent awareness of God, due to pride or rebellion against him. The "seed of religion," Calvin argued, is naturally implanted in every person by God, making knowledge of God universally accessible. Sin may dull this sense, and often distort or even suppress it, but it is never fully erased. It provides a basis for the gospel when people hear the message of Christ being preached.

Plantinga follows John Calvin and other Calvinist thinkers of the past by echoing the thought "that humans may well be psychologically so constructed by their Maker that, when they undergo certain kinds of experiences, a belief in God is naturally and non-inferentially[11] the result."[12]

The nineteenth-century German theologian Friedrich Schleiermacher (1768–1834), often regarded as the father of modern theology, underlined in a similar way that there is something in all human beings that reflects an immediate awareness of our dependence on something infinite, which he identified as God. He emphasized the "feeling of absolute dependence" (German *Gefühl der schlechthinnigen Abhängigkeit*) as the core of religious experience. This intuitive sense of being connected to the divine, Schleiermacher believed, underpins all religious life.[13]

General Revelation

If God exists (as, I think, is reasonable to believe), this idea of an innate awareness of God and/or feeling of somehow being dependent on Something/Somebody much bigger than we ourselves, makes good sense. And it makes sense to take this a step further. If this God exists and if we somehow owe our existence to him, we may expect to find at least some traces and signals of this connection with the divine in all of

10. Calvin, *Institutes*, 1.3.3.
11. That is, it does not depend on any argument as further proof.
12. Wood, *Epistemology*, 162.
13. Van der Kooi and Van den Brink, *Christian Dogmatics*, 164.

us.[14] The creation story in the Bible points to a trace of the divine in all of us, which is defined as "the image of God." In Gen 1:27 we read, "So God created mankind in his own image, in the image of God he created them." This "image of God" concept has been interpreted in many different ways, but it is in line with the ideas of prominent theologians (as, for instance, Calvin and Schleiermacher) that there is something in human beings that links them to God. It is therefore also reasonable to expect that the God who has given human beings this sense that he exists would want to strengthen this "sense of divinity" or "feeling of absolute dependence" in the beings he created. This is where the *concept of revelation* makes its entry. The idea of revelation implies that there are "truths" that are made known from "above" to us who are "below." But what, exactly, does revelation mean and involve?

The author of the letter (or perhaps *essay* is a better word) to the Hebrews emphasizes that God made himself known in a very special way in Jesus Christ. However, besides this divine self-revelation in the person and ministry of Jesus Christ, God "spoke" to "our ancestors . . . at many times and in various ways" (Heb 1:1). In systematic theologies this reference to "various ways" is reflected in the common division of revelation into *general* and *special* revelation. General revelation has to do what we see in nature, in history, and in the workings of our conscience. The written word (the Bible) and the incarnate Word (Jesus Christ) form the special revelation.

Revelation enables us to know things about God. This applies, as we shall discuss later in this chapter, most *specifically* to God's revelation in Christ. Jesus affirmed this when he said, "Anyone who has seen me has seen the Father" (John 14:9). However, *general* revelation also provides us with knowledge of God. That, of course, raises questions about the nature of this knowledge. Or, to use two technical theological terms, is this knowledge of God primarily *epistemological* or *soteriological*? Which means, does this general revelation simply add to our theoretical knowledge about God—who he is, his attributes, and his characteristics—or is this knowledge first of all related to God's love and his desire to save us, and to restore the relationship with us after it was marred by sin and evil?

The verb *to know* has different connotations in the Bible, but the most basic meaning is embedded in language that is linked to a relationship.

14. Van der Kooi and Van den Brink, *Christian Dogmatics*, 184.

Knowing goes beyond intellectual understanding but emphasizes an intimate relational connection. This is already apparent on one of the first pages of the Bible, when we read that Adam "knew" Eve (Gen 4:1 KJV). In Jer 31:34, speaking of the new covenant between God and his people, God promises that "all shall know me," signifying the possibility of a direct personal relationship with him.

We should not be disappointed if we feel that this *general* revelation does indeed remain general, and does not answer many of the theological questions we might have about God. We must realize that this general revelation has a different function. It does not primarily provide propositional information about God but lays a basis for all people, everywhere, and at all times, for recognizing God in the things we see and experience. It is intended by God to make people realize he is there, and that "he is not far from any one of us" (Acts 17:27).

Nature

For most people, spending time in nature is a meaningful experience that can arouse a range of emotions in them. Walking in a forest or along a beach can provide us with relaxation and inner rest, being away from our hectic job, and no longer hearing the constant drone of heavy traffic. It can overwhelm us when darkness has fallen and we look at the starry sky, or when we visit a mountainous area and enjoy a panoramic view of snow-covered mountain tops. The birder never gets tired watching the incredible variety of birds, large and small, and the botanist is delighted when finding a plant species he has never seen before. Ralph Waldo Emerson, the American author, theologian, and philosopher (1803–1882), once said, "Nature always wears the colors of the spirit."[15] In other words, looking at nature is more than receiving a range of sensory impressions and is more than the thousand or more pictures some of us have on our smartphones as mementoes of where we have been. Nature touches us in a different, more profound—spiritual, and at times mystical—way. This is expressed in the famous verses in the psalm that speak of the power and beauty of nature:

> The heavens declare the glory of God;
> the skies proclaim the work of his hands.
> Day after day they pour forth speech;

15. Emerson, *Nature*, 14.

> night after night they reveal knowledge.
> They have no speech, they use no words;
> no sound is heard from them.
> Yet their voice goes out into all the earth,
> their words to the ends of the world. (Ps 19:1–4)

This psalm, traditionally attributed to King David (ca. 1000 BC), is a stunning poetic declaration of God's majesty as manifested in the natural world, which is "the work" of God's hands. The beauty of creation is a nonverbal testimony of the greatness of the Creator-God. This sense of God's greatness is universal and transcends human barriers of culture or language, as it continues nonstop to speak to us, "day after day" and "night after night." These verses in Ps 19 do not contain specific doctrinal truths, but they reflect the foundation for recognizing God's existence and power, stimulating us to search further for truth about God. Nature is an important aspect of God's general revelation, which also touches people who have had no access to the special revelation in the Bible, and who have not yet been reached by the gospel of Christ.

The same message is found in Paul's letter to the Christians in Rome. People cannot claim that they have never been made aware of God's presence, since some knowledge about God has been made known to all people: "What may be known about God is plain to them, because God has made it plain to them. For since the creation of the world God's invisible qualities—his eternal power and divine nature—have been clearly seen, being understood from what has been made, so that people are without excuse" (Rom 1:19, 20).

Many theologians have commented on these verses that are so central to discussions of natural theology. They have insisted that reason and observance of the natural world can lead us to a knowledge of God. The medieval theologian Thomas Aquinas (d. 1274) based his arguments for the existence of God, in particular the so-called cosmological argument,[16] on this passage. Paul stressed that ignorance is not a valid excuse for not honoring God, because the revelation of God in creation is universally accessible to all.

16. The *cosmological argument* for the existence of God is based on the idea that there must be a first cause or necessary being that explains the existence of the universe. The argument comes in several forms, but all versions are grounded in the principle of causation or contingency.

However, nature does not only impress us because of its beauty and harmony, providing us with a sense of awe and wonder. The ongoing process of climate change has consequences for nature that do not fill us with marvel and delight, but rather with fear and uncertainty. Natural catastrophes often create large-scale chaos, death, and decay. In many places in the world, ecosystems that "normally" ensure harmony and biodiversity are under threat or worse. In the animal world we see forms of life that make us wonder, did God really create also the almost other-worldly creatures that we see in documentaries and pronounce them "very good" (Gen 1:25)? And what about the cruelty we see in nature, among small and large animals? Certain species of parasite wasps lay their eggs inside the body of live hosts, such as caterpillars or spiders. The larvae hatch and feed on the body of their host from the inside. Male lions, after finding a new female companion, are known to kill the cubs that were sired by the previous male. Numerous examples could be given of how the food chain is often characterized by extreme cruelty. So, what does this tell us about God—does this aspect also reveal something about his love and goodness? The answer to this enigma must be sought in the entrance of sin and evil into this world, which has impacted our entire existence and all natural features of our planet. (Many questions, of course, remain—one of them whether death in any form would ever have made its entry in the natural world, if sin had not occurred.) Yet, despite the disorder and ugliness that resulted from sin, nature—even in its far-less-than-originally-perfect form—still in many ways "declares the glory of God."

History

Some theologians, in particular the German theologian Wolfhart Pannenberg (1928–2014), have pointed to history as a locus where God has revealed himself in a general way. People who look at history without any bias, these theologians say, will recognize patterns that must be attributed to acts of God. This applies in particular to the history of Israel. Some theologians argue that history reflects God's providential guidance. This, they say, can be seen in the rise and fall of empires, moral progress, and the role of religious movements. Other theologians, however, point to the ambiguity of historical events, which are often open to multiple interpretations. They also tend to place question marks with regard to moral progress. If it is true that history can give us some insights into God's acting in this world, Christians will need to point to an extremely important caveat: the theological significance of specific events and trends in history must always be interpreted through the lens of special revelation to be more fully understood.

Conscience

Perhaps the most telling aspect of general revelation is the role of conscience—the inner compass that guides us in choices between things that are good and things that are evil.[17] The apostle Paul seems to refer to such an inner moral guide in Rom 2:14–15. This moral compass, he said, is not only present in those who have become Christians, but is also found with those who have not yet been influenced by the gospel: "Indeed, when Gentiles, who do not have the law, do by nature things required by the law, they are a law for themselves, even though they do not have the law. They show that the requirements of the law are written on their hearts, their consciences also bearing witness, and their thoughts sometimes accusing them and at other times even defending them."

This passage indicates that all people—regardless of whether or not they have become Christians—possess a degree of moral awareness, and that no one can, in view of God's judgment, claim complete ignorance of the divine standards of justice and righteousness. Anthropologists confirm the thesis that there appears to be a moral awareness—a distinction between what is considered good and what is considered bad—in all people. This awareness may vary depending on culture, upbringing, and one's personal history. There is, apparently, a difference between a *strong* conscience and a *weak* conscience (1 Cor 8:7). We also read in Scripture about the possibility of systematically ignoring this inner compass, so that it ceases to function properly. In his letter to his protégé Timothy, Paul mentions people "whose consciences have been seared as with a hot iron" (1 Tim 4:2). Nevertheless, the argument that this well-nigh universal moral consciousness points to a divine moral guide remains quite convincing. The medieval so-called moral argument was one of the traditional "proofs" for the existence of God. It is no longer, to the same extent, seen in that same light, and, like all other proofs for God's existence, it is often more convincing to those who already believe in God than as a road towards such belief.

17. C. S. Lewis emphasizes this in his book *Mere Christianity*, 21–32.

The knowledge of God that comes to us through general revelation is important, but it may be easier for believers to recognize its value than it is for many who classify themselves as atheists or agnostics. Moreover, this general knowledge has severe limitations. What people see in nature, in history, and in themselves may lead them to seriously consider that there is *a god*, a something or someone far superior to any of us humans, existing in some other unseen dimension, but this does not lead them any further—namely, to *the God* of the Bible, who is also the Father of the Lord Jesus Christ. General revelation points to a higher power but does not reveal how one can establish a relationship with the One who is our Creator and who wants to save us from our mortality that results from the sin problem.

Special Revelation—the Bible

Christians believe that the Bible is a very unique book, because it contains God's revelation to us humans—not the kind of general revelation we discussed on the previous pages, but a *special* revelation in which we encounter the true and only God, who made himself known as the Creator and the Covenant-God for Israel, and as the "God and Father of all mankind." Christians believe the Bible is so special because God was directly involved in its origin. We are told, "Above all, you must understand that no prophecy of Scripture came about by the prophet's own interpretation of things. For prophecy never had its origin in the human will, but prophets, though human, spoke from God as they were carried along by the Holy Spirit" (2 Pet 1:20–21).

The apostle Peter introduced this statement by first underlining that the church has a message that is "completely reliable" (v. 19). This reliability is assured because it is rooted in a source that has divine credentials. The humans who played a role in the genesis of the Bible, did not record their own ideas, but they "spoke from God" under the influence of the Holy Spirit. Another key text about the origin of the Bible is 2 Tim 3:16. Many Bible translations use the word *inspiration* to describe the process that made the Bible a unique book. But some Bible translations do a better job in catching the meaning of the original text, as for instance the New International Version, which reads, "*All Scripture is God-breathed* and is useful for teaching, rebuking, correcting and training in righteousness" (italics added).

That the Bible is "God-breathed" does not mean that, way back in the past, it miraculously and suddenly appeared in its final form, comparable to what happened when Joseph Smith in 1823 allegedly discovered the golden plates near Palmyra, New York, from which the Book of Mormon was to be translated. The Bible came to us through a long and complicated process that still has many mysteries for us. The original languages, from which translations of the entire Bible or portions of it into some 3,600 other languages were made, are Hebrew (most of the Old Testament), Aramaic (part of Daniel and sections in Ezra), and *Koinē*-Greek (the New Testament). The Old Testament, with its thirty-nine "books," contains historical parts, law codes, prophetic books, poetic sections, and other so-called writings. The New Testament is a collection of twenty-seven different literary items. It consists of the four Gospels, a historical treatise called Acts of the Apostles, a series of letters from the apostle Paul and from a few other apostles, and it concludes with an apocalyptic document called the Revelation of John.

Thousands of ancient documents with parts of the original text (sometimes major portions of the Scriptures and sometimes tiny fragments, with every size in between) have been painstakingly compared by scholars in their efforts to reconstruct the most reliable text that would be as close as possible to the original. Unfortunately, there is no autograph (a document written by the original author) of any part of the Bible. The ancient documents were copies, and often copies of copies of copies, and establishing what is closest to the original has been a painstaking detective work in which a large number of scholars have participated.

But before these documents were produced in various places in the ancient world—frequently in the scriptoria of medieval monasteries—the biblical texts were written by a substantial number of different authors over a period of many centuries. Subsequently, these writings went through the hands of redactors, were collected, and were put in a particular order. Eventually a consensus grew about what should be part of the sacred Scriptures.

In the nineteenth century, in particular, scholars attempted to establish the textual history of the Old Testament. For most Old Testament scholars, the traditional belief that the Pentateuch—the five "Books of Moses": Genesis, Exodus, Leviticus, Numbers, Deuteronomy—was written by Moses was no longer credible. The so-called documentary hypothesis, originally developed by Julius Wellhausen (1844–1918), stated that the Pentateuch was composed from multiple sources, which were later brought together in the final text. One of the key elements of this theory was based on the use of different names for God. Some sections of the Pentateuch use YHWH (Yahweh) as the name of God (attributed to an author code-named J), while in other sections God is referred to as Elohim (attributed to an author code-named E). Different theological emphases and styles further suggested that the various sections were produced by these authors at different times, while other parts of the Pentateuch (focusing on the law and reflecting the centralized worship in Jerusalem) were usually identified as written by the Deuteronomist (D), and some later sections as written by a "priestly" author (P). A redactor (R) later combined these sources into the Pentateuch, smoothing over contradictions and inconsistencies.

This hypothesis has further evolved over time, and remains influential in biblical studies, although nowadays it receives far less attention than before. One of the elements of this hypothesis of different sources had a major impact on discussions about the creation vs. evolution debate. Scholars wondered what to do with the fact that Genesis offers, in fact, two quite distinct creation stories (Gen 1:2—2:3 and Gen 2:4–25). One story was thought to have been authored by the Jahwist (J) and the other by the Elohist (E), and this, of course, raised numerous questions about the similarities and the dissimilarities between the two accounts.

Another prominent example of a part of the Bible that many scholars no longer regarded as having just one author is the prophetic book of Isaiah. Many experts concluded that chapters 1–39 were written by a prophet with that name, but that the rest of the book (chapters 40–66) was later added by a writer usually referred to as the Deutero-Isaiah, while some suggested that a third author (the Trito-Isaiah) wrote chapters 55 to 66.

Of special importance to Seventh-day Adventists is the question of the dating of the book of Daniel. Was this book of the Bible written by a historical person with that name during the Babylonian captivity in the sixth century BC, or did it originate in the second century BC as the work of an unknown author who used the name Daniel as his pseudonym? The answer to this question has a direct impact on some of Adventism's key teachings. The early (sixth century) dating has led Adventists to apply the prophecies in this Bible book to a successive range of world empires and to the rise and dominance of a religio-political power, which will remain active until the end of time. A second-century dating (which, it seems to me, has considerably stronger papers) supports a very different reading and places the prophecies of Daniel squarely in the Graeco-Roman world of King Antiochus Epiphanes (reigned 175–164 BC), with his vicious attacks on the worship of Yahweh in Jerusalem.

The problems described above, and other critical issues, have regularly been addressed by the Adventist Church. The fear that these critical conclusions will undermine the historicity of the Bible and the miraculous nature of many biblical events led to the rejection of this historical-critical approach to Scripture. This rejection received its most comprehensive form in a document that the church adopted in 1986 during a meeting with global representation in Rio de Janeiro.[18]

Adventists have through the years been much more concerned about critical theories regarding the origin of the Old Testament than about critical research into the birth of the New Testament.[19] It is generally accepted (also by Adventist scholars) that the Gospel of Mark served as an important source for both Matthew and Luke, and that these two authors further used a common source of sayings of Jesus (referred to as Q, from the German word *quelle*, "source"). In addition, it is generally believed that each of these two Gospel writers were acquainted with a unique source, referred to with the letters M and L respectively.[20] The issues around the dating and authorship of individual New Testament books have not caused much turmoil among Adventist theologians—probably because none of their doctrinal convictions were seriously impacted by matters of dates, authorship, and internal dependencies.

Inspiration

Taking into consideration what we learned from 2 Pet 1:21—namely, that "prophets, though human, spoke from God, as they were carried along by the Holy Spirit"—we must explore how the human and the divine cooperated in the origin of the Bible. As we also already saw, the Scriptures are

18. McIver, "Historical-Critical Method." For the text, see General Conference, *Bible Study*.

19. See, e.g., Nichol et al., *Seventh-day Adventist Bible Commentary*, which contains a detailed article that rejects the higher criticism of the Old Testament (5:147–75), while its treatment of critical issues in the New Testament is much less forceful (5:175–86).

20. See, for instance, Rodríguez, *Andrews Bible Commentary*, 1213.

"God-breathed," meaning that they are the result of *inspiration*. But what does this inspiration entail? Were the individual *words* of all sixty-six Bible books inspired and, as it were, "dictated" by the Holy Spirit to the men who wrote down what they miraculously "received"? Or were the authors inspired in the sense that their *thoughts* were guided to the things they were to write down, using their own style, with their own specific vocabulary, while at liberty to reflect the cultural context of their time?

In our Christian thinking we meet a number of paradoxes[21] that leave us with serious questions. We will meet a few of them as we proceed to the following chapters. Looking at the doctrine of the Trinity we will be confronted with the puzzling question of how God can be simultaneously one and three. We will see that, if we overemphasize God's three-ness, we risk losing sight of his one-ness, and when we place too much emphasis on God's one-ness, we easily compromise his three-ness. When we study the natures of Jesus Christ we meet another paradox: Christ is said to be fully human but also fully God. How can it be? Again, if we overemphasize one element of the equation, we run into major problems with regard to the other element. We find a rather similar paradox in the doctrine of inspiration, which demands that we keep the human and the divine factors in balance. If we ignore the human element in the origin of the Bible and mainly speak about what God did, we end up with a theory that does not fit the clear facts that research has established. On the other hand, if we reduce the Bible to a purely human product, we rob it of its authority and of most of its spiritual potential. However paradoxical it may be, *the Bible is both human and divine.*

How does inspiration work? Verbal inspiration is a popular theory among conservative Christians. And even though the Seventh-day Adventist Church has never officially endorsed the concept of verbal inspiration, in practice many of its members (and also some of its more conservative professional theologians) operate on the basis of this theory or something very close to it. Of course, this word-for-word inspiration—if it were true—could only apply to the original text and not to translations into other languages. Many conservative Christians in the English-speaking world, however, treat the King James Version (1611) as if it is (close to)

21. The dictionary definition of a *paradox* is a seemingly absurd or contradictory statement or proposition that, when investigated, may after-all prove to be well founded or true. *Oxford English Dictionary* (2nd ed.), s.v. "paradox."

verbally inspired and tend to claim too much for the divine component. This is true also for several revered seventeenth-century translations in other European languages.

The concept of verbal inspiration is closely linked to that of *inerrancy*—that is, the idea that the Bible does not contain any error. When the proponents of verbal inspiration are faced with inconsistencies in the Bible, they tend to speak of "apparent" contradictions and try to find (often fanciful) ways of circumventing the difficulties. They cannot concede that some statements might be historically dubious or clashing with other passages.

The theory of verbal inspiration is closely linked to the fundamentalist movement. Although the terms *fundamentalist* and *fundamentalism* have a more general application, they are mostly applied to a trend in modern Christianity. Fundamentalism may be defined as a movement that emerged in the early decades of the twentieth century "with the aim of defending conservative Protestantism against the challenges of theological liberalism, higher criticism of the Bible, evolution and other modernisms to be judged harmful to traditional faith."[22] A series of brochures, written mostly by scholars at the prestigious Princeton Theological Seminary in New Jersey, came to be known as the *Fundamentals*, which gave the emerging movement the name *fundamentalism*. A major percentage of these fundamentals were about inspiration, inerrancy, and related topics. Adventist leaders of this period were, in general, quite positive towards the fundamentalist movement and often applied the epithet *fundamentalist* to themselves. However, in summaries of Adventist beliefs the terms *verbal inspiration* and *inerrancy* were avoided. Malcolm Bull and Keith Lockart made this insightful observation: "Adventist theology has developed in parallel with the mainstream. It was at its most distinctive during a time of great diversity; it became fundamentalist in the era of fundamentalism and softened with the rise of evangelicalism."[23]

The theory of *thought inspiration* gives the author a much greater role than he is allowed to play in the theory of *verbal inspiration*, which basically reduces the writer to a secretary who recorded what the Holy Spirit whispered in his ear. When we approach the Bible without any preconceived

22. Weber, "Fundamentalism," 461; see also my brochure *Seventh-day Adventism and Fundamentalism*.

23. Bull and Lockart, *Seeking a Sanctuary*, 91.

ideas about the nature of inspiration and are open to learning how the words of the Bible came to the authors, and how they then transmitted them, we find no basis to support verbal inspiration.

For me, thought inspiration is the only credible option. When we begin to read the Bible, we meet named and anonymous authors, who employed their own characteristic language and style. They did not hide the particulars of their culture and their contemporary worldview. They believed in a flat earth and reflected a cosmology that we would today characterize as naive or primitive. They wrote against the background of an era that was blatantly patriarchal, and accepted slavery as normal. Their accounts of warfare betray no awareness of the Geneva Conventions. In many cases the ethical standards they display are no longer our Christian norms. But this is how the word of God has come to us!

In her later years, Ellen G. White came to view inspiration in terms of thought inspiration, as the following two quotes clearly illustrate:

> It is not the words of the Bible that are inspired, but the men that were inspired. Inspiration acts not on the man's words or his expressions but on the man himself, who, under the influence of the Holy Ghost, is imbued with thoughts. But the words receive the impress of the individual mind. The divine mind is diffused. The divine mind and will is combined with the human mind and will; thus the utterances of the man are the word of God.[24]

> The Bible points to God as its author; yet it was written by human hands; and in the varied style of its different books it presents the characteristics of several writers. . . . Written in different ages, by men who differed widely in rank and occupation, and in mental and spiritual endowment, the books of the Bible present a wide contrast in style, as well as a diversity in the nature of the subjects unfolded. Different forms of expression are employed by different writers; often the truth is more strikingly presented by one than by another. . . . As presented through different individuals, the truth is brought out in its various aspects.[25]

The writers of the Bible (whoever they were) were thoroughly human, but they were "carried along" by the Spirit. Their (human) words were *theopneustos*—in other words, "God-breathed." Paradoxically, the Bible is simultaneously human and divine. Only by keeping this constantly in

24. White, *Selected Messages*, 1:21.

25. White, *Great Controversy*, v–vi.

mind, and by keeping the human and the divine elements in careful balance, can the Bible be a unique guide for all aspects of our lives and a trustworthy and rational basis for Christian doctrine.

It makes a great deal of difference whether one opts for verbal inspiration or thought inspiration (also known as dynamic inspiration). Perhaps one of the strongest arguments against the kind of verbal inspiration that is defended by many fundamentalists is the fact that Jesus did not align himself with that theory. Had he been convinced of the word-for-word inspiration of the Hebrew Bible, he would never have deviated from that text and would not have used the Greek-language Septuagint but the exact Hebrew words of the Old Testament authors.[26]

The Canon

The term *canon*, literally meaning "measuring stick,"[27] is used to describe the boundaries of the writings that are considered sacred and must therefore be recognized as belonging to the Scriptures. The Old Testament canon developed over centuries. Its earliest parts, such as units of the Pentateuch, circulated orally before they were written down. By the fifth century BC, the Torah was regarded as authoritative and gradually became the foundation of Jewish identity and worship. The writings of the major prophets (Isaiah, Jeremiah, Lamentations, Ezekiel, Daniel) and those of the minor prophets were collected and assembled over time. By the second century BC, they were by and large accepted as Scripture. The group of the so-called Writings (Psalms, Proverbs, Job, etc.) took longer to stabilize. Some books, like the Psalms, were used in worship early on, but others (e.g., Ecclesiastes, Esther) were not as smoothly adopted. Around the time of the destruction of the temple (in AD 70) the Jewish communities recognized the twenty-four books of the Hebrew Bible—the same books that Christians recognize as their thirty-nine Old Testament books, but in a slightly different order and after splitting some writings that are combined in the Hebrew Bible. There is no solid historical evidence for the oft-repeated statement that at the council of Jamnia in ca. AD 90 the rabbis formally decided on the close of the Old Testament canon.

26. That point is made by several authors, among them the renowned biblical scholar F. F. Bruce in his *New Testament Documents*.

27. Cross, *Oxford Dictionary*, 227.

One of the early translations of the Old Testament in the Greek language was the Septuagint (often designated as LXX). It dates from the third and second century BC, as the product of the Jewish community in the Egyptian city of Alexandria that had become Greek speaking. Besides the writings that were included in the Hebrew canon it also contains the Apocrypha (see below). Jesus's primary language was Aramaic, but he likely spoke at least some Greek, as did many contemporary Jews in Palestine. Apparently Jesus was acquainted with the text of the LXX, as we note, for example, when he quoted from Isa 61 during his visit to the synagogue in Nazareth (Luke 4:16–19). The apostles and early Christians frequently quoted from the Septuagint rather than from the Hebrew text, thereby showing their lack of support for verbal inspiration.

The New Testament canon also developed gradually over several centuries. Early Christian communities recognized certain writings as inspired and therefore authoritative. The earliest New Testament writings that began to circulate were Paul's letters, dating from the fifth and sixth decades of the first century AD, which were addressed to churches in particular cities (Rome, Corinth, Ephesus, Thessaloniki, Philippi, and Colossae), regions (Galatia), and individuals (Timothy, Titus). The Gospels (Matthew, Mark, Luke, and John) followed soon afterward, besides some other writings that found their way into the New Testament: Acts, Revelation, and some short general epistles by Peter, John (possibly the apostle), and Jude.

Some of these New Testament parts were soon generally accepted, but doubts lingered for quite some time about the value of Hebrews, James, and Revelation. The Canon of Muratori (also called the Muratorian Fragment) is the earliest known list of New Testament books, dating from around the late second century (ca. AD 170–200). By the fourth century there was, however, almost complete consensus about the canon of the New Testament. We owe the first complete list of the New Testament books to the church father Athanasius (AD 367). The canon was affirmed by various fourth-century councils and soon further solidified. Thus the New Testament canon emerged through the recognition of apostolic origin, widespread church usage, and theological discernment, ensuring its role as Christian Scripture.

Besides the writings that became part of the Old Testament and the New Testament there is a collection of writings known as the *Apocrypha*. They did not become part of the Hebrew canon but, as already noted, did find their way into the Septuagint. They were written between 300 and 100 BC, during the intertestamental period, which was a crucial era for the development of Jewish thought and theology.

The following writings are usually included among the Apocrypha: 1 and 2 Esdras, Tobit, Judith, Wisdom of Solomon, Baruch, additions to Daniel, and additions to Esther. But the best known parts of the Apocrypha are probably 1 and 2 Maccabees, which give a historical account of the Jewish revolt against the Seleucid Empire (167–160 BC),[28] led by the Maccabees, and of the origin of the Hanukkah feast.[29]

The Roman Catholic Church confirmed the canonical status of the Apocrypha during the Council of Trent (1546). Besides the Eastern Orthodox churches and the Anglican Church, many Lutheran denominations and a few other Protestant churches (notably some Methodist groups) also added these writings to the sixty-six canonical books. Early Seventh-day Adventist leaders—among them Ellen G. White—sometimes quoted from the apocalyptic writings, in particular from 2 Esdras,[30] but refrained from doing so later on.[31]

How to Read the Bible

It is crucial that we not only give clear assent to the Protestant principle of *sola Scriptura* (the Bible alone) but that we also let this principle guide us in the *practice* of our theological enterprise. Protestants reject the Roman Catholic teaching that tradition must play an important role when we want to discover the meaning of Scripture.[32] The *sola Scriptura* principle discards this Catholic lens through which the Bible is supposedly to be viewed. However, Protestants must ask themselves how loyal they have historically been to this principle. (I already mentioned in the introduction of this

28. The Maccabees were a group of Jewish rebel warriors who took control of Judea, which at the time belonged to the Seleucid Empire, a part of the partitioned Greek empire that from 63 BC came under Roman rule.

29. Hanukkah is a Jewish festival commemorating the reconquest of Jerusalem and the subsequent rededication of the temple, at the beginning of the Maccabean revolt.

30. Ellen White wrote in 1849 that the Apocrypha were important and should be read carefully: "I saw that the Apocrypha was the hidden book, and that the wise of these last days should understand it." *Manuscript Releases*, 66. See further Graybill, *Visions and Revisions*, 35–36.

31. Korpman, "Brief History," 56–65.

32. Purgatory is a Catholic teaching that is not supported by the canonical Scriptures, but rests mainly on a passage in the second book of Maccabees (12:39–45).

book that many theologians have a problem in distancing themselves from creeds and confessional documents.) The *sola Scriptura* principle remains, as we shall see below, a very real challenge for Seventh-day Adventists in view of their high regard for the writings of Ellen G. White, in combination with their profession of total loyalty to the Protestant principle that all theology must be fully based on the Scriptures.

Linked with the *sola Scriptura* principle is that of *tota Scriptura*. This concept stresses that not just selected parts, but the entire Bible must be considered in our theological interpretations. This implies that doctrinal statements must not be based on isolated passages, using a pick-and-choose method, but on the full biblical witness. Does this mean that all parts of the Bible have the same degree of relevance for our spiritual life? The reality seems to be that most Christians recognize a personal canon within the canon of the Bible. For them the four Gospels tend to be more meaningful than the Old Testament narratives about the warfare between Israel and its neighbors, and the Pauline letters seem to have greater significance than, for instance, the laws concerning ritual purity and the various genealogies. This preference for certain parts of the Bible is a rather general phenomenon. But in developing a doctrine or forming a solid opinion on a particular topic, we must make sure that we are not selective in where in the Bible we search for support or clarification.

Bible readers do well to read complete sections of the Bible, rather than engage in a form of Bible study that jumps back and forth from one text to the other and combines statements without sufficient consideration for their context. Reading *about* the Bible, to learn more about the historical and cultural context of the different parts of Scripture, or even learning Hebrew and biblical Greek, is very helpful, but it should not replace the actual—regular and systematic—reading of the Bible itself. Since Reformation times, Protestants have firmly believed that every person, with or without formal theological training, can benefit from reading the word of God. They have stressed that the same Spirit who "carried" the authors "along," is also at work when people open their Bibles with the intense desire to be spiritually blessed. After Jesus's ascension, God gave the Holy Spirit to compensate for the loss of Jesus's actual presence. Referring to this, Jesus said the Spirit "will teach you all things and will remind you of everything I have said to you" (John 14:26). This Spirit, Paul declared, "is from God, so that we may understand what God has freely given us." The Spirit explains "spiritual realities with Spirit-taught words" (1 Cor 2:12–13).

Interpretation

Many theologians have claimed that the Bible must be its own interpreter. Martin Luther (1483–1546) was adamant: "*Scriptura sui ipsius interpres*" (Scripture is its own interpreter).[33] Rejecting allegorical interpretations of the Bible, John Calvin (1509–1564) wrote in the preface to his *Commentary on Genesis*, "Let us know that the true meaning of Scripture is the natural and obvious one and let us embrace and abide by it resolutely."[34] Following in Calvin's footsteps the Dutch Reformed theologian G. C. Berkouwer stated, "Scripture interprets itself not because of some external methodological principle, but because of its divine origin and unity."[35] William Miller (1782–1849), the leader of the Millerite movement, determined that he would not consult any other books except his concordance, since the Bible must interpret itself.[36]

Progressive Revelation

But, in allowing Scripture to interpret itself, we must take into consideration that the Bible displays *progressive revelation*. This is the term for the theological concept that God has revealed his will and character, and his redemptive plan, *gradually* rather than all at once. This idea acknowledges that God's revelation to humanity is unfolded step by step, often in response to historical circumstances and a growing human understanding. Subsequent revelation clarifies, expands, and sometimes even reinterprets earlier revelations. God's revelation in Christ is the ultimate way in which God revealed himself (Heb 11:1–2).

The plan of salvation at first lacked many details that were later revealed. Immediately after the fall God promised that he would restore what had been lost (Gen 3:15), but next to nothing was said about how he would do this. God's covenant with Abraham (Gen 12:1–3) was foundational, but its implications were not fully understood until later. The

33. Luther, *De servo arbitrio*, 606.

34. Calvin, *Commentary on Genesis*, 79.

35. Berkouwer, *Holy Scripture*, 307.

36. Knight, *Millennial Fever*, 35, 36.

detailed legal and sacrificial system, described at length in the Old Testament, prefigured what Christ would eventually accomplish. That is why Paul interpreted the Law as a "guardian" leading to Christ (Gal 3:24), showing that earlier laws were part of a progressive revelation pointing to Jesus. Linked with this, we see how the understanding of the coming of the Messiah developed over time.

The progressive nature of the biblical revelation was also clearly seen in its teachings about the nature of death. Early texts speak of the Sheol as a shadowy underworld (Eccl 9:10; Job 7:9–10). Later prophetic writings more clearly introduce the hope of a resurrection (Dan 12:2), which reaches full clarity in the New Testament with Jesus's resurrection and Paul's teaching on eternal life (1 Cor 15).

Our Bible reading must be Christocentric. The culmination of God's revelation is found on Calvary and in the coming of the Spirit. This must always be in the back of our minds as we read about God's dealings with his people and with humanity.

We must never lose sight of the fact that the Bible writers were humans who lived in a particular era and were part of a particular culture and social context. This critical fact must guide us, especially when we try to find answers to the ethical questions that confront us in the twenty-first century. Those who adhere to a theory of verbal inspiration and are blind to the clear evidence of the progressive nature of divine inspiration are often inclined to apply the customs and norms of Old Testament times one-on-one to today's situation. They tend to ignore that our present context and current challenges are in many cases very different from what people experienced in Bible times. The fact that times have changed makes it necessary to search for the underlying principles that may guide us even today when we deal with the status of women and various gender issues, and with the difficult questions surrounding both the beginning and the end of life, as well as a range of social, legal, and economic aspects of (post)modern life. Or, to put it in one single, but all-embracing, statement: *We must read and interpret all Old Testament directives from the perspective of Jesus's Sermon on the Mount.*

Much in the Bible deals with *history*. However, when reading the historical sections of the Bible, several features need to be factored in. The first eleven chapters of Genesis cover an extremely long time and deal with events that are beyond "normal" historical research. These narratives (about the creation, the fall, the lists of individuals with extremely long lives, the "table of nations," the tower of Babel, and the flood) are often referred to as *protohistory*, which, many believe, contain profound theological messages rather than historical facts. To mention another point, some parts of the Bible are duplicates. They report history from different perspectives and are, therefore, bound to show some differences. An example of this is the parallel reporting in 1 and 2 Chronicles and the books of Samuel and 1 and 2 Kings. We also note that in the narratives of the reigns of the kings of Judah and Israel the amount of attention given by the author(s) mostly depends on whether a king did what was "right" or what was "evil" in "the eyes of the Lord" (e.g., 1 Kgs 15:11; 2 Chr 17:3–4; 2 Kgs 18:3, 6; as opposed to 1 Kgs 14:8; 16:30–33; 2 Kgs 24:19–20).

The authors of biblical histories "exercised a great deal of freedom in the organization, revision and invention of materials to render an account of their national past."[37] However, the most important characteristic of biblical history is that the Bible presents us with *the story of salvation*. It is a story of a drama that, as far as human involvement is concerned, plays out in actual history. But it is not written as the kind of history that we encounter in ordinary history books. It is history that is written and edited from a particular perspective. It is *salvation history*.

Plurality of Interpretations

How do we reconcile the belief of men like Luther and Calvin, that the Bible must be its own interpreter, with the undeniable reality that there is an enormous plurality of interpretations of the Bible, leading to a multitude of doctrinal differences between theologians and denominational entities?

Friedrich Schleiermacher (1768–1834), whom we mentioned earlier, was a noteworthy figure in the transition from modernity to postmodernity. He suggested that students of the Bible should take a new look at the methods they use. Many Bible scholars who were Schleiermacher's contemporaries focused on such questions as: What do the Hebrew and Greek words mean? What do we know of the literary structure of the text? How was the text transmitted to us? Schleiermacher argued that this was largely missing the point. The crucial issue is how do we get *behind* the text? The question is not primarily what did

37. McKenzie, *How to Read the Bible*, 46.

the original author mean when he wrote his words but how can what the author wrote so many centuries ago still be relevant for me today? So, the primary question is not what did the text *originally* mean but, rather, what does the text mean *today*, for *me*?

Other, later, authors also wrestled with this issue. Wilhelm Dilthey (1833–1911), a German historian, psychologist, and sociologist, emphasized that our understanding of a text can never be complete. We read it, not as it was originally written, but against the horizon of history. We can therefore never claim that we have fathomed the full meaning. We must be content with our *interpretation*. We read, and we try to understand what it once meant. But then we have the job of *interpreting* it in such a way that the people of today can grasp what it says for them in their own present world.

More recently, men like the German philosopher Hans Gadamer (1900–2002) and the French Protestant theologian and philosopher Paul Ricoeur (1913–2005) expressed themselves in similar veins. Gadamer stressed the role of later interpreters. He speaks of a fusion of the horizon of the original author with that of the interpreter. The meaning of the text is not exhausted by what the author intended to say but emerges in the dialogue with the interpreter. Paul Ricoeur, likewise, paid ample attention to questions of hermeneutics (the science of interpreting a text). Although he is more positive than many of his colleagues in his field about our human ability to arrive at the essential meaning of a text, he also warns that much humility is needed, since we face serious obstacles and limitations.

These and other authors prepared us for the postmodern notion that in dealing with texts, *it is all about interpretation*. In fact, some would argue that there are as many interpretations as there are readers. A statement to that effect is often attributed to Stanley Fish (b. 1938), an important literary theorist, who argued that meaning is not inherent in a text but is constructed by readers within a community who share certain convictions. The well-known postmodern philosopher Jacques Derrida (1934–2004) held a very similar view.

Although the approach of the persons I refer to above (and that of many others) points to some important features that have often received insufficient attention, it does not follow that all interpretations are equally correct or defensible. Common sense tells us that the very fact that many of these interpretations contradict each other indicates that not all of them can simultaneously be true. But it does eliminate the idea of a "plain reading" that supposedly will lead every honest reader to the same conclusions.[38]

Hermeneutics

In biblical and theological studies attention has, in a significant measure, shifted from historical-critical concerns (about the origin, sources, and transmission of the biblical text) to a focus on the meaning of the text as we have it before us. The current trend is to read the Bible as a theological and literary whole, concentrating on its message rather than primarily analyzing its origins. The theory, principles, and methodology of the interpretation of texts—in particular of the *biblical* text—is called *hermeneutics*. (It is closely related to *exegesis*, which is the actual practice of interpreting a specific text and applying the hermeneutical principles.)

A fundamental concept in hermeneutics is the so-called hermeneutical circle. The term was probably first used by Schleiermacher, though the concept itself has a longer history and was further developed by him and others. The hermeneutical circle holds that understanding a text arises through a reciprocal movement between the parts and the whole: individual words and sentences are interpreted in light of the broader context of the text, its historical background, and its purpose, while this broader understanding is continually revised through closer attention to the text's components.[39] This approach challenges the notion of absolute objectivity but is widely accepted as the best way to determine the meaning of a text for the reader in our time.

The presence of an element of subjectivity is not an obstacle to a meaningful engagement with the Bible, but rather a positive element that makes Bible reading not only a beneficial communal practice but also a very personal spiritual experience, as it allows Scripture to speak to us in our present individual situation. This, inevitably, affects our theological projects. The Dutch theologian and missiologist Stefan Paas (b. 1969) maintains that theology is always, at least to some extent, autobiographical.

38. The concept of plain reading has, in recent times, frequently been used by some top Seventh-day Adventist leaders in support of a rather fundamentalist approach to the Bible, which would point to a recent literal, six-day creation and a recent, global flood.

39. For a balanced description of the hermeneutical circle, see Grondin, *Introduction to Philosophical Hermeneutics*,140–90.

The good news of the gospel is that God comes to us and reveals himself to each one of us. Paas argues that God can only meet us in the domain of our own experience, since every religious experience is received through our social, cultural, and religious conditioning. "We meet God as cultural beings, in and with and under our experiences."[40] This, Paas further opines, implies that we always read the Bible through our own lens. (For me this means that I must realize that I inevitably read the Bible as an elderly white male, through the lens of my specific Adventist and Dutch background.) Many downplay this inevitability and insist that we must do away with our personal lens or, at the very least, carefully clean it, so that our vision is not clouded by any dirt and dust that has stuck to it as we journeyed along. Metaphors, of course, always have their limitations. To what extent we can adjust the focus of our lens, change its color, or find an effective cleaning agent for it, will remain open to debate. I strongly believe that one critical point is not subject to any doubt: *We cannot at will completely do away with our lens.* A lot of misunderstanding, even controversy and misery, has resulted from an inability or unwillingness to accept this fact. Insisting that we must—and can—do away with our personal lens, or must all look through an identical lens, which is provided by a particular theological current or a corpus of denominational leaders, carries the danger that a faith community is transformed into a cult, rather than functioning as a living organism.

In his intriguing book *Reading the Bible from the Margins*, liberation theologian Miguel A. De La Torre (b. 1968) takes this point a little further, in a direction that really hits home.[41] How we read the Bible, he says, is also greatly influenced by our socioeconomic status. Traditional (mostly Western) interpretations tend to reflect the prejudices of people in power who want to justify their privileges and often maintain systems of oppression, while marginalized groups in society are more likely to see how the Bible stresses God's interest in justice and liberation.

God Revealed in Christ

Having looked at God's special revelation in his written word, we now return again to the foundational passage about God's revelation at the beginning of the book of Hebrews: "In the past God spoke to our ancestors

40. Paas, *Vrede op Aarde*, 36; my translation.

41. De La Torre, *Reading the Bible*.

through the prophets at many times and in various ways, but *in these last days he has spoken to us by his Son*, whom he appointed heir of all things, and through whom also he made the universe" (1:1–2; italics added).

Christians believe Jesus is God's ultimate revelation, because he is God in human form. His life, teachings, death, and resurrection reveal God's character—his love—in a way that surpasses all previous revelations. In a discussion with the disciples Jesus told them that he would leave them and go to his Father's house, but would come again, Philip asked him to reveal the Father to them. Jesus told the disciples that they had in fact already seen the Father: "Anyone who has seen me has seen the Father" (John 14:9). Thus, *to see Christ is to see God*. If we want to know how God really is, we must realize that we see God's love, his sense of justice, his readiness to forgive, and his attention for people in all categories, reflected in the person and ministry of Jesus. "To have genuine knowledge of God, we must begin with the norm of all knowledge of God; from a Christian perspective such knowledge is exclusively the revelation in Christ."[42] In Christianity, Jesus Christ is seen as the culmination and fullness of this revelation. He is the very embodiment of God.

The apostle Paul underlined this conviction in one of the most profound Christological statements in the New Testament:

> The Son is the image of the invisible God, the firstborn over all creation. For in him all things were created: things in heaven and on earth, visible and invisible, whether thrones or powers or rulers or authorities; all things have been created through him and for him. He is before all things, and in him all things hold together. And he is the head of the body, the church; he is the beginning and the firstborn from among the dead, so that in everything he might have the supremacy. For God was pleased to have all his fullness dwell in him. (Col 1:15–19)

And this is further reinforced in the introduction to the Gospel of John: "The Word became flesh and made his dwelling among us. We have seen his glory, the glory of the one and only Son, who came from the Father, full of grace and truth" (John 1:14).

In chapter 3 we will further explore how we must understand that Jesus, through his incarnation, became fully man and how his humanity, though real, did not diminish his deity. But because his divine glory was

42. Van der Kooi and Van den Brink, *Christian Dogmatics*, 188.

shrouded by his humanness, we can become recipients of this culmination of God's special revelation.

The Spirit of Prophecy

In a book about Adventist theology the section about revelation cannot ignore that Seventh-day Adventists, while claiming to fully adhere to the Protestant principle of *sola Scriptura*, recognize another source of inspiration—namely, the writings of Mrs. Ellen G. White. Her voluminous literary production is held in high esteem by most Adventists, but there has, to my knowledge, never been any suggestion that any of her writings should be added to the canon.

Adventists point to the fact that the Bible mentions prophets who did not leave writings that became part of the canon, and also that there were several women among these prophetic voices. They further state that the gift of prophecy would re-emerge towards the end of time (Joel 2:28–29) and that among end-time believers the "spirit of prophecy" (Rev 19:10) would be manifested in a special way. This, they maintain, was realized in the ministry of Ellen White. She grew up in a segment of Methodism in which prophetic phenomena were quite common,[43] and her visionary experiences were soon recognized as divine revelations.

The current text of number eighteen of the Fundamental Beliefs of the Adventist Church reads as follows:

> One of the gifts of the Holy Spirit is prophecy. This gift is an identifying mark of the remnant church and was manifested in the ministry of Ellen G. White. As the Lord's messenger, her writings are a continuing and authoritative source of truth which provide comfort, guidance, instruction, and correction to the church. They also make clear that the Bible is the standard by which all teaching and experience must be tested (Joel 2:28, 29; Acts 2:14–21; Heb 1:1–3; Rev 12:17; 19:10).

The wording of this fundamental belief attempts to maintain a precarious balance between upholding the Bible as "the standard by which all teaching and experience must be tested" and defining the writings of Ellen White as a "continuing and authoritative source of truth."

Adventist historians confirm that the role of Ellen White in the development of Adventist doctrines has been limited, and that she called

43. Taves, *Fits, Trances & Visions*, 71–117, 158–61.

herself a "lesser light" that pointed to the "greater light" of the Bible.[44] But in reality, for many Adventists the words of Ellen White are decisive for their interpretations of biblical passages, for their approach to organizational and ethical issues, and for most aspects of their daily lives. In sermons quotes from "the spirit of prophecy" may at times be more numerous than references to the Bible. From the 1930s onward Ellen White was placed by many on a pedestal in a way she herself would most probably have objected to. The influence of Ellen White was enhanced by the publication of a range of compilations in which her statements about specific issues were published, often without proper regard for their historical context.

From early on views about the inspiration of Ellen White were diverse, and in recent decades they have become an area of strong polarization.[45] Recurrent accusations about plagiarism were downplayed by the custodians of the writings of Ellen White. But from the 1960s and 1970s onward, gradually reports about a high dependency on other authors, and about the rather extensive role of literary assistants, have caused increasing doubt about many of the claims that were traditionally made about the nature of her work. The forceful promotion of her books by the church, especially of *The Great Controversy*, has led to fierce internal disputes.

For a significant segment of the Adventist global community the discovery of many all-too-human aspects of Ellen White's ministry has done little to diminish the appreciation for her writings. They continue to see her voice as authoritative and of great relevance. Others pay, at most, lip service to her opinions and have but little regard for the legacy that Ellen White left to the church. It is difficult to project how support for the view of Ellen White as an inspired prophet—in whatever way this inspiration is defined—will develop, and how it will continue to relate to the *sola Scriptura* principle that the Adventist Church has always claimed to embrace. It remains to be seen whether ultimately the status of Ellen White within Adventism will become more like that of the founders of other denominations, as for instance Martin Luther, John Calvin, or John Wesley. Their writings are still held in high esteem by the members of the church bodies that see them as their spiritual

44. White, "Signal of Advance"; *Selected Messages*, 3:30.

45. In recent decades many books on this topic have been published. Among the most noteworthy are: Aamodt et al., *Ellen Harmon White*; McAdams, *Ellen White*; Knight, *Ellen White's Afterlife*; and Anderson, *Reclaiming the Prophet*.

forebears without, however, regarding them as inspired, as official Adventist teaching claims for Ellen White.

One thing is, it seems to me, a pressing responsibility for the leadership of the church. Numerous issues have been raised, as time has gone by (and especially in recent decades), about Ellen White's private life and about aspects of her ministry, some even claiming that she was deceitful in the way she presented herself and in her description of how the content of her messages was revealed to her.[46] She has been described as being at times quite manipulative in her dealings with church leaders,[47] and it was revealed that, when she died, she left a considerable debt to be sorted out by her heirs and the church's leadership.[48] As I have tried to follow various publications, I have concluded that many attacks on Ellen White have been needlessly aggressive and often rather selective in the arguments that are presented. Yet, there are many questions that cannot be ignored and need honest answers. If those answers are not given, the confidence of many church members in the continuing relevance of Ellen White's writings will be seriously undermined, and many may even decide that they no longer want to be part of a denomination that is unwilling to be transparent about such an important aspect of its identity.

Having discussed at some length the various aspects of general revelation and of God's special modes of revelation, we will now, in the next chapter, turn to the foundational question of what has been revealed about the *One*, whom Christians recognize as the *triune* God of Father, Son, and Holy Spirit.

46. Daily, *Ellen G. White.*

47. Valentine, *Prophet and the Presidents.*

48. Valentine, *Struggle for Prophetic Heritage.*

Chapter 2

The Triune God

FROM TIME IMMEMORIAL, PEOPLE have worshiped a range of deities. The Greeks had their gods on Mount Olympus, including Zeus, Hera, Poseidon, Hades, Athena, Apollo, Artemis, and Aphrodite. Influenced by the Greeks, the Romans developed their own pantheon, with gods such as Jupiter, Juno, Neptune, Venus, and many others. The Egyptian pantheon was dominated by gods like Ra, Osiris, Isis, and Anubis. Even today, the English names of the days of the week reflect the deities of early Germanic peoples: Tuesday is named after Tyr, the Germanic god of war; Wednesday after the chief Germanic god Woden (or Odin), the god of wisdom and knowledge; Thursday after Thor, the god of thunder; and Friday after Freyja, the goddess associated with love and fertility. In the present day, more than a billion Hindus worship Brahma, Vishnu, and Shiva, along with thousands of other gods.

In addition to polytheistic religions in past and present, the world's three major monotheistic religions—more precisely called Abrahamic religions—are Judaism, Christianity, and Islam. In Judaism, the oldest of these three, monotheism gradually emerged from an earlier stage of monolatry (the worship of one god while recognizing the existence of others) to pure monotheism. In early Israelite religion, the existence of other gods was acknowledged, while Yahweh was regarded as the national deity. During the time of the judges and the early kings, Israelite religion often coexisted with the worship of Canaanite deities such as Baal and

Asherah. The first major shift towards exclusive monotheism appeared in the reforms of King Josiah (seventh century BC), which centralized the worship of Yahweh in the Jerusalem temple. During and after the Babylonian captivity in the sixth century BC, a deeper understanding of Yahweh as the sole, universal God became central to Jewish religious thought. The Shema became the defining statement of Jewish faith: "Hear, O Israel: The Lord our God, the Lord is one" (Deut 6:4).

The word *Shema* is Hebrew for "hear," and it became the name for the prayer that begins with this word. According to most scholars it was written in the seventh century BC. The Shema affirms the absolute oneness of God, which became the central tenet of the Jewish faith. The verse that follows in Deut 6 commands loving God with all one's heart, soul, and strength. Observant Jews recite the Shema in their morning and evening prayers and place the words of the Shema, written on parchment, inside a mezuzah (a small case affixed to the doorpost) and in the tefillin (small black leather boxes with straps, containing scrolls of parchment inscribed with these words from the Torah).

God Has a Name

Names are important in the Bible, and it should therefore not surprise us that God also has a name. In fact, he has a range of different names. The word *god* is not a proper name but a general designation for a higher power. It corresponds to the Hebrew words *El* and the plural *Elohim*, which occur about two hundred and twenty-five hundred times, respectively, in the Old Testament, and to the Greek word *theos*, from which our term *theology* is derived. The word *El* can stand alone, but it is often linked to one of several other terms, thereby forming various proper names. For example, God is referred to as *El-Roi*, "the God who sees" (Gen 16:13), or *El-Shaddai*, "God the Almighty" or "God the Awesome" (Gen 17:1). Also, the term *Adonai* (Lord), although not a proper name like *Yahweh*, is often used to emphasize the sovereignty of God.

We must turn to the story of Moses to learn more about God's name. When God called Moses to go on his behalf to the Egyptian Pharaoh, Moses was far from eager to accept that assignment. What happened next is recorded in this passage:

> Moses said to God, "Who am I that I should go to Pharaoh and bring the Israelites out of Egypt?"

> And God said, "I will be with you. And this will be the sign to you that it is I who have sent you: When you have brought the people out of Egypt, you will worship God on this mountain."
>
> Moses said to God, "Suppose I go to the Israelites and say to them, 'The God of your fathers has sent me to you,' and they ask me, 'What is his name?' Then what shall I tell them?"
>
> God said to Moses, "I AM WHO I AM. This is what you are to say to the Israelites: 'I AM has sent me to you.'"
>
> God also said to Moses, "Say to the Israelites, 'The LORD, the God of your fathers—the God of Abraham, the God of Isaac, and the God of Jacob—has sent me to you.' This is my name forever, the name you shall call me from generation to generation." (Exod 3:11–15)

Those reading this story for the first time may find this a rather enigmatic answer to Moses's question about God's identity. Moses desperately wants to know on whose behalf he is to go to Pharaoh. God tells Moses to say to the ruler of Egypt, "I AM has sent me to you." Later, God adds, "The LORD [YHWH], the God of your fathers, has sent me to you." The word *LORD* is a rendering of YHWH—a form of the Hebrew verb "to be," suggesting "I AM" or "I WILL BE." In Hebrew, this name carries present and future nuances.

The name Yahweh, which appears more than five thousand times in the Bible, is based on this verb from Exod 3:14. Because Hebrew was originally written without vowels, this name was spelled YHWH—the four letters commonly referred to as the *tetragrammaton* (literally, "four letters"). Out of deep respect for God's holy name, people in Old Testament times avoided pronouncing it. When they came to God's name in the Scriptures, they replaced Yahweh with Adonai (Lord). In the Middle Ages, scribes added vowels to the Hebrew consonants, combining the vowels of Adonai with YHWH (YaHoWaiH). This is how we got Jehovah.

Commenting on the biblical book of Exodus, Old Testament scholar Jon Dybdahl (1942–2023) emphasized that God was not trying to play with words, or to give an evasive answer, when he called himself the *I AM*. There was too much at stake for that. Nor did God intend to define his divine being, or his eternal existence. By calling himself "I AM" or "I WILL BE THERE," God emphasized that he would always be there for his people as their almighty protector.[1] "You are never alone. You can always count

1. Dybdahl, *Exodus*, 55–56.

on me—now and in the future." That name gave Moses the courage to go to the Pharaoh. That name still also tells us, "I am all that you need, and all that the world needs," or, to use the famous expression of the German American theologian Paul Tillich (1886–1965), I am the Ground of your Being, on which everything in the universe depends.[2]

Israel believed that this God was the Creator of everything, as the author of the first chapter of Genesis affirms in its opening verse: "In the beginning God created the heaven and the earth" (Gen 1:1). This belief is repeated in the heart of the Ten Commandments: "For in six days the Lord made the heavens and the earth, the sea, and all that is in them" (Exod 20:11). Numerous other passages in the Old Testament echo the deep conviction that God is the Maker of everything, as for instance in the Bible book Isaiah: "Do you not know? Have you not heard? The Lord is the everlasting God, the Creator of the ends of the earth" (Isa 40:28).

Israel also saw their Creator-God as their permanent Sustainer, as is expressed in several psalms that are attributed to King David: "Cast your cares on the Lord and he will sustain you; he will never let the righteous be shaken" (Ps 55:22). "Surely, God is my help; the Lord is the one who sustains me" (Ps 54:4). And in the Bible book of Isaiah we read, "Even to your old age and gray hairs I am he, I am he who will sustain you. I have made you and I will carry you; I will sustain you and I will rescue you" (Isa 46:4).

Yahweh was also recognized by the people of Israel as their lawgiver: "For the Lord is our judge, the Lord is our lawgiver, the Lord is our king; he will save us" (Isa 33:22). And he was, above all, the God who had made a covenant with his people, guaranteeing them his constant care and protection. God's promise to Abraham about his enduring commitment to being the God for all his descendants, remained a foundational theme throughout Old Testament history: "I will establish my covenant as an everlasting covenant between me and you and your descendants after you for the generations to come, to be your God and the God of your descendants after you" (Gen 17:7).

Speaking About the Christian God

The God of the Old Testament believers is also the God of the Christians. Since the birth of the church the Christian believers and their

2. Tillich, *Systematic Theology*, vol. 1, in Bruinsma, *Our Awesome God*, 86–88.

leaders have been anxious to become better acquainted with their God. Who and what God is became the foundational question of all theology. But repeatedly, Christian voices stressed that it is, in fact, impossible to give a fully satisfying description of God. These voices referred to what is called the *ineffability* of God. This is the idea that God is far beyond human comprehension, and that, therefore, human words will always be inadequate to describe God.

This concept of the ineffability of God is found in many religious and philosophical traditions and suggests that any attempt to define God with human words will fall short. God, it is argued, exists beyond space, time, and human experience, which makes direct knowledge impossible. In line with this, many theologians (and, in particular, mystics) have opted for a "negative theology" (in Latin, the *via negativa*). Instead of saying what God *is*, this approach defines God by what he *is not*.

Others disagree with this premise that we can say nothing substantial about God. The Roman Catholic cardinal Henri de Lubac (1896–1991) stated this in no uncertain terms when he said, "Nothing is worse than a premature 'negative theology.'" And he added, "The ineffability of God is only another name for the absolute transcendence." We must do what we can to say something about our God. "Silence comes at the end—not at the beginning."[3]

We have enough reason to reject the proposition that we can say nothing about God, since, as we saw in the previous chapter, God did reveal himself in various ways. However, having said this, we should always keep in mind that God can never be brought down to our level. To quote Cardinal de Lubac once more, a God "whose thoughts are our thoughts and whose ways are our ways: such a God has proved useless in practice and has become the object of justified ressentiment."[4]

Christians believe that God is "above" the world and "other" than the world. Our priority is to discover how he *relates* to the world.[5] When we speak about God, our words do not have the exact same meaning as when we apply these words to our human environment. But saying that our words are meaningless when applied to God would also imply that God's written word is void of any revelation. When we speak of God, we use *analogical* language. That is, our words point to a *similarity* between

3. Lubac, *Discovery of God*, 121.

4. Lubac, *Discovery of God*, 176.

5. Vick, *Speaking Well of God*, 82.

our own world and God's world. We can say something about God because creation reflects him (*analogia entis*, the analogy of being), but we must always remember the infinite distance between God and us. This avoids the extremes of making God too human (too anthropomorphic) or making him so unknowable that we cannot talk about him at all.

In our speaking about God and his relationship with us, we follow the Scriptures in using many different metaphors that do provide symbolic rather than literal information. Metaphors reveal something, without providing us with a full picture. Saying that God is a rock (Ps 18:2) does not mean that God is an object of stone, but it emphasizes his stability, strength, and reliability. Referring to God as a shepherd (for instance in Ps 23) suggests guidance and protection, rather than implying that God has herds of actual sheep.

In his love for human beings, God stooped down to our level. He did so in the most complete and ultimate way in the incarnation of Jesus Christ, when he became flesh and lived among us (John 1:14). This accommodation is also seen in the multitude of metaphors that the Bible uses in connection with God.[6] Numerous metaphors describe God's physical characteristics. He is said to have a voice (John 5:37), eyes (Ps 11:4), a mouth (Deut 8:3), an arm (Exod 15:16), a heart (Gen 6:6), and several other physical parts. Of course, these descriptions are not literal. Jesus told the Samaritan woman at the well that God is Spirit (John 4:24).

There is a tension between these metaphorical depictions and the divine attribute of omnipresence. Nonetheless, these anthropomorphic characteristics tell us something about God's power and majesty, and about his nearness and his desire to relate to us. These same characteristics are also seen in the many texts that express God's emotions. Like humans, God rejoices (Isa 62:5; 65:19), but he also sorrows (Ps 78:40), and can be provoked (Jer 7:18–19). Above all, he loves his creatures and is compassionate. Moses encountered the Lord, who is the "compassionate and gracious God, slow to anger, abounding in love and faithfulness" (Exod 34:6). Dozens of different verbs describe God's activities. These are just a few examples: he investigates (Gen 18:21), he forgets (1 Sam 1:11), he smells (Gen 8:21), he heals (Ps 103:3), and he cleanses (Ps 51:2).

In addition, there are many other metaphorical descriptions of God. He is likened to a bridegroom (Isa 61:10), a husband (Isa 54:5–6), a warrior (Exod 15:3), and is linked to many different occupations.

6. See Gulley, *God as Trinity*, 56–60.

Other descriptions are taken from nature. God is also compared to a lion (Isa 31:4), a torch (Rev 21:23), a shadow (Ps 91:1), and so on. All of these metaphors help us to get some glimpses of who God is and what kind of God he is for us.

Many of these metaphors refer to God as *male*. In our speaking about God we tend to follow the biblical convention of using the pronouns *he*, *him*, and *his*. Also in this respect, however, we must realize that this reflects our human limitations when describing God. Feminist theologians make an important point when they tell us that our speaking of God often reflects a male bias.[7] They rightly emphasize that the Bible at times also employs female images of God. Isaiah 49:15 refers to God as a woman tenderly breastfeeding her infant. In Ps 123:2 God is portrayed as the chief woman of a household, and in Luke 15:8–10 as a woman sweeping the floor in search of a lost coin.[8]

Our Father

No metaphor about God is as well-known as that of "Father." When we pray the Lord's Prayer (Matt 6:9–13), we begin by addressing God as "our Father in heaven." In Old Testament times people were quite reticent in calling God their father. As a rule, in the ancient world people worshiped a large number of gods and goddesses who had all kinds of interrelationships and could reproduce enthusiastically. They had a mother or father role in a way that resembled sexual relationships in the human world. The God of Israel, however, was quite different, Nevertheless, he is occasionally referred to as "father." In Exod 4, we read—as we saw already above—how Moses had to tell the king of Egypt to free the people of Israel from their captivity. Moses here speaks on behalf of the Father-God about Israel as God's son. Isaiah 64:8 is another example in the Old Testament where God is presented as a father: "Yet, you Lord, are our Father. We are the clay, you are the potter; we are all the work of your hand." It is abundantly clear that this is symbolic language. We are not literally clay, but are moldable as clay in God's hands. God is not a literal father, but he is compared to an ideal human father, full of care for his children. This is

7. See the chapter on feminist theology in Smith, *Handbook of Contemporary Theology*, 241–58.

8. Smith, *Handbook of Contemporary Theology*, 249–50.

what is also emphasized in Ps 103:13: "As a father has compassion on his children, so the Lord has compassion on those who fear him."

In the New Testament, God's fatherhood is emphasized much more strongly. The apostle Paul wrote to the believers in the city of Rome that they are children of God if they are led by the Spirit. "The Spirit you received brought about your adoption to sonship. And by him we cry, 'Abba, Father'" (Rom 8:14–15). Paul repeats this in his letter to the Christians in Galatia: God "sent the Spirit of his Son into our hearts, the Spirit who calls out 'Abba, Father.' So now you are no longer a slave, but God's child; and since you are his child, God has also made you a heir" (Gal 4:6–7). Shortly before his death on the cross, Jesus used the same words when he prayed that, "if possible," this hour might pass from him: "Abba, Father . . . take this cup away from me" (Mark 14:35–36).

Abba is the word for "father" in the Aramaic language. Aramaic is a sister language of Hebrew that was long used as the primary language in large parts of the Middle East. Jesus spoke Aramaic. Over time, the New Testament took shape in the Greek language, but experts have done their best to verify what Jesus might originally have said when he spoke to people in Aramaic. When he instructed his disciples how to pray, he began with the words "Our Abba!" It was an intimate phrase to characterize the special bond between God and man. It is actually quite unimaginable that we may address the Ruler of the universe as such. There is no reason for fear or uncertainty. He is there for us, just as an earthly father—that is, someone who indeed deserves the appellation *father*—is expected to always be there for his children. But "Abba" emphasizes not only *intimacy*, but also the aspect of *obedience*. We do well to read the paragraph in Rom 8, where Paul uses the word *Abba*, in its entirety:

> Therefore, brothers and sisters, we have an obligation—but it is not to the flesh, to live according to it. For if you live according to the flesh, you will die; but if by the Spirit you put to death the misdeeds of the body, you will live. For those who are led by the Spirit of God are the children of God. The Spirit you received does not make you slaves, so that you live in fear again; rather, the Spirit you received brought about your adoption to sonship. And by him we cry, "Abba, Father." The Spirit himself testifies with our spirit that we are God's children. Now if we are children, then we are heirs—heirs of God and co-heirs with Christ, if indeed we share in his sufferings in order that we may also share in his glory. (vv. 12–17)

There are people for whom referring to God as Father feels uncomfortable, since they have experiences with a human father that were extremely unpleasant. It has been suggested that it might therefore be better to refer to God as Mother. But the same objection applies, for not all human mothers are loving and caring. In calling God our Father, we recognize that no human parent can match the love and constant care of the heavenly Father, but there are, fortunately, many fathers who do, to some extent, reflect the fatherhood of God.

Many people find it difficult to confidently answer yes to the question whether they are indeed a true child of God. However, we must have the confidence that we can address God without hesitation as "our Abba." John's first letter is very clear: we are called "children of God and that is what we are" (3:1). "Now we are children of God" (3:2).

The Lord's Prayer does not begin with "*my* Father." This is because the title "*my* Father" is uniquely reserved for Jesus. He is the only one who can say "my" Father without any qualifications. God is "*our*" Father—that is, he is the Father of all his children, who are equally dear to him. Again, we must remember, the word *father* is a human word we use, for lack of a better one, to signify the unspeakably close relationship between God and us.

Where Is God?

One of the Christian beliefs about God is that he is not confined to any space, but that he is *omnipresent*. That God is everywhere does not imply that God is identical with all that exists, and that there is no distinction between the divine and the cosmos, as supporters of pantheism maintain. King David was aware of God's omnipresence, as we read in these poetic words: "Where can I flee from your presence? If I go up to the heavens, you are there; if I make my bed in the depths, you are there. If I rise on the wings of the dawn, if I settle on the far side of the sea, even there your hand will guide me, your right hand will hold me fast" (Ps 139:7–10). Jeremiah echoes the same message: "'Am I only a God nearby,' declares the Lord, 'and not a God far away? Who can hide in secret places so that I cannot see them?' declares the Lord. 'Do I not fill heaven and earth?' declares the Lord?" (23:23–24).

Our Father is "in heaven" or "in the heavens." When we say those words as we pray the Lord's Prayer, we must remember that time and space are categories that belong to our earthly reality. God is not bound to any particular location, for even the entire universe cannot contain him (1 Kgs 8:27). King Solomon was aware of this when he prayed at the dedication of the temple he had built. God wanted to come and dwell in that temple, but this was not to be understood in a literal sense. Solomon realized that God cannot be confined to a particular locale.

Yet, the Bible often refers to heaven as the *place* where God has his habitat. This raises the question where and what this heaven is. Already in the first verse of the Bible we read about heaven: "In the beginning God created the heavens and the earth" (Gen 1:1). In Old Testament thinking, man lives on a flat earth. The "waters" are below the surface of the earth and the heavens are above it. God, we read in the creation story, separated "the waters" below the earth from those above it, and the "vault" of waters above the earth he called "sky" (Gen 1:8). In this layered universe, heaven (or sky) is first and foremost the atmosphere; above it is the space where the heavenly bodies move in their orbits. Far above that is the place where God "dwells." The apostle Paul, in his letter to the Corinthians, tells of a vision he received. He says he was taken away "to the third heaven." That was the "paradise," where he heard "inexpressible things, things that no one is permitted to tell" (2 Cor 12:2–4). Did Paul have the unique privilege of visiting the heavenly place where God "dwells"? The apostle himself was left with several unanswered questions. Did it happen "in the body" or "out of the body"? Paul did not know. "Heaven" remained a mysterious concept even for him after this experience.

During three rather controversial audiences in 1999, Pope John Paul II declared that heaven should not be seen as a *location*, but rather as a *way of being* of the spirit or the human soul. Words having to do with *place*, according to this former pope, are not at all adequate to describe the reality at issue here, because *place* is a category that is part of the present order. The pope added that his view was not really new but has long been defended by many in the church. Quite a few theologians agree with the pope, while others, along with a lot of "ordinary" believers, have serious reservations. Who is right? It seems there is no fully satisfactory answer. However, Pope John Paul II certainly made an important point in stating that human words can never adequately catch the heavenly reality.

The fact remains that a great many people cannot possibly imagine heaven without thinking of a concrete place, somewhere in the universe.

Among Seventh-day Adventists the constellation of Orion has frequently been mentioned as the area in the universe where God has his abode. This was a suggestion from church pioneer Joseph Bates (1792–1872), who through his earlier work as a sea captain had some knowledge of astronomy. He believed that the new Jerusalem would descend from that part of the universe.[9] Ellen G. White mentions an "open space in Orion, whence came the voice of God."[10] It is important for most Seventh-day Adventists to insist that heaven is a location somewhere in the universe. According to the book of Hebrews, Jesus Christ currently ministers in a heavenly sanctuary as our high priest. Many can only conceive of this heavenly sanctuary in terms of a concrete place that resembles the biblical sanctuary, with its two apartments. They would find it impossible to imagine this essential part of Adventist beliefs without a spatial concreteness. In discussing the passages in Hebrews that refer to the heavenly sanctuary, Adventist theologian Jean-Claude Verrecchia, however, comments, "Yes, there is a sanctuary in heaven. Jesus has entered it. But the sanctuary should not be conceived of as a building, as a space located in any geography. It is into the very presence of God that Christ has entered on our behalf."[11]

The fact is that God's celestial abode has remained invisible to the most powerful telescopes in the world, including the Hubble Space Telescope, which until recently orbited Earth for some twenty years and could penetrate deep into the universe, and the even more powerful James Webb Space Telescope, launched in December 2021. Even if we assume, as many scientists do, that our universe is just one of a countless number of universes, it remains impossible for our human brain, which functions in a three-dimensional world, to define the concept of heaven as a place, somewhere in space. But, on the other hand, it does not do justice to the heavenly reality if we reduce "heaven" to a *mode of being*. The concrete language of the Bible presupposes much more than that—though it is beyond all human imagination and understanding. Therefore, it may be best to continue speaking of heaven as a *place*, as long as we realize that we use this word for lack of a better term to describe the inexpressible reality of God's presence. Perhaps the metaphor "heart" is used in a similar way. When we ask the Lord to

9. Knight, *Joseph Bates*, 138.

10. White, *Early Writings*, 41.

11. Verrecchia, *God of No Fixed Address*, 135.

come and dwell in our heart, we do not think of a supernatural invasion of an Invisible Being into the muscle that pumps the blood around in our bodies. Yet, we mean something very real and deep when we invite Christ to "live" in our "heart." This term also refers to a place, but it is not meant literally. Nevertheless, it remains very profound. Heaven is a reality beyond the limitations of time and space of our created and sin-fallen world. It represents perfect harmony with the divine.

What Is God Like?

The Angelic Pilgrim, Angelus Silesius (1624–1677), originally named Johann Scheffler, was a German mystic, poet, and religious thinker who once said, "The better you know God, the more you agree that you are less and less capable of expressing it."[12] Being fully aware of this (and we will keep stressing that point), we must nevertheless try to find words to say something of significance about God, so that we can relate to him. With this firmly in mind, we move on to a discussion of God's attributes and his characteristics. The term *characteristics* is mostly used to describe how God acts, notably in his relationship to us humans—for example, in his faithfulness and his patience. The "attributes" of God refer to his essential qualities that define who he is. These attributes consist of two categories: *incommunicable* attributes and *communicable* attributes. The latter category of attributes (love, mercy, justice, holiness) can, to a limited extent, be reflected by humans. The incommunicable attributes define how God differs from us. We will briefly look at each of these attributes.

Simplicity

This is a classical theological concept that tells us that God is totally different from us, or anything we know. We are composed of many different parts and may be able to live on without some of these parts. God is not composed of parts. His characteristics and attributes are not separate elements that together make up who God is. And, therefore, we can never play off certain properties of God against other properties. God's characteristics, such as love, power, and wisdom, are not separate qualities he possesses but are identical to his very being. They belong indivisibly

12. Lubac, *Discovery of God*, 118.

together, and God would not be God "if he did not possess all these attributes in the simplicity and perfection of his essence."[13]

Self-Existence (or Aseity)

Human beings are in many ways dependent on others, but God is totally independent. God *is* life and *gives* life. He does not owe his life to anything else. God chooses to be involved with this world, but he is in no way dependent on it. This concept stresses God's absolute self-sufficiency and autonomy.

Immutability and Impassibility

These two words have Latin roots: immutability is derived from the verb *mutare*, to change; impassibility derives from *passio*, meaning suffering or passion.[14] The two previous attributes (simplicity and self-existence) may seem rather abstract and philosophical, but God's immutability and impassibility are aspects that strike home much more directly. Both terms express the principle that God cannot change. This is certainly a biblical concept. The prophet Malachi cites these unambiguous words of Yahweh: "I the Lord do not change" (3:6). The apostle James is just as straightforward: "Every good and perfect gift is from above, coming down from the Father of the heavenly lights, who does not change like shifting shadows" (1:16). The fact that God does not change is the basis for our trust in him. If he were as liable to change in his opinions and affections as his creatures, this trust would quickly evaporate.

There are, however, several difficult issues in connection with God's immutability. Scripture presents many examples that God *can change* and, in fact, has done so repeatedly in the past. God can "repent" of actions that he intended, and he may decide to cancel what he had planned. Jeremiah reports how the Lord commanded him to visit a local potter, where the divine way of operating would become clear to him: "So, I went down to the potter's house, and I saw him working at the wheel. But the pot he was shaping from the clay was marred in his hands; so the potter formed it into another pot, shaping it as seemed best to him. Then the word of the Lord came to me. He said, 'Can I not do with you, Israel, as

13. Horton, *Christian Faith*, 229.

14. Peckham, *Divine Attributes*, 44–46.

this potter does?' declares the Lord. 'Like clay in the hand of the potter, so are you in my hand, Israel'" (18:1–6).

Just as a potter can reshape clay as he desires, God may change his mind, and shape and reconsider the fate of nations according to his will. A striking example of how God changed his mind is found in the story of Jonah. When the inhabitants of Nineveh repented, God cancelled the predicted destruction of the city. That God is immutable does not mean that he cannot opt for a new strategy. "That God is true to himself and unchangeably faithful to his people" does not mean "that he is incapable of being affected by the sufferings of his people."[15] That God is impassible means that his emotions do not affect who he is in his very being. In that sense he cannot suffer, but *he* "suffers" when *we* suffer, and he suffered in the most profound way when, as the incarnate Son, he agonized and died on the cross. Theologian Dietrich Bonhoeffer (1906–1945), who was executed in a German concentration camp, wrote, "Only a suffering God can help."[16] Another German theologian, Jürgen Moltmann (1926–2024), was convinced that a God who is incapable of suffering is an inadequate and imperfect God.[17]

It has been argued that having emotions means being subject to change. This is true for humans, who must deal with suffering, but it does not apply to God. "Humans are often overcome and defeated by suffering, but God is never overcome or defeated. Rather, God ultimately defeats suffering through voluntarily and temporarily taking on suffering, without divesting himself of any divine attributes."[18] One might say that it is part of God's unchanging self that he is deeply affected by the experiences of his creatures and that he suffers with them.

When speaking of God's changelessness, we must briefly refer to the so-called process theology. This approach to theology is rooted in the philosophy of Alfred North Whitehead (1861–1947), an English mathematician and philosopher, who viewed reality as dynamic and ever-changing rather than static. By implication, this line of thought rejects the classical idea of an unchanging, all-controlling God. Instead, process theology portrays God as deeply involved in the unfolding of the universe. Everything, including God, is in a state of *becoming*. God does

15. Bloesch, *God the Almighty*, 92.

16. Bonhoeffer, *Letters and Papers*, 300.

17. Moltmann, *Gekreuzigte Gott*, 230.

18. Peckham, *Doctrine of God*, 52.

not dictate outcomes but influences possibilities, respecting the free will of creatures, while he himself is also affected by what happens in his creation.[19] Process theology is the soil in which open theism developed, a theological current that, as we shall see below, is especially relevant in connection with God's omniscience—the belief that God knows everything. One of the main theologians who defends open theism is Adventist systematic theologian Richard Rice.[20] He states, "For open theism the ways in which God may choose to act within the world, and to interact with human beings, are much richer and far more subtle than either mere persuasion or dominating control."[21]

Eternity and Omnipresence

We touched on God's omnipresence—that is, the belief that God is everywhere at the same time—when we discussed the concept of heaven. *Omnipresence* is the theological term to underline that God is not restricted to a particular location, while at the same time his limitless presence does not imply some sort of pantheism that identifies God with all that exists. Norman Gulley states that "the whole God is present in the entirety of space. He is no more partially present in some parts of space than he is absent in any part of space."[22]

As with the concept of omnipresence, and God's relation to space, human minds struggle to make sense of the concept of eternity and God's relationship to time. There never was, nor will there ever be, a time when God was, and is, not. The fifth-century Christian thinker Boethius gave a definition of eternity that has been a favorite of many later theologians: eternity, he said, is "the whole simultaneous and perfect possession of boundless life."[23] In a psalm that is attributed to Moses, God is praised with the words, "From everlasting to everlasting you are God" (Ps 90:2).

There has been much debate over the question of whether God's relationship with time is best expressed by the term *eternity* or by saying that God is *timeless*. If God is timeless, he exists outside time and knows no past, present, or future. Thus, God "lives" in an eternal now. The idea

19. Smith, *Handbook of Contemporary Theology*, 150–64.

20. See Rice, *Future of Open Theism*.

21. Rice, *Future of Open Theism*, 117.

22. Gulley, *God as Trinity*, 68.

23. Quoted in Horton, *Christian Faith*, 253.

of a timeless God would seem to underscore his immutability, but it may be better to say that God somehow experiences *unending time* in a dynamic interaction with his creation.

Sovereignty and Omnipotence

Here again we meet two terms that defy human comprehension. God's status as our Creator is proof of his sovereignty and unlimited power. Unfortunately, the idea of God's sovereignty has at times been so defined that it lost its connotations of grace and love. In Calvin's theology it could serve as the basis for his "contentious" doctrine of double predestination.[24] God's absolute sovereignty allowed him to decide, even before people were born, who would eventually be saved and who would be eternally lost. This is a terrible caricature of God's character. Says Rice, "We need to examine the theme of divine power and sovereignty in the light of the biblical emphasis on God's love."[25] And, "Hard as it is to grasp, the idea that supreme love is the ultimate power in the universe is the heart of the Christian portrait of God."[26]

For humans, who are so limited in what they are able to do, omnipotence is a baffling notion. The question is often asked whether, if God can do anything, he can create a stone that is so heavy that he cannot lift it. Such questions overlook the common-sense condition that God can do everything that is *logically possible*. He cannot draw a square circle. "We do not honor God by attributing nonsense to him or detract from his glory by denying it."[27]

Edward Vick (1929–2024) emphasizes that God's power is "the power of love." He adds, "Omnipotence does not imply unlimited force and brute strength."[28] The good news is that God's power guarantees that he can fulfill his purposes. This means that his kingdom will come, and his divine will shall be done.[29]

24. See Thuesen, *Predestination*. Ellen G. White calls the doctrine of predestination a "horrible doctrine" with "hideous aspects." *Spirit of Prophecy*, 352.

25. Rice, *Reign of God*, 61.

26. Rice, *Reign of God*, 63.

27. Rice, *Reign of God*, 81.

28. Vick, *Speaking Well of God*, 101–2.

29. Vick, *Speaking Well of God*, 103.

Omniscience

From time to time we meet people who amaze us with their astounding scope of knowledge. But even the most educated and erudite men and women will readily admit that there are many things they do not know. They are not *omniscient*—literally, knowing everything. But Christians confess that God has no such limitation. He knows everything *that can be known*. It is important to add these last four words: *that can be known*. God has a perfect knowledge of the past. And also of the present. According to Prov 15:3, "The eyes of the Lord are everywhere, keeping watch on the wicked and the good." And Heb 4:13 affirms, "Nothing in all creation is hidden from God's sight. Everything is uncovered and laid bare before the eyes of him to whom we must give account." This goes so far that God is also perfectly aware of our inner motives. The psalmist recognizes, "You know when I sit and when I rise; you perceive my thoughts from afar. You discern my going out and my lying down; you are familiar with all my ways. Before a word is on my tongue you, Lord, know it completely" (Ps 139:2–4).

But does God also know the future? Does he know what I will do tomorrow? And what decision I will arrive at next month? In asking these questions we touch on the issue of free will. Many classical theologians will argue that man does indeed have a free will, but also that the omniscient God knows how a person is going to use that free will. Open theists wonder whether we can truly maintain that we have a free will if in fact it is already, ahead of time, certain how we are going to act. God's knowledge, they say, is limited to what is actually knowable, and God must (humanly speaking) also wait and see what we are going to decide.

Opponents of open theism object that it limits God, but Richard Rice and other open theists deny this and say that it would not be correct to state that they limit God's knowledge, because his knowledge includes every *possible* object of knowledge. It simply cannot include what is logically unknowable, because it has not yet happened. In his sovereignty God created a world in which he does not decide everything, but in which he shares power with his creatures and "creatively responds to their choices."[30] Rice states that many value open theism precisely because it "accentuates, not diminishes, how truly glorious God is."[31]

30. Rice, *Future of Open Theism*, 132.

31. Rice, *Future of Open Theism*, 135.

Another facet that is connected with God's omniscience is the nature of prophecy. To what extent does God not only know our individual future, but also the future of rulers and empires? Open theism suggests that God knows all possibilities and responds in real time. Many prophecies are conditional, while others reflect God's unchanging purposes (e.g., Christ's return at the end of time). Open theists argue that God can predict the future with accuracy, based on his wisdom and knowledge of human tendencies, but that he does not determine every detail. In this view, prophecy is not rigid predestination but part of a relational, unfolding history between God and humanity.

God Is Infinite

When theologians speak of God's holiness, goodness, justice, mercy, and love they often link these concepts with the word *infinite*. Human beings can only reflect these divine characteristics to a limited—a *finite*—extent. This enables us to grasp some of the essence of these qualities, but at the same time we realize that God is all these things in a different, much more elevated way—in other words, in an *infinite* way that leaves us in our finiteness straining for words.[32]

Holiness

When asked what the word *holy* means, most people will suggest such terms as *sinless*, *good*, *superior*, or *virtuous*. And, indeed, all these shades of meaning, and more, are applicable. Sometimes people also connect negative connotations to holiness. Some "very holy" people tend to irritate us, especially when we see a discrepancy between what they say and how they act.

In the Bible the word *holy* refers to what is good and honorable, but its root meaning is *separation* from all that is unclean and from everything that is of mere passing significance. A piece of land, a mountain, or a building can be holy. This is true also of utensils, garments, and many other objects. People in God's service are holy. They are in a special class for a special purpose. In all these cases the basic idea is that these persons or objects are separate from everyday use or normal

32. See also Bruinsma, *Our Awesome God*, 81–85.

activities. This gives us an idea what we mean when we say that God is holy. He is indeed in a special category, by himself.

Hundreds of times the Bible refers to God as the "Holy One" (e.g., Prov 9:10; Hos 11:9; 1 John 2:20). Isaiah employs the same term when the prophet quotes the divine question, "'To whom will you compare me? Or who is my equal?' says the Holy One" (40:25). In other texts God is referred to as "the Holy One of Israel" (e.g., Isa 1:4; 5:19, 24; 43:14) or is acclaimed as "majestic in holiness" (Exod 15:11). The angels sing "Holy, holy, holy" (Rev 4:8), and Jesus calls God the "holy Father" (John 17:11), and teaches us to pray that God's name be "hallowed"—in other words, made holy (Matt 6:9).

"God's holiness is his majestic purity that cannot tolerate moral evil." It is "his separateness from what is unclean and profane."[33] It is "God's innermost nature, embracing power, eternity, and glory."[34] God's holiness makes God completely different from all gods. This is most compellingly underlined by the German theologian Rudolf Otto (1869–1937) in his unique book *Das Heilige* (The Sacred), which was published in 1917.[35] For Otto, the sacred is the essence of every religion, including Christianity. He discusses the experience of *das ganz Andere* (that which is totally different), which may arouse both fear and fascination. But it is also *numinous*, which means that it radiates a mysterious power. His stress on the nonrational aspect of human awe for the majestic holiness of God gives his observations extra significance.

The Bible also speaks of God's anger (e.g., Rom 1:18; Nah 1:2) and his jealousy (e.g., Exod 34:14; Deut 4:24). This anger and jealousy are qualitatively different from human emotions. They are not separate characteristics of God, but "the radical outworking of God's holiness when it comes into contact with what is unclean."[36] Bloesch comments, "God is jealous for the sake of our preservation and salvation. He is wrathful for the sake of our redemption from the powers of sin."[37]

33. Bloesch, *God the Almighty*, 140.

34. Bloesch, *God the Almighty*, 139.

35. Rudolf Otto's book *Das Heilige* was published in English under the title *The Idea of the Holy*.

36. Bloesch, *God the Almighty*, 143.

37. Bloesch, *God the Almighty*, 145.

God Is Love

God is also described as good, merciful, and compassionate. And he is defined as righteous and just and, above all, as love. When we say that God is love (1 John 4:8, 16), and that he *also* has these other characteristics we are mistaken. God does not have a range of other qualities in addition to his love. Somehow, all these characteristics are expressions of his love. God's matchless love is perfect and does not need to be complemented by other qualities. Exodus 34:6–7 is one of the most comprehensive statements in the Bible about this ineffable love: "The Lord, the Lord, the compassionate and gracious God, slow to anger, abounding in love and faithfulness, maintaining love to thousands, and forgiving wickedness, rebellion and sin. Yet he does not leave the guilty unpunished."

And Ps 103:8–13 paints much the same picture:

> The Lord is compassionate and gracious,
> slow to anger, abounding in love.
> He will not always accuse,
> nor will he harbor his anger forever;
> he does not treat us as our sins deserve,
> or repay us according to our iniquities.
> For as high as the heavens are above the earth,
> so great is his love for those who fear him;
> as far as the east is from the west,
> so far has he removed our transgressions from us.
> As a father has compassion on his children,
> so the Lord has compassion on those who fear him.

The Greek language has several words for love. *Agape* is the word that occurs many times in the New Testament to denote the totally selfless love that God has for his creatures. It is a kind of love that is always willing to serve and to give. It is epitomized in the greatest love-gift ever given: God gave "his one and only Son" to this world (John 3:16).

To affirm that God is love, and that all God's characteristics and attributes are somehow embedded in, and part of, this agape-love, may be theologically correct, but it does not answer the question of many Christian believers how this loving God could ever allow his people to wage bloody wars and how he could demand gruesome punishments when his rules were ignored, or allow terrible natural disasters to take place.

And it does not remove the anguish when death is at our door, and we see our loved ones suffer pain and agony. The theological term for the attempt to vindicate God in response to this problem of suffering and evil is *theodicy*, literally doing justice to God. I found the following succinct definition very helpful: theodicy is the defense of God's goodness and omnipotence in view of the existence of evil.[38]

Richard Rice provides a survey of various approaches to this topic.[39] According to one view, all suffering and misery is in some way part of God's plan for humankind. Those who think along these lines say that often we may not understand why God would approve or allow horrible events to occur, but he makes no mistakes, and we must trust that in his good time all things will eventually fall into place. Others maintain that God is not to blame for the suffering in the world. It is the result of man's free will. God did not want robots, but created beings that would love and serve him from their own free will. God took the risk that things might turn sour, but that does not make him responsible for our wrong choices and thus for all the suffering we see in the world. Still others suggest that we may not be able to find explanations for the suffering we see and experience, but we can appreciate the fact that the things that happen to us have the potential of stimulating our inner growth and helping us to mature spiritually.

Seventh-day Adventist Christians have traditionally pointed to the cosmic war between good and evil, and to this ongoing struggle between the powers of light and the powers of darkness in which humans also play their role. They refer to this cosmic conflict as *the great controversy*. The advocates of open theism (with Rice as one of its main representatives) opt for a different kind of response. They tell us, as we saw earlier in this chapter, that God is not omniscient and not all-powerful in the classical sense of those terms. God does not know exactly how we will decide to use our free will, and by taking our free will utterly seriously, he does not have the possibility to intervene when we make wrong decisions.

The book by Richard Rice is of great value because it provides such a cogent survey of the various options regarding the issue of theodicy and then deals with the strong and the weak points of each of them. It provides much added value through the way in which the author deals with the personal dimension of the problem. Human suffering is not just

38. *Merriam-Webster*, s.v. "Theodicy."

39. Rice, *Suffering and the Search*.

a philosophical and theological *problem* (in fact, Rice prefers the term *mystery*). Sooner or later it affects all of us very personally. Rice proposes that we might combine aspects from the various theodicies and distill "fragments of meaning" from the different approaches and thus find comfort and support when we are struck by personal disaster.[40]

The dilemma of God's love and the existence of so much misery and evil in the world is part of a larger set of questions about the origin of evil, man's free will, and God's dealings with sin through the gift of his Son. We shall come to these matters in due time.

God as Trinity

First John 5:7 seems to be quite clear about the triune nature of the Godhead: "There are three that bear witness in heaven, the Father, the Word, and the Holy Ghost; and these three are one." This text is quoted from the King James Version and not from the New International Version, which is used throughout this book. The reason for quoting it from the King James Version is that this verse (the so-called *Comma Johanneum*) does not appear in the New International Version and in most versions that are more recent than the King James Version. The consensus among scholars is that this verse is a gloss—that is, a later insertion, intended to give support to the Trinity doctrine. It is not found in any early manuscript. Does this mean that the doctrine of the Trinity misses a solid biblical basis? From Reformation times onward some Christian communities have held that position. Today, besides the worldwide Watchtower Society (Jehovah's Witnesses), the Unitarian Universalist Association, with over one thousand congregations in the US, is the best-known antitrinitarian denomination.

Adventism is officially committed to the doctrine of the Trinity. The second of the twenty-eight fundamental beliefs is solidly trinitarian:

> There is one God: Father, Son, and Holy Spirit, a unity of three coeternal Persons. God is immortal, all-powerful, all-knowing, above all, and ever present. He is infinite and beyond human comprehension, yet known through His self-revelation. God, who is love, is forever worthy of worship, adoration, and service

40. Rice, *Suffering and the Search*, 137–64.

> by the whole creation. (Gen. 1:26; Deut. 6:4; Isa. 6:8; Matt. 28:19; John 3:16; 2 Cor. 1:21, 22; 13:14; Eph. 4:4–6; 1 Pet 1:2.)[41]

Several of the leaders in early Adventism—among them James White and Uriah Smith—had their roots in an antitrinitarian group called the Christian Connection.[42] The rejection of the Trinity doctrine was quite general in Adventism's early years. "The development of the Trinity doctrine demonstrates that sometimes doctrinal changes require the passing of a previous generation. It took over 50 years for the doctrine of the Trinity to become normative within the Adventist Church."[43] Though, apparently, still reluctant to use the term *Trinity*, Ellen G. White expressed in 1905 what by then had become accepted Adventist teaching: "There are three living persons in the heavenly Trio . . . the Father, the Son and the Holy Spirit."[44] However, since the 1990s antitrinitarianism is again on the rise in Adventism, especially in some groups on the fringes of the church and in their online media.[45] We see in these circles a strong sentiment that Adventists need to go back to the theological convictions of the pioneers of their movement, while it is also frequently alleged that the doctrine of the Trinity is an unbiblical invention by the Roman Catholic Church.

There is, however, strong biblical support for the concept of the Trinity, even though the word itself is nowhere found in the Scriptures. (That in itself is hardly a problem, since this is true for more theological terms that serve us well as symbols for a fullness that remains inexpressible.) The most prominent New Testament passages to support the Trinity are found in the Gospel of Matthew and in 2 Corinthians: "Therefore, go and make disciples, baptizing them in the name of the *Father* and the *Son* and the *Holy Spirit*" (Matt 28:19; italics added); and, "May the grace of the Lord *Jesus Christ*, and the love of *God*, and the fellowship of the *Holy Spirit* be with you all" (2 Cor 13:14; italics added).

Other texts also show that the doctrine of the Trinity expresses the all-pervasive pattern of divine action in the New Testament. There is a oneness in three-ness in the "totality of God's saving presence and power."[46]

41. General Conference, "What Do Adventists Believe?," no. 2.
42. Campbell, "Christian Connexion."
43. See Burt, "History," 139.
44. White, *Evangelism*, 615.
45. Whidden et al., *Trinity*, 8.
46. McGrath, *Christelijke Theologie*, 265; my translation.

This is clear from the following passages:

> There are different kinds of gifts, but the same *Spirit* distributes them. There are different kinds of service, but the same *Lord*. There are different kinds of working, but in all of them and in everyone it is the same *God* at work. (1 Cor 12:4–6; italics added)

> Consequently, you are no longer foreigners and strangers, but fellow citizens with *God's* people and also members of his household, built on the foundation of the apostles and prophets, with *Christ Jesus* himself as the chief cornerstone. In him the whole building is joined together and rises to become a holy temple in the Lord. And in him you too are being built together to become a dwelling in which God lives by his *Spirit*. (Eph 2:19–22; italics added)

> But when the kindness and love of *God* our Savior appeared, he saved us, not because of righteous things we had done, but because of his mercy. He saved us through the washing of rebirth and renewal by the *Holy Spirit*, whom he poured out on us generously through *Jesus Christ* our Savior. (Titus 3:4–5; italics added)

There are more New Testament texts that mention this same threefold divine manifestation; for example, 2 Cor 1:21–22; Gal 4:6; 2 Thess 2:13–14; and 1 Pet 1:2. Moreover, there are already traces of the Trinity doctrine in the Old Testament. God is referred to as personified in three different ways: as Wisdom (e.g., Prov 1:2–23; 3:19; 9:1–6); as the Word of God (e.g., Ps 119:89; Isa 55:1–11); and as the Spirit of God (e.g., Isa 42:1–3; Ps 104:30; Ezek 36:27; 37:1–14).

Further evidence for a Trinity of three fully equal persons is found in the fact that the Bible often gives Jesus Christ, the Son, names and attributes that indicate he is fully God, on the same level as the Father—or, as the early church expressed it, that he is "very God of very God."[47] And the Holy Spirit is definitely also more than an impersonal influence. In several instances the Holy Spirit is described as on a par with the Father and the Son. He has attributes and participates in actions that make him clearly a fully divine person.

The creation story contains an interesting allusion to the fact that more than one person was involved in the origin of life on our planet.

47. Nicene Creed, line 2.

Note also the plural in the sentence: "Let *us* make man in *our* image, in *our* likeness" (Gen 1:26: italics added). Some claim that the plural "us" and "our" foreshadow the Trinity concept, while others prefer to explain it as a reference to God and his angels in a heavenly council, or as a "plural of deliberation."[48] However, in different places the Bible attributes the creation of the world to the Father (Ps 102:25) as well as to the Son (Col 1:16; Heb 1:10) and to the Spirit (Gen 1:2; Ps 104:30).

Father, Son, and Holy Spirit are all referred to as *God* (Matt 11:25; John 6:27; Rom 1:7; John 1:1, 14; Titus 2:13; Heb 1:8; Acts 5:3–9). All three are depicted as omniscient (Rom 11:33; Rev 3:23; 1 Cor 2:11), and each is presented as equal to the others (Matt 28:19; John 10:30; 2 Cor 13:14: Eph 4:4–6).

Nicaea and Chalcedon

We already mentioned the Adventist fundamental belief that deals with the Trinity. It begins with the words, "There is one God: Father, Son, and Holy Spirit, a unity of three coeternal persons." The authors of this statement were not the first theologians who searched for suitable words to fit the biblical data, which we reviewed above, into a doctrinal formula that would satisfy all. Most of that work was already done in the early centuries of the Christian era and resulted from the deliberations during a number of ecumenical church councils, most notably those of Nicaea in 325 and Chalcedon in 451.

From May 20 until June 19 of the year 325, bishops from across the Roman Empire met in Nicaea (modern-day Iznik, in Turkey), at the request, and under the chairmanship, of the newly converted Emperor Constantine. They assembled to address several theological disputes that were endangering the unity of the church. One of the most urgent threats was the heresy of Arianism—the denial of the full divinity and eternity of Jesus Christ. This theory was successfully propagated by Arius, a priest from Alexandria, who had gained a very substantial following. The church leaders who assembled in Nicaea rejected the theological ideas of Arius and agreed on the so-called Nicene Creed, which became a foundational document for the Christian church. The conclusions of Nicaea were further refined during later meetings—the First Council in Constantinople

48. Turner, *Genesis*, 23.

in 381 and the Council of Chalcedon in 451. The results were accepted by almost all segments of Western and Eastern Christianity.

The conclusions of these important conventions may be summarized as follows:

- God is one in essence. There is one divine nature, substance, or being.
- God exists in three persons—Father, Son, and Holy Spirit.
- The three persons are distinct, but equal.
- The Son is eternal and not created.
- The three persons are coeternal.

A problem remained with respect to the Holy Spirit. The church of the East believed that the Spirit "proceeds" from the Father, while the Western church maintained that the Spirit "proceeds" from the Father and the Son ("filioque"[49]).

A key term in this description of God as Trinity is the word *person*. We must remember that the church leaders and theologians of the early centuries used the Greek language before the church in the West adopted Latin as its lingua franca. The word *hypostasis* was introduced in the Greek discussions about God. It had different meanings in ancient Greek but acquired the meaning of "individual reality,"[50] and had the connotation of a distinct mode of manifestation. It was rendered in Latin as *persona*, which was originally used to refer to theater masks or theater figures or roles. This *persona* is not identical with our concepts of *person* or *personality*. But, once again, we are confronted with the limitations of our human vocabulary. What the early Christian leaders wanted to emphasize was that the divine personhood was not less than human personhood but rather surpassed it.

As time passed, various ideas emerged about the three-ness and the one-ness of the Godhead and the relationship between the three persons that were studied and subsequently rejected by various church councils. These "heresies" (deviations from orthodoxy) tended to go in two directions. Some theories overemphasized the distinctiveness of the

49. This term, meaning "and from the Son," would continue to play an important role, notably in the ultimate schism between Rome and Constantinople in 1054.

50. Cross, *Oxford Dictionary*, 673.

three persons and tended towards forms of *tritheism*—that is, a belief in three gods rather than one God. On the other hand, a lack of regard for the distinct personhood of Father, Son, and Spirit inspired forms of *modalism*. The defenders of modalism held that God is one person who manifests himself in different modes or roles, rather than being three distinct persons (Father, Son, and Holy Spirit). This view was ultimately rejected as heretical by the early church. In the next chapter we will touch on other heresies that relate to the natures of Christ and the relationships between the three members of the Godhead. In the chapter on the Holy Spirit, the relationship between the Spirit, on the one hand, and the Father and the Son, on the other, will be discussed. This matter would play an important role in the eventual schism between the Western church and the Eastern church in 1054.

Our Salvation

There are numerous studies about the Trinity in which a much more detailed picture is given of the many related issues than is possible within the confines of this book. These theological works usually allow ample space to two overall approaches to the Trinity doctrine. This concerns the question whether we must mostly concentrate on the *ontological* aspect of the Trinity or on the *economic* aspect. The ontological approach has to do with the *being* of God. It is quite philosophical and focuses on who God *is*—on his attributes and characteristics. The economic approach tries to chart the roles of the three persons of the Trinity in our redemption. We do well to realize that the Bible says very little about the ontological nature of God and draws our attention mostly to the economic Trinity and the role of each divine person in the plan of salvation. But regardless of whether we choose the first or the second approach, we will always have to admit that God is infinitely greater than we are, and that each answer we find produces a thousand new questions.

Hopefully, this chapter has helped many readers to realize anew, or more fully, the greatness, majesty, and love of our Creator-God. But, at the very moment when we think we have defined an aspect of the triune God, we must in all humility step back and remember that our human words remain totally inadequate to describe who and what God is. However, while taking that step back, we must be deeply grateful that we can have a loving relationship with this indescribable God and can worship him and serve him with all that we have and are. The great medieval theologian St. Anselm expressed what is, no doubt, the prayer of many who have read this chapter: "Lord, I do not try to reach your heights, for I do not put my intelligence on your level. But I long for a glimpse of the truth which my heart loves and believes in."[51]

51. St. Anselm, *Proslogion*, cited in Lubac, *Discovery of God*, 116.

Chapter 3

Jesus Christ—Fully God and Fully Man

AROUND AD 116, A Roman historian named Tacitus wrote in his *Annals*, "Christ, from whom the name [Christians] had its origin, suffered the extreme penalty during the reign of Tiberius at the hands of one of our procurators, Pontius Pilatus."[1] Two other Roman authors—Suetonius (ca. AD 69–122) and Pliny the Younger (ca. AD 61–113)—also mentioned Jesus as a historical figure. And so did some Greek and Jewish authors, most notably the Jewish historian Flavius Josephus (AD 37–ca. 100) in his work *Antiquities of the Jews* (ca. AD 93).[2]

These sources confirm that there was indeed a man called Jesus, who caused serious upheaval in Palestine at the time when Pilate was the Roman governor, and that this Jesus was eventually executed. But for detailed information about the person and life of Jesus we must look elsewhere.

1. Tacitus, *Annals of Imperial Rome*, 15.44.

2. For a complete survey of the non-Christian sources that refer to Jesus, see Habermas, *Ancient Evidence*, 87–108.

What Do We Know?[3]

The apostle John wrote his Gospel towards the end of the first century. Jesus called him to be his disciple while he was employed in the fishing business of his father. He was with Jesus during his earthly ministry. He stood at the foot of Jesus's cross, but he had also seen the resurrected Christ with his own eyes. He proclaimed the gospel of his risen Lord. Towards the end of his long life he spent time in political exile on the small Greek island of Patmos, before his life ended in nearby Ephesus. This is his powerful testimony: "In the beginning the Word already existed" (John 1:1 NLT). "The Word became flesh and made his dwelling among us. We have seen his glory, the glory of the one and only Son, who came from the Father, full of grace and truth" (John 1:14).

When John wrote these words, the apostle Paul had a few decades earlier already written to the believers in Philippi about this same magnificent fact of Jesus's incarnation—God entering human flesh. For Paul this was the ultimate demonstration of self-sacrificing love: "Though [Jesus] was God, he did not demand and cling to his rights as God. He made himself nothing; he took the humble position of a slave and appeared in human form. And in human form he obediently humbled himself even further by dying a criminal's death on a cross" (Phil 2:6–7 NLT).

These statements by John and Paul were testimonies of faith. For them (and many others), Jesus, the son of a carpenter from Nazareth, had become the Christ of faith. How did this happen? On what basis did their faith—and, for that matter, the faith of the Christ-followers in the twenty-first century—rest? Can we discover how much of the Jesus-story was a historical reality? This question was asked, more than ever before, by a group of (mostly German) New Testament scholars in the nineteenth century, in the so-called quest for the historical Jesus. They wanted to find out *wie es eigentlich gewesen war* (what had actually happened).[4] The famous Albert Schweitzer (1875–1965)—a medical doctor in a missionary hospital in Lambaréne, in the African country of Gabon, and a gifted New Testament theologian—wrote his doctoral dissertation about the history of this search for the historical facts of the life and ministry

3. In this chapter I have adapted a few sections from the chapter "How Human Was Christ?" in my book *In All Humility*, 49–68.

4. This was a play on the famous dictum of historian Leopold von Ranke (1795–1886) about writing history "wie es eigentlich gewesen ist" ("how it actually happened").

of Jesus.[5] In the post–World War II era, some scholars returned to this project during the so-called new quest, though they were somewhat less skeptical in their approach. In the 1980s the Jesus Seminar was popular in the United States. A group of scholars examined, passage by passage, the New Testament material about Jesus to determine what was in all probability authentic and what was not.

It is not difficult to understand why both scholars and ordinary believers ask questions about the historicity of the Gospel narratives. The story of Jesus begins with the virgin birth and ends with the account of Jesus's resurrection, with many miracle stories in between. Are we here in the sphere of trustworthy reporting or, at least partly, in the domain of myth? We must readily admit that the Gospels are not ordinary history. The work of Luke may come closest to what we would call *research*. He begins his Gospel with referring to eyewitnesses who wrote accounts of "the things which have been fulfilled among us." Luke himself had not been among these eyewitnesses, but in order to present the "most excellent Theophilus"[6] with an "orderly account" of the story of Jesus, he had "carefully investigated everything from the beginning" (Luke 1:1–3).

The Gospels

The four Gospels[7] were written by different authors, at different times, and for different audiences. They each have their own background and perspective. The Gospels of Matthew, Mark, and Luke—the Synoptics—manifest, as we saw in chapter 1, a clear literary relationship, but also rely on sources that are unique to each of them. By combining the information of the four Gospel accounts we can arrive at a reasonably full picture of Jesus's ministry. But we hear very little about the early years of Jesus and there are major gaps in what we are told of his public ministry of

5. Albert Schweitzer's *Von Reimarus zu Wrede: Eine Geschichte der Leben-Jesu-Forschung* (*From Reimarus to Wrede: A History of Life-of-Jesus Research*), later translated as *The Quest of the Historical Jesus*. It was first published in 1906 by J.C.B. Mohr in Tübingen, Germany. The first English translation was published in 1910 by A. & C. Black in London.

6. Theophilus may have been a person of high status, possibly a Roman official or a wealthy patron.

7. Besides the four Gospels that have been included in the New Testament, there are several apocryphal Gospels as, for instance, the Gospel of Thomas and the so-called Infancy Gospels.

approximately three years. This conclusion about the duration of Jesus's public ministry is based on data in the Gospel of John, notably the references to the various Jewish feasts that Jesus attended. Had we only possessed the three synoptic Gospels, we might have concluded that Jesus's public work had been of much shorter duration.

The four Gospels not only differ in content but at times also show some inconsistencies. For instance: the number of women in the resurrection narratives differs sharply. Luke mentions five women, Mark three, Matthew two, and John one, while women do not feature at all in the version of the story that Paul was familiar with. And, to mention another irregularity, according to John it was still dark when the women reached the tomb, while Mark tells us that the sun had already risen.[8]

The Gospels contain several other discrepancies, apart from differences in chronology, literary style, and theological emphasis. Matthew traces Jesus's lineage through Joseph back to Abraham, while Luke traces it back to Adam, with a list that includes other names. Remarkably, the nativity stories are quite different when we compare the Gospels: Matthew describes the visit of the magi and Herod's massacre; Luke includes the shepherds and the census but omits Herod's role. Other examples could be added.

For John Macquarrie (1919–2007), a Scottish-born Anglican theologian, the differences in the reporting by the four Gospel writers do, in fact, add to the authenticity of their stories.[9] There is no sign of later attempts to eliminate the differences, as might have been expected. Others who have studied the different Gospels in detail have concluded that the details tend to supplement each other, rather than being contradictory. Dorothy L. Sayers (1893–1957), who made fame as a gifted writer of detective novels, was also a competent theologian. She opined that supernatural events may well appear differently to different observers.[10]

N. T. Wright (b. 1948), a New Testament scholar and former Anglican bishop, emphasizes that alleged or real discrepancies between the Gospels do not indicate that nothing really happened. "Indeed, they are a reasonable indication that something remarkable occurred, so remarkable that the first witnesses were bewildered into telling different stories about it."[11] Several authors have emphasized that, if the

8. See my book *I Have a Future*, 66–67.

9. Macquarrie, "Keystone," 9–24.

10. See Mascall, "Did Jesus Really Rise," 62.

11. Wright, *Surprised by Hope*, 54.

accounts had been pure fabrications, there would have been plenty of time between the alleged events and the writing to ensure that the stories would be in full harmony!

In fundamentalist circles considerable effort has at times been made to downplay the differences between the Gospels. The doctrine of biblical inerrancy has led many to argue that *apparent* contradictions stem from human misunderstanding rather than textual flaws. They have often constructed "harmonies of the Gospels" that merge the four accounts into a single narrative, smoothing over inconsistencies.[12] Most nonfundamentalist commentators will reply that many elements in these harmonies are not convincing, and that these constructs are not needed to produce a story that is sufficiently coherent and, more importantly, deeply inspiring.

Jesus in Other New Testament Writings

The Gospels were written in response to the questions people with all sorts of different backgrounds were asking about Jesus—who he was, what he did, and why he suffered and died. The four Gospel accounts are the main sources for what we know about Jesus's life on this earth. We will focus mostly on these four reports. But, in addition, there is some extra information in other New Testament books.

The second book by Luke—the book of Acts—relates how the apostles proclaimed the risen Christ on the basis of their experiences with him. In the New Testament letters Paul and others applied the teachings of Christ to the daily life of the believers in the churches that had been established. They indicated how many Old Testament passages found their fulfillment in Christ and laid the basis for the branch of theology that is commonly referred to as Christology—the study of the doctrine of Christ.

Somewhat surprisingly, Paul rarely quotes Jesus's teachings directly. The Lord's Supper (1 Cor 11:23–26) and teachings on love (Rom 12:9–21; 1 Cor 13) reflect Jesus's influence, but Paul does not systematically recount parables or moral teachings.

It has also been remarked by many that Paul never directly mentions the empty tomb. However, his teachings about the bodily resurrection do strongly imply it! Paul's picture of Christ is primarily

12. In Nichol et al., *Seventh-day Adventist Bible Commentary*, such a "Harmony of the Gospels" is included. See 5:194–203.

theological. He focuses on his divine role and his work as our Savior, whereas the Gospels primarily aim to provide a narrative account of his life, teachings, and actions.

The book of Hebrews presents Christ as the ultimate revelation of God, the eternal Son, and the heavenly High Priest. He is superior to angels, Moses, and the Levitical priesthood. He fulfilled the Old Testament sacrifices through his once-for-all atonement. Jesus intercedes for believers in the heavenly sanctuary and provides them with access to God. He is presented as the mediator of a new and better covenant.

The last Bible book is not the Revelation *of John*, but rather the "revelation *from Jesus Christ*" (NLT), or the revelation *of* Jesus Christ (NRSV). In the book of Revelation, Christ is depicted as the victorious, divine King and Judge. He is the Alpha and Omega, the Lamb who was slain, but reigns as the triumphant Lion of Judah. He appears as the glorified Son of Man, with eyes like fire and a voice like rushing waters. Christ holds the keys of death and Hades, walks among his churches, and leads the armies of heaven. As the righteous Judge, he defeats evil, ushers in God's kingdom, and reigns forever. Ultimately, he is the Bridegroom, bringing his redeemed bride into the new Jerusalem for all eternity.

The Incarnation and Jesus's Early Years

Let's go back to the story of Jesus in the Gospels. Jesus was born under very uncomfortable circumstances in Bethlehem, after his teenage pregnant mother, together with her—presumably quite a bit older—future husband, had travelled there because of a summons for a census by the Roman authorities. The events surrounding Jesus's birth are narrated in some detail in Matthew and Luke, although they mention different aspects. The stories emphasize the supernatural character of Jesus's entry into this world. Luke 1:26–38 recounts how the angel Gabriel visited Mary, announcing that she will conceive a son by the Holy Spirit. The child must be named Jesus, and "will be called the Son of the Most High" (Luke 1:32). Matthew tells his readers that a young girl, Mary, who had not yet had sexual relations with her husband-to-be, Joseph, had become pregnant through the Holy Spirit (Matt 1:18–25). An angel reassured Joseph in a dream that the child was conceived by the Holy Spirit. It fulfilled the prophecy of Isaiah: "Behold, the virgin shall conceive and bear a son, and they shall call his name Immanuel" (Matt 1:23; Isa 7:14).[13]

Can people in our day and age still believe in the virgin birth? It demands faith, certainly. But must we not expect that something very extraordinary was bound to happen, if it is true that God decided to become incarnate and to be the Immanuel—God with us? Karl Barth stated very poignantly that the miracle of the virgin birth is a sign that Jesus Christ does not have his origin in humanity, but in God. He is the new beginning that humanity itself could never bring forth.[14]

The doctrine of the Trinity implies the preexistence of Jesus. He is God, and God is eternal. Father, Son, and Spirit are coeternal, and therefore we must conclude that there never was a time when anyone of the three persons of the Godhead did not exist. The prologue of John's Gospel borrows the gnostic term *Logos*[15] (Word) as the name for the divine Emissary who came to this planet. "In the beginning was the Word, and *the Word was with God, and the Word was God. He was with God in the beginning*. Through him all things were made; without him nothing was made that has been made. . . . *The Word became flesh and made his dwelling among us*. We have seen his glory, the glory of the one and only Son, who came from the Father, full of grace and truth" (John 1:1–3, 14; italics added).

Oscar Cullmann (1902–1999) pointed to the crucial importance of this passage in the first chapter of John's Gospel: "The title [Logos] expresses very forcefully an important aspect of New Testament Christology—the unity in the historical revelation of the incarnate and preexistent Jesus."[16]

13. Matthew applies the prophecy of Isa 7:14 ("The virgin will conceive and give birth to a son, and will call him Immanuel") to the virgin birth of Jesus Christ. It should be noted that the original word in the Hebrew text (*almah*) frequently simply denotes a young woman or a girl who is not necessarily a virgin. However, the Septuagint has the word *parthenos*, which almost always means "virgin."

14. Barth, *Doctrine of the Word*, 172.

15. Gnosticism was a diverse set of religious and philosophical movements in the early Christian era that emphasized the secret knowledge (*gnosis*) needed for salvation. It viewed the material world as flawed or evil, created by a lesser deity (the Demiurge), and taught that the true God could only be known through spiritual enlightenment. The gnostics perceived "Logos" as a divine intermediary between the unknowable God and creation. John, in the prologue to the Gospel, tells his readers that Christ is the true Logos, who connected the world with God.

16. Cullmann, *Christology*, 258.

A key passage about the incarnation of the preexistent second person of the Trinity is found in Paul's letter to the church in Philippi, which speaks of the *kenosis*—the self-emptying—of Jesus:

> In your relationships with one another, have the same mindset as Christ Jesus: Who, being in very nature God, did not consider equality with God something to be used to his own advantage; rather, he made himself nothing by taking the very nature of a servant, being made in human likeness. And being found in appearance as a man, he humbled himself by becoming obedient to death—even death on a cross!
>
> Therefore, God exalted him to the highest place and gave him the name that is above every name, that at the name of Jesus every knee should bow, in heaven and on earth and under the earth, and every tongue acknowledge that Jesus Christ is Lord, to the glory of God the Father. (Phil 2:5–11)

Jesus "made himself nothing" by taking the very nature of a servant, being made in human likeness. He came as a helpless babe, was part of a Jewish family in his role as the son of a carpenter (Matt 13:55), together with brothers and sisters (Mark 6:3). He grew up and developed from infancy to young adulthood (Luke 2:40, 52; Heb 5:8). Just like other Jewish boys he was circumcised (Luke 2:21) and joined his parents as a twelve-year-old on a visit to the temple in Jerusalem. And when John the Baptist called people to repentance and baptized them in the River Jordan, Jesus also stepped forward and underwent this baptism by full immersion, in order "to fulfil all righteousness" (Matt 3:13–17; Mark 1:9–11; Luke 3:21–22). It was the occasion when he was anointed by the Spirit (John 1:32). Luke emphasized this element: "Jesus, full of the Holy Spirit, left the Jordan and was led by the Spirit into the wilderness" (Luke 4:1–2).[17]

Jesus came to this world to deal with the sin problem and thus, more specifically, with the devil, the instigator of sin and evil. Before he began his ministry at the age of around thirty years, Jesus faced a special confrontation with Satan. In this first battle with the evil one, "the true state of things"—namely, that Christ is the Victor—was already becoming clear.[18] Jesus showed that it was possible to withstand the temptations of the devil. If he had not withstood the suggestions of the evil one, he would have

17. For a fuller description of the close connection between the Spirit and Jesus, see Horton, *Christian Faith*, 552–86.

18. Van der Kooi and Van den Brink, *Christian Dogmatics*, 331.

been disqualified as the sinless Savior, and his mission to redeem humanity through a perfect sacrifice would have collapsed.

In these temptations everything was at stake. Christ's temptations were not make-believe pieces of theater. They were 100 percent real (Matt 4:1–11). And, yes, they were fundamentally the same for Jesus's contemporaries, as they are for us who live in the first half of the twenty-first century. But when we are confronted with major crises in our lives, we must always react on the basis of our human limitations. Christ, however, remained God—even during his incarnation. At any moment he could have invoked his divine powers to save himself from every predicament. When Satan suggested to Jesus that he should throw himself from the roof of the temple, Jesus could, indeed, have commanded a legion of angels to provide him with a soft landing in the temple court. But he knew that we would not have that possibility in similar circumstances. Had he succumbed to this temptation by calling upon divine resources that are not at our disposal, he would no longer have been our perfect example and could no longer be our Savior. "It seems from a simple reading of the Bible that irrespective of the constitution of his human nature, Jesus was tempted far beyond how any other person can ever be tempted. Most of his temptations are not even temptations to us, because we lack the ability to respond to them successfully."[19] The good news is that Jesus could have sinned when he was tempted, but that he did not!

Hebrews 4:15 tells us that Christ was tempted "in every way just as we are." How must we then understand that statement? We need not understand the text in the sense that Christ's temptations were *identical* to ours. That could hardly be the case. Contemporary life presents us with temptations earlier generations never knew. And there were, undoubtedly, temptations in the ancient world, in the Middle Ages, and even less than a century ago, that we no longer face. However, the urges and sensations behind our temptations have always existed, and in fundamental ways humanity has always faced similar temptations.

Announcing the Kingdom

"The idea of the 'kingdom of God' dominated the ministry of Jesus. It was the central topic of his preaching, and his miracles were object lessons

19. Knight, *Matthew*, 69.

intended to illustrate its reality and its character."[20] For theologian Richard Rice the topic of God's kingdom is so central that he based his entire systematic theology on this theme and called it *The Reign of God*.

The kingdom of God does not refer to a territory but has to do with God's ruling activity—his reign. George Ladd, in his classic book *Crucial Questions About the Kingdom of God*, defines the kingdom with these words: "The kingdom of God is the sovereign rule of God, manifested in the person and work of Christ, creating a people over whom he reigns, and issuing in a realm or realms in which the power of his reign is realized."[21]

John the Baptist "came preaching in the wilderness of Judea and saying: 'Repent, for the kingdom of heaven has come near'" (Matt 3:2). Shortly after this, "Jesus began to preach: 'Repent, for the kingdom of heaven has come near'" (Matt 4:17). He "went throughout Galilee, teaching in their synagogues, proclaiming the good news of the kingdom" (Matt 4:23; Luke 4:43). Jesus also instructed his twelve disciples, when he sent them out to preach, to proclaim this message about the coming kingdom (Matt 10:7). In fact, the gospel of the kingdom was to be preached in the entire world (Matt 24:14).

The dual nature of this divine rule was consistently emphasized. The kingdom is an eschatological reality and will come at the end of time, but, in a sense, it is also already present. We read in Luke 17:21 that the kingdom is among us, *in our midst*. The King James Version translates it as, "The kingdom of God is *within you*." The original Greek text allows for both renderings. The kingdom is an inner spiritual reality and was present in Jesus's ministry. And through acts of love, justice, and worship, the church anticipates, and is called to foreshadow, the coming fulfillment of God's rule. The kingdom is not yet present in its fullness and perfection. Or, to use a theological term, the kingdom is only *proleptically* present in the here and now. The word *proleptic* comes from the Greek *prolepsis*, meaning "anticipation."[22] Jesus's life, death, teachings, and acts of love demonstrate the kingdom's presence in advance of its full realization. As a result, God's kingdom is both *already* and *not yet*. It is not fully realized, but God's Lordship is universal, and every aspect of our life, in the here and now, is subject to his sovereignty. Ladd states, "Jesus

20. Rice, *Reign of God*, 13.

21. Ladd, *Crucial Questions*, 80.

22. *Oxford English Dictionary* (2nd ed.), s.v. "prolepsis."

was continually concerned with two emphases in the portrayal of the eschatological drama: Its ultimate accomplishment, and its immediate application. The ultimate realization will involve the perfect realization of God's reign in all creation; and the immediate application involves the personal realization of God's reign within the lives of men by which they are prepared to enter the future kingdom."[23]

Jesus explained the characteristics of the kingdom by means of a range of parables, which all begin with "the kingdom of God is like . . ." For instance, it is like the mustard seed that starts small but grows into a large bush (Matt 13:31–32); it is like a hidden treasure (Matt 13:44); or like a particular kind of fishing net (Matt 13:47–50). And Jesus made a series of other comparisons. But his most extended discourse about the kingdom focused on the ethics of the kingdom. The kingdom values were the main topic of the Sermon on the Mount (Matt 5–7; Luke 6:17–49).

The radical nature of these sayings of Jesus led some to conclude that the requirements that were placed on the followers of Jesus were impossible to comply with. Some theologians, as for instance Albert Schweitzer, saw the kingdom values of the Sermon on the Mount as an "interim ethic."[24] Schweitzer was of the opinion that Jesus was (mistakenly) convinced that his kingdom would come very soon, and that these ethical principles would only apply to the short interim period before his return. For other theologians the kingdom values remain a moral vision for Christians of all ages. Bonhoeffer insisted that we must live out Jesus's instructions in a radical way, despite the costs.[25] Martin Luther saw it as a mirror reflecting our sinfulness and thereby driving us to Christ's grace.

Some of the statements in the Sermon on the Mount are clearly nonliteral and hyperbolic. For instance, "If your right eye causes you to stumble, gouge it out and throw it away" (Matt 5:29). However, it is clear that the teachings of Jesus (here and elsewhere in the Gospels) provide us with the lens through which the moral teachings, which Jesus's followers inherited from Old Testament times, must now be viewed. We must not just be concerned about the external rules but, first of all, about the spiritual principles behind these rules. In the Sermon on the Mount Jesus gives a new meaning to the Ten Commandments. His spiritual

23. Ladd, *Crucial Questions*, 97.

24. Schweitzer, *Quest of the Historical Jesus*, 352.

25. See Bonhoeffer, *Cost of Discipleship*.

illuminations must guide present-day Christians in their approach to pro-life and gender issues and other modern ethical dilemmas, such as dealing with migration, the treatment of refugees, and amassing wealth. They must also guide us as Seventh-day Adventist Christians in our approach to the Old Testament directives that we still regard as valid for today. In our Sabbath keeping, for instance, legalistic tendencies should be replaced by a conscious effort to follow Christ's approach to the Sabbath. We must be inspired by his emphasis on the spiritual significance of the Sabbath and focus on grace rather than on outward strictness to ensure full compliance with the letter of the law.

The Gospel narratives tell us about the many miracles Jesus performed. The question naturally arises by what power Jesus performed his miracles. Before him the prophets in Old Testament times sometimes performed miracles, and so did the apostles after Jesus left the earth. Were Jesus's miracles similar in nature to those of the prophets and the apostles? Ellen G. White suggested that there was a special element, and that Jesus employed his deity when he healed people and even raised a few people from death. She commented, "It was by faith and prayer that he wrought miracles. He depended upon his Father's power. In himself, he possessed no power to heal. But *divinity flashed through humanity* when he spoke the word, and the afflicted ones were made whole."[26] Theologians have different opinions about this aspect of Jesus's ministry. Some believe that he did indeed exercise divine power on such occasions, while others insist that, because Jesus had fully emptied himself and put his divine power aside, he depended, like the apostles, on the power of the Holy Spirit that is also available to all humans who are close to God. In any case, we can conclude that Jesus never used his divine powers to perform miracles for his own benefit. Had he done so he would no longer be our perfect role model.

Suffering, Death, and Resurrection

A major part of the Gospel narratives is devoted to the final week of Jesus's ministry, his arrest and trial, his death on the cross, his rest in the tomb, his resurrection, and the subsequent appearances. In the Pauline writings the emphasis is, as we already noted, also on these aspects of

26. White, *Ministry of Healing*, 37.

Jesus's life. The meaning of Jesus's suffering and death is, of course, the fundamental topic of soteriology: the plan of salvation and the doctrine of the atonement. The miracle of Jesus's resurrection is the basis of Christian eschatology. Paul emphasized in 1 Cor 15 that the idea of a resurrection of God's people at the end of time becomes utter nonsense if the resurrection of Jesus Christ is not a historical reality.

Admittedly, belief in the historicity of Christ's resurrection demands a leap of faith, since there is no hard historical evidence. In the first century the world did not yet dispose of CCTV systems that could have recorded what happened in and near the tomb where Jesus's body had been laid. But if we want to explain the origin and rapid growth of the apostolic church, we must assume that something extraordinary did take place.[27] N. T. Wright put it succinctly in these words: "The disciples were hardly likely to go out and suffer and die for a belief that was not firmly anchored in fact."[28] Many other authors have stressed the same point. Peter, who in Jesus's darkest hour had avowed that he did not even know the man who was arrested and tried by the Jewish elite, changed into the apostle who, only a few weeks later, proclaimed to a large multinational and multicultural crowd in Jerusalem that Christ was alive. The doubting Thomas came to believe that the Lord was truly risen. He eventually became a missionary to India, where even today some four million "Thomas Christians" are a testimony to his radical conversion. There is good reason to think that most, if not all, of the original apostles, except John (who for several years was banished to the Greek isle of Patmos), met with a martyr's death. What could have propelled the apostles to pursue a career that would end in opposition, torture, and an ignominious death? How do we explain that James, one of the half-brothers of Jesus, became a prominent leader in the early church, while earlier he had flatly rejected Jesus's ministry? (John 7:5; Acts 15:14–21). The explanation lies in the extraordinary, incontestable Easter event.

This is echoed by a rather unexpected voice—namely, that of the Jewish theologian and Israeli historian Pinchas Lapide (1922–1997). He did not become a Christian, but he did firmly believe that the resurrection of Jesus was a historical reality. It is, he said, the only explanation for the birth and further rise of Christianity. He confronts his readers with these pressing questions: "How can it be explained that, against all

27. See Bruinsma, *I Have a Future*, 64–87.

28. Wright, *Resurrection*, 73.

plausibility, his adherents did *not* finally scatter, were *not* forgotten, and that the cause of Jesus did *not* reach its infamous end at the cross?"[29] Lapide concluded that the explanations of many resurrection-denying theologians fail miserably to explain "the fact that the solid hillbillies from Galilee . . . were changed within a short period of time into a jubilant community of believers."[30]

Jesus as Savior, Prophet, Priest, and King

In the Old Testament, the role of the Messiah (Hebrew *Mashiach*, meaning "anointed one")[31] is central to Jewish hopes and expectations. Messianic expectations in Old Testament and intertestamental times were diverse in nature. The Hebrew Bible presented different kinds of messiahs: a Davidic king who would rule justly (2 Sam 7; Isa 9), a suffering servant (Isa 53), a prophet like Moses (Deut 18:15), and an apocalyptic Son of Man (Dan 7). During the Second Temple period, these ideas further evolved. Some expected a warrior-king to overthrow foreign rulers, while others envisioned a heavenly figure (1 Enoch). The Qumran community anticipated two messiahs—one priestly, one kingly. By Jesus's time, many awaited a political deliverer, though some expected an apocalyptic judge or a spiritual leader.

We find predictions in the Old Testament that were intended as so-called messianic prophecies—or were later interpreted as such. These prophecies describe the Messiah's birth, and his life, mission, suffering, and triumph. Key passages include Gen 3:15, which hints at a coming redeemer; Isa 7:14, understood as foretelling a virgin birth; Mic 5:2, predicting his birthplace in Bethlehem; and Isa 53, detailing the experiences of a suffering servant. Other significant references include Ps 22 (Jesus's crucifixion) and Zech 9:9 (Jesus's entry into Jerusalem).

That Jesus saw himself as the Messiah is clear, for instance, from his conversation with the Samaritan woman at the well (John 4:7–14). He also did not beat around the bush when he stood before the Sanhedrin, just prior to his execution, and the high priest asked him, "Are you the Messiah, the Son of the Blessed One?" Jesus replied, "I am," and then cited Dan 7:13, implying his divine authority: "You will see

29. Lapide, *Resurrection of Jesus*, 123.

30. Lapide, *Resurrection of Jesus*, 129.

31. *Merriam-Webster Collegiate*, s.v. "Messiah."

the Son of Man sitting at the right hand of the Mighty One and coming on the clouds of heaven" (Mark 14:61–62). Jesus at times used some titles with messianic implications but, on the other hand, we find that he was often quite reticent in pushing this messianic claim. The fact that at times he purposefully hid his true identity (most prominently in the Gospel of Mark) is usually referred to as the "Messianic Secret." The Jewish expectation of the Messiah was often linked to a military or political liberator. Jesus distanced himself from these expectations, emphasizing a different kind of kingdom.

The Greek translation of Messiah is *Christos*, which also means "anointed one."[32] Christians believe Jesus Christ fulfilled the messianic prophecies, bringing salvation and God's kingdom, and making *Christos* his defining title rather than just a surname.

Jesus is called both the Son of God and the Son of Man, reflecting his divine and human natures. The title *Son of God* emphasizes Jesus's divine origin and his unique relationship with his Father. In the Old Testament, the title *son* is used for Israel (Exod 4:22) and kings (Ps 2:7), but Jesus's sonship is unique. In the New Testament he is conceived by the Holy Spirit (Luke 1:35) and identified as God's Son at his baptism (Mark 1:11). He shares in God's nature (John 10:30) and has authority over the creation (Col 1:15–17). Calling Jesus the Son of God affirms his role as the Messiah and divine Savior.

The *Son of Man* title highlights Jesus's humanity and mission on earth. It appears over eighty times in the Gospels, often in reference to Jesus's suffering and death (Mark 8:31). It also connects with Dan 7:13–14, where the "Son of Man" receives an everlasting kingdom. By using this title, Jesus subtly revealed his divine authority and role in God's kingdom without directly provoking opposition. *Messiah* and *Son of God* were titles that had strong political and revolutionary overtones in first-century Judaism, whereas *Son of Man* did not have that association and pointed rather to Jesus's role as a suffering servant (Mark 8:31). The title refers to Jesus's suffering, death, and resurrection (Mark 10:33–34) and his future return in glory (Matt 24:30). By using this title, Jesus revealed both his humility, his close bond with humanity, and his heavenly authority.

In a number of passages, particularly in the Gospel of John, Jesus is described with the Greek term *monogenēs*. In the King James Version this

32. Liddell and Scott, *Greek-English Lexicon*, s.v. "Christos."

is translated as "only-begotten." John 3:16 is a prime example of this: "For God so loved the world, that he gave his only begotten Son, that whosoever believeth in him should not perish, but have everlasting life." Other examples are John 1:14, 18; 3:18; and 1 John 4:9. This translation as "only begotten" has caused considerable misunderstanding. Many have thought it suggests that Jesus did have a beginning, since he was "begotten." Most more recent translations opt for another rendering of *monogenēs*, "unique" or "one of a kind," or they translate it as "the one and only Son," which more accurately represents the underlying Greek text.[33] Dutch theologian Gerrit Cornelis Berkouwer (1903–1996) stated the term *monogenēs* is an expression that indicates "in a very special manner, that which is unique and is incomparable in Christ."[34] *The Seventh-day Adventist Bible Commentary* interprets the word *monogenēs* along the same lines. It has nothing to do with status or order of birth but points to absolute uniqueness.[35]

Other titles that are central to our understanding of the person and work of Jesus Christ are *Priest* and *King*. The *priest* title emphasizes Jesus's role as the ultimate mediator between God and humanity. In the letter to the Hebrews Jesus is described as the great High Priest (Heb 4:14–16), who offered himself as the perfect sacrifice. The key differences with the priesthood of the Old Testament sanctuary are that the sacrifice of Jesus needed no repetition, as it was "once for all" (Heb 10:10–12), and that Jesus did not bring his sacrifice on his own behalf: "Such a high priest truly meets our need—one who is holy, blameless, pure, set apart from sinners, exalted above the heavens. Unlike the other high priests, he does not need to offer sacrifices day after day, first for his own sins, and then for the sins of the people. He sacrificed for their sins once for all when he offered himself" (Heb 7:26–27).

Jesus's eternal and universal priesthood is compared with that of the mysterious priest-king Melchizedek (Gen 14:18–20; Ps 110:4; Heb 7) to underline that it was not based on lineage but on divine appointment and was universal and eternal.

As king, Jesus is the promised Davidic ruler (2 Sam 7:12–16; Luke 1:32–33). He proclaims the kingdom and stresses that his rule is not political but spiritual (John 18:36–37). "Jesus promised and produced

33. Rodríguez, *Andrews Bible Commentary*, 1413.

34. Berkouwer, *Person of Christ*, 175.

35. Nichol et al., *Seventh-day Adventist Bible Commentary*, 5:902–3.

the reign of God."[36] Above all, he is presented in the New Testament as the triumphant king who will return in glory to judge and to reign (Rev 19:11–16).

The title for Christ that was to dominate the Christian vocabulary is *Lord*. The Greek term *Kyrios*, while used broadly in everyday Greek, functioned in Jewish Scripture as the standard translation of the divine name YHWH, and thus its use for Jesus underlines his divine status. The apostle Paul confessed that "every tongue" on earth will acknowledge that "Christ is Lord [*Kyrios*], to the glory of God the Father" (Phil 2:11). In a somewhat more elaborate way Paul writes to the Christians in Corinth about the meaning of this title: "For even if there are so-called gods, whether in heaven or on earth (as indeed there are many "gods" and many "lords"), yet for us there is but one God, the Father, from whom all things came and for whom we live; and there is but one Lord [*Kyrios*], Jesus Christ, through whom all things came and through whom we live" (1 Cor 8:5–6).

Oscar Cullmann states that the designation *Lord* "far exceeds the dignity of an ordinary teacher," but becomes "the expression of an absolute total claim."[37] The title *Kyrios* was at times used by Roman emperors, who insisted that they be worshipped because of their superhuman status. Thus, when Christians called Jesus the *Kyrios*, it could easily be seen as a subversive claim, asserting that not the Caesar but Jesus Christ possessed absolute authority. To recognize Christ as the Lord of all facets of our life demands a deep spiritual insight. "No one can say, 'Jesus is Lord,' except by the Holy Spirit" (1 Cor 12:3).

One other title of Jesus holds special significance for Seventh-day Adventists. With a few other communities (most notably the Watchtower Society) they believe that Jesus Christ may be identified with the archangel Michael.[38] The name *Michael* occurs five times in the Bible to denote a high celestial being (Dan 10:13, 21; 12:1; Jude 9; Rev 12:7). There is no explicit identification with Jesus, but Adventist authors have equated Jesus with Michael after comparing their roles. That Michael is described as an angel does not mean that he must be a created being, but that he is a

36. Rice, *Reign of God*, 166.
37. Cullmann, *Christology*, 205.
38. Biblical Research Institute, "Is Michael Another Name."

"messenger," which is the root meaning of the term *angel*.[39] The name *Michael*, so it is argued, emphasizes the fact that Christ is the supreme leader of the heavenly host. It is possible that early Adventist leaders brought this view with them from their earlier association with a restorationist group called the Christian Connection. Both James White[40] and Uriah Smith[41] defended the position that Michael was another name for Christ in his preincarnate status. Both were members of the Christian Connection before turning to Adventism. It does not seem that this identification of Michael with Christ adds anything of significance to our understanding of the person and work of Jesus.

The Christological Controversies

In the previous chapter we saw how the early church struggled to define the essence of the Trinity: how to do justice to the one-ness and the three-ness of the Godhead. The other issue that kept minds and emotions occupied in the early centuries was the *nature* of Christ. Already in New Testament times some people had questions about the deity of Christ, while others wondered about the true humanity of the Savior. The gnostics were adamant that it would be impossible for a divine being—as a pure spirit—to be associated with evil matter (human flesh)! They thought that in his incarnation Christ assumed a phantasmal, make-believe body. He only *appeared* to be a human being. In the latest strands of the New Testament we already find protests against this mode of thinking. That is why John could write in his second general epistle, "Many deceivers, who do not acknowledge Jesus Christ as coming in the flesh, have gone out into the world." John has nothing good to say about people who spread this kind of false teaching. Anyone who does this is a "deceiver and the antichrist" (2 John 7).

Another early controversy was Adoptionism, which held that Jesus was merely a man whom God adopted as his Son. It thereby undermined his divine nature.

The long and intense controversies about the natures of Christ were a major threat to the unity and well-being of the Christian church. It

39. *Oxford English Dictionary*, "angel."

40. White, "Signs of the Times," 2–3.

41. Smith, *Thoughts on Daniel*, 245, 301–2, 546.

caused a tremendous amount of tension between different groups of believers. As we already noted, the early church councils were important in settling important trinitarian issues, but the process also demonstrated how difficult it apparently was to describe who and what Jesus Christ is. And it only got more and more complex when the church had to deal with the disputes about the two natures of Christ—how the human and the divine natures were related and impacted each other. In the previous chapter we already referred to Arius, the priest from Alexandria, who argued that Jesus was a created being, not coeternal with the Father. This view was condemned at the Council of Nicaea (325), which affirmed that Christ was of the same essence (*homo-ousios*) as the Father. The debates continued, leading to the Council of Constantinople in 381, which condemned the teachings of Apollinaris (ca. 310–390). This Christian theologian and bishop of Laodicea taught that in Jesus Christ the divine Logos replaced the rational human mind. This attempt to explain the union of Christ's divine and human nature was condemned. The council reaffirmed that Christ had a rational human soul.

In the fifth century, a new controversy erupted over how Christ's divine and human natures interacted. A central figure in this phase of the development of the Christological doctrine was Nestorius (ca. 386–450), a theologian and archbishop of Constantinople. His views were condemned at the Council of Ephesus in 431, but Nestorianism would long remain an important strand of Christianity, in particular outside of Europe.[42] It played a crucial role in the spread of Christianity across the Middle East, Persia, central Asia, India, and even China.

Nestorius opposed the use of the title *theotokos* for Mary and suggested instead the term *Christotokos*. He believed the first term would lead to the false idea that Mary gave birth to Jesus's divine nature. But his main contention had to do with the two natures of Christ—namely, that the divine and the human natures were not mixed but closely associated. His opponents accused him of dividing Christ into two separate persons—one divine and one human—rather than maintaining the unity of Christ's person. The Council of Ephesus condemned the views of Nestorius, who, after being deposed, spent the rest of his life in a monastery in Egypt. Among the main opponents of Nestorius was Cyril of Alexandria who was adamant that Christ was one person with two natures,

42. In his book *Migration and the Making of Global Christianity*, Jehu J. Hanciles, a professor at Emory University, documents the significant role of the widespread migration of Nestorians in the missionary outreach of the church.

united in the so-called hypostatic union. Some modern scholars think that Nestorius may not actually have taught the heretical two-persons Christology that was attributed to him, but rather that his ideas were misunderstood or misrepresented by his opponents.

Soon after this, Eutychius (ca. 375–454), an abbot in Constantinople, caused considerable upheaval with his view that Jesus's human nature was in fact absorbed in his divine nature, leaving him with only one (divine) nature. This theory was condemned at the Council of Chalcedon (AD 451), which established the famous Chalcedonian definition: Christ is *one person in two natures, fully divine and fully human, without confusion or division.*[43] Others proposed that Jesus had only one divine will rather than a human and a divine will. This view was rejected at the Third Council of Constantinople (AD 680–681). Though the Monophysite (one nature) view was rejected, it contributed to long-lasting theological and ecclesiastical divisions that persist to this day in Eastern Orthodox Churches (e.g., in the Coptic, Armenian, and Ethiopian Orthodox Churches).

The Two Natures of Christ

These various controversies shaped Christian doctrine, leading to the foundational creeds that still dominate Christology. The above summary of the most important Christological debates in the early church is an important background when we try to evaluate the biblical data concerning the natures of Christ and, in particular, of his human nature. The prolonged and fierce debate and controversy of the early centuries should raise a red flag if any Seventh-day Adventist Christian (or anyone else, for that matter) proposes some simplistic, definitive definition of the human nature of Christ. In any case, they must be careful not to do so on the basis of a selective reading of the biblical material in combination with some, equally selective, statements by Ellen G. White.

One of the most serious internal theological issues in the Seventh-day Adventist Church is the polarization that has arisen around the so-called Last Generation Theology (LGT).[44] M. L. Andreasen (1876–1962) is

43. Wikipedia, "Chalcedonian Definition."

44. In recent years three significant books have been published that provide a critical evaluation of LGT. The most complete survey of the issues surrounding LGT is *God's Character and the Last Generation*, edited by Jiří Moskala and John Peckham. This 2018 book features contributions from twelve Andrews University professors.

often mentioned as the person who rekindled this theory that already had long antecedents in Adventist history. Since his time, LGT has become an influential current in the more conservative segments of Adventism. One of the main tenets of this current is that, just before the end of time, there will be a "generation" that achieves sinless perfection. The thought that Jesus Christ will not return to this earth before that stage has been reached is mainly based on a single statement made by Ellen G. White: "Christ is waiting with longing desire for the manifestation of himself in his church. When the character of Christ shall be perfectly reproduced in his people, then he will come to claim them as his own."[45]

The question arises whether sinful human beings can ever reach sinless perfection. The reply of the LGT believers is that perfection is indeed within human reach, because Christ was perfect while he had the same human nature as Adam had *after* the fall (and as we have). With this same kind of human nature Jesus succeeded to keep sin at a distance. The "last generation" will have that same experience.

Below we will discuss in some detail what we know about the dual natures of Christ, and especially about his human nature. We will conclude that the view of the LGT believers is untenable. The idea that perfection is possible inevitably leads to legalism and serious mental anguish on the part of many who struggle to reach their perfectionist goal.

Christ's Divinity

What does the Bible tell us about the two natures of Christ? The matter may be less straightforward than is often suggested. We find not only some "easy" texts but also statements that are more difficult to understand and, possibly, also contain elements that appear to contradict other Bible passages.

The official Adventist teaching stresses that Jesus is fully God and fully man. Fundamental belief number four begins with these words: "God the eternal Son became incarnate in Jesus Christ. Through him all things were created, the character of God is revealed, the salvation of humanity is accomplished, and the world is judged. Forever truly God,

---

Two other books are Knight, *End-Time Events and the Last Generation*, and Bruinsma, *In All Humility*. In the section of this chapter on the natures of Jesus, I have relied on my book about LGT.

45. White, *Christ's Object Lessons*, 69.

he became also truly human, Jesus the Christ. He was conceived of the Holy Spirit and born of the virgin Mary."[46]

The words *fully God* imply that Christ has always existed. There never was a time when Christ was not. He was "with God" and he "was God" (John 1:1). Full divinity implies eternity. The Old Testament prophet Isaiah not only spoke of the child that was to be born as the "Prince of Peace," but also called him "the Mighty God" and "the everlasting Father" (Isa 9:6). Peter confessed that Jesus was the Messiah, "the Son of the living God" (Matt 16:16), and Thomas exclaimed, when looking into the eyes of the risen Christ, "My Lord and my God!" (John 20:28).

Together with the other members of the Trinity, Christ is the Creator of all that exists. Paul stressed that point in his letter to the church in Colossae: "For in him all things were created: things in heaven and on earth, visible and invisible" (Col 1:16). He is "the Amen . . . the ruler of God's creation" (Rev 3:14). Life itself is in him (John 1:4). Jesus has a "name that is above every other name" (Phil 2:9). Numerous times Jesus is referred to as Lord. As mentioned earlier, in the Septuagint this word Lord (*Kyrios*) was the title commonly reserved for God the Father. It is essential that we recognize Jesus Christ as the Lord. Paul asserted that if we confess that Jesus is Lord, we will be saved (Rom 10:9). And speaking of the return of Jesus Christ at the end of history, the apostle wrote, "We wait for the blessed hope—the appearing of the glory of our great God and Savior, Jesus Christ" (Titus 2:13).

Because Jesus was fully God, the disciples did not just treasure his memory after he had ascended to heaven—but "they worshiped him" (Luke 24:52). Even before this, Jesus had accepted worship from his followers. After he had walked on water and climbed back into the boat, "the disciples worshiped him" (Matt 14:33 NLT). And when Jesus had risen and appeared to his disciples, "they worshiped him" (Matt 28:9, 17). For people with a Jewish background to worship any other being than the only God was an unthinkable abomination. There is an abundance of evidence that in the early church, worship centered on the Lordship of Jesus Christ, and the hymns that were used in their worship testify to the belief of the early Christians that Christ was of equal status with the Father.[47]

46. General Conference, "What Do Adventists Believe?," no. 4.

47. Young, "Jesus," 116–19.

What Does the Bible Say About Christ's Humanity?

I could have quoted more Bible texts that emphasize Christ's full divinity. He is, indeed, our *Lord* and our *God*! But there is another side to the picture. *God became man*. And so, we not only find passages in the New Testament that identify Jesus as *God*, but we also read about the *man* Jesus Christ, as, for instance, in 1 Tim 2:5: "For there is one God and one mediator between God and mankind, the man Christ Jesus!"

The men and women who associated on a daily basis with Jesus, when he was among them, had no doubt that, whatever he was, he was a human being in the fullest possible sense of the word. When, contrary to the customs of his day, Jesus asked a Samaritan woman to give him a drink, she voiced her amazement with these words: "You are a Jew and I am a Samaritan woman" (John 4:9). This woman made an important point about Jesus's humanness. He was like a "normal" Jew of his day. We have no portrait or selfie of Jesus, but of one thing we can be quite sure: he did not look like a blond Viking or a young, white American adolescent, such as we see on so many illustrations in children's Bibles and on posters. Jesus was the Son of God. But he was also born of a human mother in the Middle East (Gal 4:4). Like every other human being, he had a body, a soul, and a spirit. When facing his imminent death, Jesus's soul was "troubled" (John 12:27), and when he was about to die, he said, "Father, into your hands I commit my spirit" (Luke 23:46).

Jesus came as a helpless infant and grew up as a normal child. Like any other human being, he could be hungry (Matt 4:2) or thirsty (John 19:28). He needed sleep (Matt 8:24) and could be tired (John 4:6). He knew of sadness, as the shortest text in the Bible tells us that "Jesus wept" when hearing about the death of his friend Lazarus (John 11:35). And, of course, the ultimate proof of his humanness was that he could suffer and die.

Several New Testament passages mention that Christ "took" human nature. Paul wrote that Jesus came in "human form" (Phil 2:7 NLT). But in his letter to the Romans, the apostle is more specific: God "sent his own Son in a human body like ours—except that ours are sinful" (Rom 8:3 TLB). And the author of Hebrews agrees: "He had to be made like them, fully human in every way" (Heb 2:17). So, what does this "in every way" mean? It certainly indicates that he can understand our situation, the same author underlines, because he "has been tempted in every way, just as we are," with the crucial difference that he never yielded to sin (Heb 4:15). Whatever may be said, and whatever questions may be asked about Jesus's human nature, one thing is clear: he never sinned!

Did Jesus Adopt a *Sinful* Human Nature?[48]

Jesus was fully man. But did he perhaps have an advantage by not having the same inherited inclination, or propensity, towards sin as we have? Or must we conclude from words like "being in every respect like us" that he also shared in the sinful aspect of our nature that has, ever since Adam's transgression, been passed on from one generation to the next? The biblical material is not so clear-cut as some want us to believe.

Romans 8:3 is a key verse. In the New King James Version, which is the favorite translation for most LGT supporters, we read, "For what the law could not do in that it was weak through the flesh, God did by sending his own Son in the likeness of sinful flesh." Some commentators point out that the "likeness" of sinful flesh does not necessarily mean the "sameness" of human flesh, with its inherited tendencies towards evil. Others contend that Heb 7:26 points us in another direction by affirming that Jesus was "separate from sinners." But others again, with the LGT supporters among them, think that Rom 8 leaves us with the definite impression that Jesus's humanity did include the inherited propensities towards sin.

Raoul Dederen (1925–2016), one of the most respected Adventist theologians of the last century, wrote in his chapter about Christ in the *Handbook of Seventh-day Adventist Theology*,

> He came "in the likeness of human flesh" (Rom 8:3). He took human nature in its fallen condition with its infirmities and liabilities and bearing the consequences of sin; but not its sinfulness, he was truly human, one with the human race, except for sin. He could truly say "He [Satan] has no power over me" (John 14:30). . . . Jesus took human nature, weakened and deteriorated by thousands of years of sin, yet undefiled and spotless. "In him," writes John, "there is no sin" (1 John 3:5).[49]

48. To say that Jesus had a sinful nature is, in fact, unbiblical and I find it reprehensible. The adjective *sinful* means full of sin and cannot be applied to the biblical Christ.

49. Dederen, "Christ," 164–65.

The pre-fall interpreters do not deny that Christ was subject to human weaknesses. His body was affected by the same bodily processes and the same physical challenges as the bodies of his contemporaries. "But they deny that Christ took or had sinful inclinations, propensities, or tendencies."[50] After a careful evaluation of the various viewpoints, Woodrow Whidden (1944–2025) makes this succinct but thoughtful statement:

> They [the expressions pre-Fall and post-Fall] are not very helpful, in that Jesus was neither completely pre-Fall nor post-Fall—as such terms would imply. On the one hand, he was pre-Fall in the sense that his humanity was not "infected" with sinful, corrupt tendencies, or propensities to sin, such as we are born with. On the other hand, he was post-Fall in the sense that his humanity was "affected" by sin, in which he never indulged. Thus he was neither completely one nor the other. In a very important sense he was both, and the all-or-nothing implications of such expressions are not helpful.[51]

The certainty that Christ took post-fall human nature rather than pre-fall human nature is an important building block of LGT. It should be clear, however, that this position is mainly arrived at by a selective use of statements by Ellen G. White that are directly or indirectly related to this matter. The truth is that, when we analyze all her pronouncements about the humanity of Christ, the picture is, at the very least, ambiguous. This should not surprise us, as she was no trained theologian, and her thinking developed over the course of her long life.

The Ultimate Paradox: Divinity and Humanity Combined

How Christ can, at the same time, be fully human and fully divine remains one of the great paradoxes the Christian believer is faced with. We saw in chapter 1 how the written word of God also presents us with an example of a fundamental paradox in the Christian faith. Paradoxically, the Bible is both divine and human. Overemphasis on the human aspect will destroy the authority of the Bible. On the other hand, a lack of recognition of the human element will easily lead us to a distorted theory of inspiration.

50. Whidden, "Humanity of Christ," 694.

51. Whidden, *Ellen White*, 15.

What is true of the *written word* also applies to the *living Word*. When dealing with the two natures of our Lord, we are confronted with the ultimate paradox. How can anyone be simultaneously fully divine and fully human? How are these two natures united—blended—in one Person? We tread on holy ground, a terrain full of pitfalls for finite human minds. If we focus exclusively on the divine nature of Christ, we may unwittingly follow in the footsteps of the heretics of ancient times, who made his human nature into some kind of make-believe humanness. In other words, it would mean that we accept the idea that he *appeared* to be human and *played the role* of a human being, while he was never fully one of us. If, on the other hand, we lay stress on his humanity to the extent that we lose sight of his full divinity, we end up with a Christ who has no life in himself, and, as he cannot give what he does not possess, he cannot make us partakers of his eternal life. Thus, when we destroy the balance between Christ's divinity and his humanity, we no longer have a true Savior.

Must we then leave our intellect behind us when we contemplate this difficult topic? Must we be prepared to simply accept what many see as nonsensical statements? Or is this the place where, in all humility, we take off our shoes, recognizing that we tread on holy ground, and where, aware of our creaturely finiteness, we reverently bow before the mystery that confronts us? Note that this is what Ellen White suggested in 1898:

> The humanity of the Son of God is everything to us. It is the golden chain that binds our souls to Christ, and through Christ to God. This is to be our study. Christ was a real man; he gave proof of his humility in becoming a man. Yet he was God in the flesh. When we approach this subject, we would do well to heed the words spoken by Christ to Moses at the burning bush, "Put off thy shoes from off thy feet, for the place whereon thou standest is holy ground." We should come to this study with the humility of a learner, with a contrite heart. And the study of the incarnation of Christ is a fruitful field, which will repay the searcher who digs deep for hidden truth.[52]

52. White, "Search the Scriptures," para. 6. This statement is also found in Nichol et al., *Seventh-day Adventist Bible Commentary*, 7A:443.

The Uniqueness of Jesus Christ

Christ is unique. There has never been anyone like him. The biblical testimony underlines both his divine and his human nature. It is clear that Christ became fully man; he was like his contemporaries in Galilee and could blend into the crowds in Jerusalem. But he never sinned.

Perhaps we would have liked the New Testament to be more specific and more systematic in its witness regarding the divine and the human natures of Christ and would have liked to see some definitive statements about the nature of Christ's sinlessness that would have stopped all further debate. However, the New Testament "was not consumed with theological speculation about the divine and the human natures in Jesus. Statements about Jesus' person came indirectly in the context of worship and pastoral exhortation." We must remember that the New Testament is not a theological treatise; it is a testimony of salvation history.[53]

We must stand in awe and humility before the greatest miracle of all times. God became man. It has only happened once, and it will never happen again. That is what we must always keep in mind when we discuss the natures of Christ, including the question of his pre-fall or post-fall humanity. No human definitions will suffice and answer all questions. In the end we must humbly confess that we cannot compare him with anyone else. He is the only One who can save us because, in a miraculous way that far exceeds our understanding, he is both God and man.

The Christ of Faith

Several prominent theologians in the nineteenth and twentieth centuries, like David Friedrich Strauss, Albert Schweitzer, and later Rudolf Bultmann, emphasized the contrast between the Jesus of history—who lived in first-century Palestine—and the Christ of faith, who became the object of Christian belief and theological reflection. Rudolf Bultmann (1884–1976) advocated a process of *demythologization* and insisted that faith does not depend on historical details but on an existential encounter with Christ. This demythologizing approach "displays a radical skepticism towards any objective understanding of the stories which it seeks to interpret."[54] It was especially directed at those parts of the New

53. Young, "Jesus," 121.

54. Macquarrie, *Scope of Demythologizing*, 17.

Testament that appear to be more or less mythical, such as the miracle stories, and not at the ethical teachings of Jesus. But critics have pointed out that it is extremely difficult to draw a line between what is supposedly mythical and what purportedly is not.

Bultmann accepts that Jesus Christ was a historical figure. But he is presented as the Son of God, "a pre-existent divine being, and therefore to that extent is a mythological figure."[55] Bultmann and his followers have emphasized that the core of the Christian faith is not an acknowledgment of historical data about Jesus, but the *kerygma*—the gospel proclamation that calls for a radical decision to acknowledge Jesus's Lordship. However, the Scriptures claim that God revealed himself in a historical reality (Luke 1:1–4). Even though there may be difficulties in a full historical reconstruction of who and what Jesus was, and what he did, without a historical foundation the gospel message is reduced to a personal, human experience rather than a saving truth.

Jesus is not just a founder of a new religion like Gautama Buddha was for Buddhism, or Mohammed was for Islam. These founders were primarily important for their teachings and not for who they were. Jesus is different:

> Jesus is not simply the one who first discovered or proclaimed its [i.e., Christianity's] belief. He is himself the basic object of its beliefs, the essential content of its doctrines. . . . For Christianity, then, it is the founder that makes his teachings important. We need to hear what Jesus said, Christians believe, because of who and what he was. At the center of Christianity lies a particular understanding of Jesus, and in the final analysis, the Christian doctrine of salvation is nothing other than the interpretation of Jesus' significance for human existence. Soteriology is Christology, we might say.[56]

55. Bartsch, *Kerygma and Myth*, 34.

56. Rice, *Reign of God*, 164–65.

Chapter 4

God the Holy Spirit

In Acts 19:1–6 a rather unexpected incident is reported. It occurred during the apostle Paul's repeat visit to the city of Ephesus in Asia Minor. He met a group of "about twelve men," who are described as "disciples." Only a small part of the conversation between Paul and these disciples has been recorded. The apostle asked these men, "Did you receive the Holy Spirit when you believed?" Their answer was as direct as it was surprising. They replied, "No, we have not even heard that there is a Holy Spirit." This event took place some twenty years after the Christian mission had started; yet, somehow, these followers of Christ had remained totally ignorant on the topic of the Holy Spirit. This gap in their knowledge was, however, soon remedied. Since these men had only been baptized with "John's baptism," they were now baptized with the Christian baptism "in the name of the Lord Jesus." Then Paul "placed his hands on them, the Holy Spirit came on them, and they spoke in tongues and prophesied." No further details are given of how exactly the Spirit "came on them," and about their gift of tongues.

Although today most Christians have at least some understandings of the Holy Spirit, it is probably true that for many this knowledge is rather limited. What is the Spirit like? What does he do in the world, and in our personal life? And how can a person tell whether he has actually "received" the Holy Spirit?

The Apostles' Creed, which most denominations (including the Seventh-day Adventist Church) accept as a basic summary of Christian teachings, has ten lines about the belief in Jesus Christ, and then just one short line that says, "I believe in the Holy Spirit." There is no further explanation about what this belief entails. In the discussions about the Trinity in the early church the identity and role of the Holy Spirit gradually received the contours of the doctrine of the Spirit. A consensus developed that the Holy Spirit is one of the three persons of the Godhead. As we further explore this, we must keep in mind what we said earlier about the human limitations in our God-talk and about the use of the term *person*. When theologians speak about the Spirit, they tend to use the pronouns *he* and *his* in full awareness that we cannot assign a gender to God. In fact, some have preferred to use *she* and *her* in recognition of some characteristics of the Spirit that most people associate with the female rather than the male person. Interestingly, the Hebrew word for spirit (*ruach*) is feminine, but the Greek word for spirit (*pneuma*) is neuter. We should not draw any conclusions from this with regard to a gender of the Spirit. In Greek the word *teknon* (child) is neuter, but that "does not suggest that Greeks viewed children as sub-personal. . . . God and the Holy Spirit transcend the human genders, so that both 'masculine' and 'feminine' qualities are ascribed to them, as biblical passages about fatherly and motherly qualities apply to them."[1]

Through the ages some theologians have emphasized feminine imagery to describe the Holy Spirit. In some Jewish literature, particularly Prov 8 and the apocryphal Wisdom of Solomon, Wisdom is personified as a woman and some early Christians linked this feminine Wisdom with the Holy Spirit. Hildegard von Bingen (1098–1179), the German Benedictine abbess, who is regarded as the first representative of German medieval mysticism, often described the Holy Spirit as a woman and a mother. So did Julian of Norwich (1343–1416), a religious recluse in medieval England. Among later authors, John Wesley (1703–1791), the founder of Methodism, sometimes used feminine imagery in describing the role of the Spirit. In modern times Elisabeth Schlüssler Fiorenza (b. 1938) and other feminist theologians have explored the feminine aspects of the Spirit. In his heartrending novel *The Shack*, author W. Paul Young brings Mack Philips, who sadly lost his little daughter through a crime, to a location connected with this tragedy. There Mack meets with

1. Thiselton, *Holy Spirit*, 121–22.

the Trinity. The three persons of the Godhead are represented in rather nontraditional ways. The Holy Spirit is presented as Sarayu (the Sanskrit word for "wind"), an Asian woman with an elusive, sparkling presence, often difficult to perceive fully.

The Biblical Picture of the Holy Spirit

Christ told his disciples that he would send the Holy Spirit to fill the vacuum that would result upon his departure from this earth. That caused many Christians to believe that the Spirit's connection with mankind effectively started when he "replaced" Jesus Christ. This view is incorrect. As "part" of the triune God, the Holy Spirit existed from eternity, and he was involved with this world and its inhabitants from the time when God created. Although the Old Testament is less explicit than the New Testament about the personhood and role of the Spirit, we find throughout the Old Testament references to the presence and the activities of the Holy Spirit. The Old Testament itself was the product of the Spirit, since "prophets spoke from God as they were carried along by the Holy Spirit" (2 Pet 1:20–21).

On the very first page of the Bible we are told that the Spirit was associated with the creation of our world. The author of Genesis informs us that the Spirit of God was "hovering over the waters" (Gen 1:2). In these first sentences of the Bible we are given notice that, "where chaos rules, with darkness covering the deep, God is present. The Spirit of God is moving, presaging God's first command [that there be light] in the next verse."[2] Psalm 104:30 also links the Spirit with creation. God's Spirit was active in bringing life and form out of chaos. The Spirit remains omnipresent, as David testified: "Where shall I go from your Spirit? Where can I flee from your presence?" (Ps 139:7).

A passage in Isa 63 reflects on the rebellion of Israel against God, their subsequent hardships, and God's past acts of deliverance and guidance through Moses. It emphasizes the role of God's Holy Spirit in leading and providing rest for his people, underscoring the relationship between divine guidance and the people's actions (vv. 10–14). In the Old Testament stories we find repeated mention of people in whom the Spirit was present in a special way. Even the Egyptian Pharaoh noticed that

2. Turner, *Genesis*, 21.

there was nobody like Joseph—"one in whom is the spirit of God" (Gen 41:38). Moses was instructed by God to lay his hands on his successor, Joshua, in recognition of the fact that he had "the spirit of leadership" (Num 27:18). When Saul was anointed by Samuel as the future king of Israel, "the Spirit of God came powerfully upon him." The story adds that Saul at that occasion received the gift of prophecy (1 Sam 10:9–10). The same wording—"the Spirit of God came powerfully upon him"—is found in the story of David's anointing (1 Sam 16:13).

In these and similar cases the presence of the Spirit was specifically related to the preparation of a person for a particular task. However, the gift of the Spirit was not bestowed without conditions. Those who were blessed by the power of the Spirit could "grieve" the Spirit (Isa 63:10), and the Spirit could therefore leave a person altogether (1 Sam 16:14). After his grievous sin with Bathsheba, King David prayed that God would not take his Holy Spirit from him (Ps 51:11).

Although the Holy Spirit is certainly not absent in the Old Testament period, he has a much more prominent place in the New Testament. He is depicted as the empowering agent during Christ's earthly life. Mary was informed by the angel Gabriel of the supernatural role of the Spirit in the unfathomable miracle that was about to take place: "The Holy Spirit will come on you, and the power of the Most High will overshadow you" (Luke 1:35). After his baptism, at the very beginning of his ministry, Jesus was "full of the Holy Spirit" and "was led by the Spirit to the wilderness," where he would be tempted by the devil (Luke 4:1). Matthew states that it was "by the Spirit" that Jesus delivered people from the demons that possessed them (12:28), and the apostle Paul affirms the role of the Spirit in the resurrection of the Lord (Rom 8:11).

In numerous places in the New Testament the central role of the Spirit in our salvation is underlined. The role of the Holy Spirit is crucial in our communication with God. "The Spirit helps us in our weakness. We do not know what we ought to pray for, but the Spirit himself intercedes for us" (Rom 8:26). "It is the work of the Spirit to rephrase the ignorant specifics of our prayers to align them more accurately with the will of God and to our real need."[3] The power of the Spirit enables the believers to become effective witnesses of the gospel truth (Acts 1:8). The Spirit also directly impacts on the functioning of the human conscience. He came to "prove the world to be in the wrong about sin and

3. Rodríguez, *Andrews Bible Commentary*, 1581.

righteousness and judgment" (John 16:8–11). The Spirit is the divine agent who facilitates the "new birth" and opens the path to eternal life in the kingdom of God (John 3:3–7, 16). He brings salvation "through the washing of rebirth and renewal by the Holy Spirit" (Titus 3:5). The Spirit also incorporates us into the church—the body of Christ. "For we were all baptized by one Spirit so as to form one body . . . and we were all given one Spirit to drink" (1 Cor 12:13).

Of special significance is the passage about the Spirit in Eph 1:13–14: "And you were included in Christ when you heard the message of truth, the gospel of your salvation. When you believed, *you were marked in him with a seal*, the promised Holy Spirit, who is a deposit guaranteeing our inheritance until the redemption of those who are God's possession—to the praise of his glory" (italics added). "A wax seal would have a sign of ownership or identification stamped in it, identifying who was attesting what was inside the container that had been sealed. . . . Paul here speaks of the Spirit as a deposit—a term used in ancient business documents to mean a 'down payment.' Those who had tasted the Spirit had begun to taste the life of the future world that God had promised his people."[4] In Rev 7:2–3 an angel "having the seal of the living God" calls upon four other angels to "put a seal on the foreheads of the servants of our God." In classical Adventist eschatology this seal, with which the 144,000 "from all tribes of Israel" are sealed, is understood as the seventh-day Sabbath. God's end-time people obey all God's commandments, but the Sabbath commandment is special because it emphasizes God's ownership of everything. Therefore, it is argued, the Sabbath is God's seal, in contrast with the "mark of the beast" (Rev 13:16–18), which symbolizes the end-time obstinacy in keeping the Sunday as the day of worship. We will return to this later in this book, but it would seem that Paul's clear identification in Eph 1:13 of the seal as the Holy Spirit should be a point of departure in any interpretation of the seal in Revelation.

A final comment in this section concerns an issue that has perplexed many people. The Bible is clear that the Lord is a forgiving God, and that forgiveness is available even for the most heinous of sins (Isa 1:18). Yet, Jesus said there is a sin that will not be forgiven—namely, "blasphemy against the Holy Spirit" (Matt 12:31–32; Mark 3:28–31; Luke 12:10). Jesus made this statement after he had healed a demon-possessed man who

4. Keener, *IVP Bible Background Commentary*, 542.

was also blind and mute. The people who witnessed this miracle were astonished; they apparently reported to a group of Pharisees what they had witnessed. When these spiritual leaders heard this, they attributed this miracle to the power of "Beelzebub, the prince of demons." Jesus indicated that, when people willingly and persistently ascribe that which is good to an evil source, they are in danger of moving outside the realm of grace. Thiselton comments, "It is difficult to see how a person who has utterly distorted and confused good and evil still has the capacity to repent."[5] "It is the Spirit that leads us to repentance and persistent rejection of him will finally make our sins unforgivable."[6]

The Third Person of the Godhead

Before ending his earthly ministry Jesus promised that he would not leave his followers as "orphans" but would send them the Holy Spirit: "I will ask the Father, and he will give you *another* advocate to help you and be with you forever" (John 14:16; italics added). The word *another* is theologically very significant. The Greek has two words for "another," namely *heteros* and *allos*. The word *heteros* means "another of a different kind," while *allos* stands for "another of the same kind."[7] In this text Jesus spoke of an "allos" advocate. In other words, Jesus promised to send Someone who is "of the same kind," who is equal in divinity with himself. The Holy Spirit would take over his role—not as a *different* kind of helper but as one *just like him*. In his highly esteemed commentary on the Gospel of John, C. K. Barret confirms this: the words that are used and "the context suggests very strongly continuity between the offices of Jesus and the Paraklete."[8]

The Spirit is called a *Paraklētos*. This term (literally meaning "one who is called alongside") was translated "Comforter" in the King James Version. "Advocate" is a better rendering, even though there is no specific legal implication.[9] The precise meaning of *Paraklētos* remains intensely

5. Thiselton, *Holy Spirit*, 43.
6. Rodríguez, *Andrews Bible Commentary*, 1251.
7. Nichol et al., *Seventh-day Adventist Bible Commentary*, 5:1037.
8. Barret, *Gospel According to St. John*, 385.
9. Green et al., *Dictionary of Jesus*, 349.

debated,[10] and "helper" may be preferable, as this aligns with the tasks of the Spirit that are mentioned in the context of this passage. Jesus said that the "Spirit will teach you all things and will remind you of everything I have said to you" (John 14:26); "he will testify about me" (John 15:26); "he will prove the world to be in the wrong about sin" (John 16:6–7); and "he will tell you what is yet to come" (John 16:13).

Jesus's reference to the Spirit as the *Paraklētos*, and to the things this helper who is like him will do, strongly underlines the personhood of the Holy Spirit. This is further confirmed by the personal characteristics that are attributed to the Spirit, such as intelligence (1 Cor 2:10–11), affections (Eph 4:30), and will (1 Cor 2:11). These things cannot be said of an impersonal influence. The same pertains to activities of the Spirit on our behalf. He commands, as is clear from the story of Philip's encounter with the Ethiopian eunuch: "The Spirit told Philip: 'Go to that chariot and stay near it'" (Acts 8:29). In other passages we learn that the Spirit teaches the followers of Jesus (John 14:26) and that he intercedes for us in prayer (Rom 8:26).

The Spirit "Fills" the Believer

The Holy Spirit is involved in every aspect of the Christian life, from our spiritual birth and throughout our spiritual pilgrimage. We are told we are no longer "in the realm of the flesh" but have moved "into the realm of the Spirit, if indeed the Spirit of God lives in you" (Rom 8:9, 13). The believer is "God's temple" in which the Spirit of God dwells (1 Cor 3:16). Paul reminds the Corinthian church members, "Do you not know that your bodies are a temple of the Holy Spirit, who is in you?" (1 Cor 6:19; see also Eph 5:18). The Spirit brings radical change in the life of the Christian: "Now the Lord is the Spirit, and where the Spirit of the Lord is, there is freedom. And we all, who with unveiled faces contemplate the Lord's glory, are being transformed into his image with ever-increasing glory, which comes from the Lord, who is the Spirit" (2 Cor 3:17–18). These words highlight the transformative power of the Holy Spirit. They emphasize spiritual freedom and the ongoing process of becoming more like Christ.

The experience of the indwelling of the Spirit is often described as a "baptism" of the Spirit. John the Baptist, the forerunner of Jesus,

10. See, e.g., Thiselton, *Holy Spirit*, 140–44.

indicated that the person on whom the Spirit descended in the form of a dove (John 1:31) would baptize people with the Holy Spirit (v. 32; see also Matt 3:11). And this person—Jesus—told Nicodemus during their nocturnal conversation that entry into the kingdom of God is on the condition that people are "born of water and the Spirit" (John 3:5). This Spirit baptism is often referred to as a "second blessing."

Christians hold different views concerning the baptism with the Holy Spirit or the Spirit baptism (or about the meaning of being "sealed" by the Spirit). In charismatic and Pentecostal circles the Spirit baptism is separated from the water baptism. It is a subsequent experience, often received after special prayer and a laying on of hands and marked by speaking in tongues (see below) and/or other spiritual gifts. Roman Catholics, Anglicans, and Orthodox Christians see *confirmation* as the moment when the Spirit is imparted. For some other groups the Spirit baptism is not a onetime event but rather an ongoing experience of renewal.

Together with many other groups, Seventh-day Adventists and most evangelical Christians believe that the Spirit baptism occurs when a person undergoes the water baptism and is incorporated into the body of Christ. For them the key text is, "We are all baptized by one Spirit so as to form one body" (1 Cor 12:13).

Perhaps we must be careful not to "force everything in one same system," say systematic theologians Van der Kooi and Van den Brink. "The New Testament sometimes refers to a certain lapse of time between the moment a person first becomes a believer and the time he or she received (the baptism of) the Spirit." They point to Acts 8:14–17 and Acts 19:1–7 as examples. "Apparently, the Spirit works with people in different ways and—independently of their character, spiritual development, or communal context—is able to give, at a certain moment in time, an important new impulse, an intensification of a conscious life in the Spirit, so that they 'grow up in every way into him who is the head, into Christ' (Eph 4:15)."[11]

Spiritual Gifts

The Holy Spirit works in us and, as we saw, impacts on all aspects of our spiritual life. These activities of the Spirit are universal. But in addition to what the Spirit does for every person who is open to this, the Bible

11. Van der Kooi and Van den Brink, *Christian Dogmatics*, 511.

mentions a number of special gifts that are widely, albeit unequally, distributed. The Spirit decides which of these gifts he will give to particular persons. "He distributes them . . . just as he determines" (1 Cor 12:11).

The apostle Paul provides us with three different lists of spiritual gifts. They partly overlap, but each list has a specific focus. In Rom 12:6–8 we find a list of *motivational* gifts. They include the gifts of:

a. *Prophecy*—providing counsel and vision
b. *Serving*—giving practical assistance and service to others
c. *Teaching*—explaining the gospel truth
d. *Encouragement*—inspiring and motivating others
e. *Giving*—of ourselves and of our resources
f. *Leadership*—gifted in administration and management
g. *Mercy*—showing compassion to those in need

In 1 Cor 12 we find a somewhat longer list, which includes several of the gifts that are specified in the list in Rom 12 (prophecy, helping, and administration), but also a number of other, so-called *manifestation* gifts. They are:

a. *Wisdom*—a special insight into God's will
b. *Knowledge*—knowing facts spiritually revealed by God
c. *Faith*—an above-average ability to trust God's presence and power
d. *Healing*—the gift of restoring sick people to health
e. *Miracles*—the ability to perform supernatural wonders
f. *Discernment*—the ability to distinguish between positive and negative spiritual influences
g. *Tongues*—speaking in an unknown language to the glory of God
h. *Interpretation of tongues*—understanding and translating the messages others have spoken in tongues
i. *Apostleship*—pioneering the planting of new churches

In Eph 4:11 Paul mentions five categories of spiritual workers, whom the Spirit may equip with a special giftedness to fulfil their assignment: *Apostles*—those who plant and oversee churches; *Prophets*—those who proclaim divine revelations; *Evangelists*—those who spread the gospel effectively; *Pastors*—those who care for and guide the believers; and *Teachers*—those who instruct in doctrine and faith.

The question naturally arises whether these gifts may be equated with talents or special skills. Can they be learned or are they perhaps, at least in part, genetically determined? It seems that spiritual gifts may enhance, or make use of, natural talents and/or build on skills people have learned in theory and practice. The gift of administration may increase and intensify the organizational skills that people already have acquired in their professional life. The Spirit may decide to endow a person who possesses a natural talent for public speaking with the gift of preaching or teaching. A study in pastoral theology may be used by the Spirit as a basis for becoming a "gifted" pastor.

Talents can be used for personal projects and for our own success; they can be put to the service of others, but they may also serve our own interests, while spiritual gifts have as their sole purpose to build up the church and serve others (Eph 4:12). Talents and skills are inherited or developed, and can be cultivated through training and experience, while spiritual gifts are distributed as the Spirit wills—they do not have their origin in ourselves but are given by the Holy Spirit. A talent becomes most powerful when surrendered to God and used in alignment with one's spiritual gifts. While all people have talents, only believers receive spiritual gifts for the work of the church and the kingdom of God.

The Spirit decides what gift or gifts an individual may receive, but this distribution does not happen without any human input. Jesus made a statement that also relates to the topic of spiritual gifts—namely, that God gives the Holy Spirit to those who ask him for his "good gifts." While this primarily refers to the Holy Spirit himself, it also suggests that seeking abilities for his work, including the spiritual gifts, is encouraged (Luke 11:13). In his discussion of the spiritual gifts, Paul encourages believers to "eagerly desire the greater gifts" (1 Cor 12:31) and "especially prophecy" (1 Cor 14:1).

Another question has to do with the time element. Were the spiritual gifts limited to the apostolic age? Or were they available for believers in all ages, and can we therefore also expect them today? Many theologians have concluded that the miraculous gifts were specifically intended for the apostolic era, to authenticate the ministry of the apostles and their associates. Among these "secessionists" (those who think the spiritual gifts ceased when the church was firmly established) were church fathers like Augustine, but also many later leaders in the Reformed tradition. On the other hand, there are also many "continuationists," who believe that all spiritual gifts, including the most miraculous ones, are still active. Justin Martyr, Irenaeus, and other early Christian writers reported miracles beyond the time of the apostles. Many contemporary Christians, in particular in the charismatic and Pentecostal branches of Christianity, report modern-day prophecies, healings, and tongues as genuine experiences. They emphasize that the Bible nowhere indicates that the spiritual gifts will end at some point in the Christian era, before Christ's return. A third group opt for a middle ground. They believe spiritual gifts *may* continue today but warn that they are often misused or counterfeited.

Those who believe that the spiritual gifts will remain operative until the end of time should, of course, take into consideration that the gifts must always serve one fundamental purpose. First Corinthians 12:7 tells us what that purpose is: "To each one the manifestation of the Spirit is given for the common good." And what is this "common good"? It is the building up of the church—the body of Christ (Eph 4:11–12). Does this mean that in some local churches, at particular moments in time, and/or in certain geographical areas in the world, particular gifts may be especially needed, while some other gifts may, under specific circumstances, not always bring the same positive results? This is, however, not for humans to determine. After all, the Spirit decides when, and to whom, he distributes the gifts.

The *gifts* of the Spirit are not identical with the *fruit* of the Spirit, even though there is a close connection. While the gifts are distributed to certain individuals and not given to all, the fruit of the Spirit is universal. "Every true Spirit-led Christian has every aspect of it."[12] The various elements of the fruit (singular) are listed by Paul in his letter to the Galatians.

Paul seems to deliberately use the singular word *fruit* and not the plural *fruits*. This suggests that the various qualities he lists are not separate, individual virtues, but rather aspects of one unified work of the Holy Spirit. In other words, the Spirit produces one fruit that manifests itself in multiple characteristics.

The fruit of the Spirit is "love, joy, peace, forbearance, kindness, goodness, faithfulness, gentleness, and self-control" (Gal 5:22–23). Much can be said about these things, but, as Adventist church historian George

12. Knight, *Exploring Galatians and Ephesians*, 139.

Knight tells us, "for that fruit to be truly fruit of the Spirit, the Christian must live it rather than merely talk about it."[13]

Adventists and Spiritual Gifts

From the beginning of their movement Seventh-day Adventists have been adamant that the spiritual gifts did not cease when the apostolic period ended, but continued through the centuries and would certainly characterize end-time Christianity. But soon after the start of their movement there were second thoughts on the part of many of the earliest Adventist believers. Some of their meetings were rather chaotic, with ecstatic phenomena that were quite controversial: loud singing, shouting, being "slain in the Spirit," occasions of faith healing, visions, dreams, and speaking in tongues.[14] This caused a great deal of apprehension but, nonetheless, an early consensus developed that the spiritual gifts were not limited to the past. During the General Conference Session of 1868 a resolution was adopted that emphasized belief in the ongoing manifestation of spiritual gifts. The resolution stated that the presence of these gifts, especially the gift of prophecy, was a distinguishing feature of the Adventist movement.[15]

As Adventism further developed, the occasional occurrence of speaking in tongues was increasingly seen as an undesirable phenomenon that led to unruly situations and could easily be counterfeited. The persistent negative attitude towards speaking in tongues was, no doubt, also associated with the rise of modern Pentecostalism at the beginning of the twentieth century and its subsequent extraordinary success in many parts of the world.

Adventist theologians are divided with regard to the nature of speaking in tongues and the interpretation of tongues. Some differentiate between a gift of speaking in known languages (which the speakers did not learn) and a gift of speaking in an unknown prayer language that needs interpretation by someone who has a spiritual gift for that specific purpose. They point to the fact that the gift that was manifested at Pentecost, as recorded in Acts 2, enabled the apostles to communicate

13. Knight, *Exploring Galatians and Ephesians*, 141.

14. Graybill, "Enthusiasm," 10–12. See also a series of articles by Arthur L. White, "Ecstatic Experiences."

15. Levterov, *Development*.

the gospel in the actual languages of people who had gathered in Jerusalem, which proved to be a tremendous evangelistic advantage. They recognize that the gift that is described in 1 Cor 14 has very different characteristics.[16] The words of the people who spoke in tongues had to be interpreted in order to be understood.

Most Adventist scholars defend the (in my view untenable) position that the gift of Acts 2 and that of 1 Cor 14 are, in fact, identical.[17] Underlying this may be a strong urge not to give credibility to a prominent phenomenon in charismatic circles that Adventists have strongly disliked ever since they themselves had some unfavorable experiences with it. They invariably emphasize in their evaluation of Pentecostal Christianity that whatever is described in 1 Cor 14 should not be elevated to a "gift" that is prominent among the spiritual gifts.

The Adventist attitude towards the gift of *healing* has been rather ambivalent. Adventists have consistently warned against the abuse of this gift and against phony claims by charismatic individuals or downright charlatans. They have from early on emphasized a holistic approach to health and health care, combining spiritual well-being with physical health practices. The fact that the denomination operates a large hospital system testifies to its commitment to the use of the medical scientific processes that are at our disposal. At the same time, the Adventist Church does recognize that even today healing by divine intervention may occur, while it consistently affirms the church's dedication to health ministry, emphasizing the importance of both spiritual and medical approaches to healing.[18] The passage of Jas 5:13–15 plays a significant role in the Adventist pastoral praxis. Although the anointing of the sick, to which this passage refers, did not achieve the status of a sacrament (or ordinance), it is a rite that is regularly performed when people who suffer from a serious illness or are terminally ill ask for it. The anointing

16. Nichol et al., *Seventh-day Adventist Bible Commentary*, 6:795–96, emphasizes the differences between Acts 2 and 1 Cor 14 and suggests that the gift of foreign languages at Pentecost was not identical with the gift of ecstatic utterances in Corinth, referred to as "tongues." W. Larry Richards (1936–2017), an Adventist New Testament scholar, held the same view. See his *1 Corinthians*, 235–36. See also Richardson, *Speaking in Tongues*.

17. E.g., Hasel, *Speaking in Tongues*; Rice, "Spiritual Gifts," 610–50; and Rodríguez, "Gift of Tongues."

18. See General Conference, "Commitment to Health and Healing."

underlines trust in the ability of God to heal the person, but it does not carry the expectation that he will always do so.

The gift of *prophecy* is, among Adventists, undeniably the most prominent—and also the most controversial—spiritual gift. As already mentioned, one of the official fundamental teachings (number eighteen) of the Adventist faith community concerns the gift of prophecy and claims that this gift was specifically manifested in the life and ministry of Ellen G. White. As with all fundamental beliefs, a series of Bible texts are added as the Scriptural basis for the belief.

> The Scriptures testify that one of the gifts of the Holy Spirit is prophecy. This gift is an identifying mark of the remnant church, and we believe it was manifested in the ministry of Ellen G. White. Her writings speak with prophetic authority and provide comfort, guidance, instruction, and correction to the church. They also make clear that the Bible is the standard by which all teaching and experience must be tested. (Num. 12:6; 2 Chron. 20:20; Amos 3:7; Joel 2:28, 29; Acts 2:14–21; 2 Tim. 3:16, 17; Heb. 1:1–3; Rev. 12:17; 19:10; 22:8, 9.)[19]

The underlying reasoning for this belief in the perpetuity of the gift of prophecy follows a few basic steps. The prophecy of Joel 2:28–29 was partially fulfilled in Jerusalem in the supernatural phenomena during Pentecost, just ten days after Jesus's ascension. This prophecy about a time when people would have dreams and visions would see its final fulfilment in the end of time through an outpouring of the Spirit, with a revitalization of the prophetic gift. According to Matt 7:15–20 believers must be aware of the danger of *false* prophets. This implies that there will also be *genuine* prophets. Christ stressed that believers must test those who claim to be prophets to verify the genuineness of their gift: "By their fruit you will recognize them" (v. 16). A similar counsel is found in 1 Thess 5:19–20: "Do not quench the Spirit. Do not treat prophecies with contempt but test them all; hold on to what is good."

So far, this seems quite straightforward, but the Adventist argumentation is met with considerable criticism when it is narrowed down to the belief in the end-time prophetic gift in the person of Ellen G. White. A key text in this process is Rev 12:17. In this chapter Satan (under the symbol of a dragon) is featured as personified evil, waging war on God's people. He is portrayed as quite successful, but ultimately there

19. General Conference, "What Do Adventists Believe?," no. 18.

will be a "rest"—or as other Bible versions render it, "a remnant"—that is, a relatively small group that remains loyal to God amid widespread apostasy. Seventh-day Adventists have traditionally self-identified as this remnant, which is characterized by two specific elements: they "keep God's commandments and hold fast their testimony about Jesus" (Rev 12:17). The statement about the keeping of the commandments is, so they argue, a very fitting description for a group of people who keep all God's commandments, including the fourth of the Ten Words that stipulates keeping the Sabbath on the seventh day of the week. The "testimony about Jesus" of Rev 12:17 is linked to Rev 19:10. In the King James Version we read, "The testimony of Jesus is the spirit of prophecy." Other versions do not always make this same direct identification, as, for instance, in the New International Version: "For it is the Spirit of prophecy who bears testimony to Jesus."

As we discussed in the chapter on inspiration, there is no doubt that Ellen White played (and plays) an important role in the Adventist Church. She was a cofounder and had a key role in the development of the Adventist educational network and health systems, and millions of people have testified that her writings have been of spiritual benefit to them. However, as time has gone by, many church members (theologians and non-theologians), have questioned the exclusive identification of their church with the end-time remnant or rest, and feel it shows unbecoming arrogance to ascribe such exclusivity to their denomination. Not surprisingly, a number of other possible interpretations of the remnant concept have emerged.[20] And, increasingly, many Adventists feel it requires too many exegetical jumps to prove from the few texts in Revelation that are usually cited that the charismatic abilities of one person can be regarded as a key characteristic of a particular denomination that claims an exclusive role in contemporary Christianity. Many are no longer prepared to take all these jumps.[21]

20. For various interpretation of the remnant concept in current Adventism, see the chapter by Frank M. Hasel, "Remnant," 159–80.

21. Sigve Tonstad is a prominent Adventist theologian who does not hold to the traditional Seventh-day Adventist view of the "testimony of Jesus," which applies it to one person. See *Saving God's Reputation*.

The Holy Spirit in the Time of the End

A few denominations teach that in the final phase of the history of the earth an unparalleled outpouring of Holy Spirit power will take place. Among these are some Pentecostal and Charismatic movements and some Holiness and Revival groups. Seventh-day Adventists are probably most outspoken about this and see this as an important aspect of the elaborate end-time scenario that they developed.[22] Ellen G. White wrote extensively about this theme. The biblical foundation is, however, rather slim. The concept of the "early" and "latter" rain (in the spring and the autumn, respectively) as a metaphor for the outpouring of the Holy Spirit is mainly derived from Joel 2:23, 28–29:

> Be glad, people of Zion,
> rejoice in the Lord your God,
> for he has given you the autumn rains
> because he is faithful.
> He sends you abundant showers,
> both autumn and spring rains, as before.
> . . . "And afterward,
> I will pour out my Spirit on all people.
> Your sons and daughters will prophesy,
> your old men will dream dreams,
> your young men will see visions.
> Even on my servants, both men and women,
> I will pour out my Spirit in those days."

As already mentioned, this prophetic passage about the outpouring of the Spirit, to be accompanied by special manifestations, such as the gift of prophecy, had its initial fulfillment in the apostolic church (Acts 2). The prophet does, however, point to the eschatological day of the Lord as the time of the final fulfillment. The latter rain will enable the end-time church to give global evangelism one final, unparalleled boost. If this interpretation is correct, it underscores the view that the Holy Spirit will also play a very special role when this present world transitions into God's new creation.

22. See, e.g., Chaj, *Preparation*, 55–64.

Chapter 5

God's Solution for the Sin Problem

In three of the four Gospels we read the story of the wealthy young man who approached Jesus with the question what he should do to receive eternal life (Matt 19:16–30; Mark 10:17–31; Luke 18:18–30). That perennial question was repeated by Martin Luther. While still a monk, he was tormented by his deep sense of sinfulness. Extreme asceticism, frequent confessions, and the strictest possible monastic discipline failed to bring him lasting inner peace. The turning point came when, through his study of the Bible—in particular of Paul's letter to the Romans—he understood that salvation did not come through his own efforts, but that "the just shall live by faith" (Rom 1:17). Before and after Luther's conversion experience the question "How can I be saved" has been asked by millions of people whose names we do not know, and it may also be lingering in the minds of some who are now reading this chapter.

In this and the next chapter we will try to answer questions about the path towards salvation. At the end of our discussion some questions will, no doubt, remain unanswered, but I hope that one certainty will stand out: it is not anything *we* can do in our own strength that brings eternal life, but it is what *God* did in giving his Son Jesus Christ as the Redeemer of mankind that guarantees us our eternal future. The key thought that will guide us through this chapter is twofold: (1) Sin has a demonic dimension, with a superhuman origin and with consequences that go far beyond our comprehension. (2) Divine love provides the solution for the sin problem in a way that also far exceeds our human understanding.

The Mysterious Origin of Evil

From a statement in Rev 12 we get a glimpse of how the conflict between good and evil originated: "Then war broke out in heaven. Michael and his angels fought against the dragon, and the dragon and his angels fought back. But he was not strong enough, and they lost their place in heaven. The great dragon was hurled down—that ancient serpent called the devil, or Satan, who leads the whole world astray. He was hurled to the earth, and his angels with him" (vv. 7–9).

This passage describes a cosmic battle in which the archangel Michael, together with his angels, defeated Satan and his "fallen" angels, after which they were eliminated from heaven. How this conflict could ever start remains an unfathomable mystery. How could "war" break out in a perfect environment? This inexplicable fact caused Paul to speak of the "mystery of iniquity" (2 Thess 2:7 KJV). The Greek word used is indeed very appropriate: *mustērion*—mystery.

The leader of the rebellion in heaven is called "the dragon," alias the "ancient serpent" or "the devil, or Satan." How can we portray the leader of this rebellion? We are familiar with the caricatural images of a creature with horns and goat's legs, often also with a tail. In Rev 12, John used the apocalyptic image of "a great red dragon with seven heads and ten horns" (v. 3) to describe the devil, and elsewhere in the Bible we encounter other symbols and metaphors.

The prophet Isaiah prophesizes about the rise and fall of the Babylonian empire. The imagery he uses leaves the distinct impression that the king of Babylon was an earthly mirror image of the instigator of all evil. He is described as the "morning star, the son of the dawn" who has fallen "from heaven." He wanted to rival "the Most High," but ultimately ends up "in the realm of the dead, in the lowest depths of the pit" (14:12, 15). We discover a similar reflection of Satan in Ezekiel's prophecy about the prince of the city-state of Tyre: "You were blameless in your ways from the day you were created, till wickedness was found in you." The period in which this evil power could assert itself would, according to the prophet, be of limited duration, for there would come a time when "you will be no more" (28:15, 19).

In the earlier parts of the Bible the devil was not portrayed as the outright adversary of God. He seemed to be somehow in God's service as the accuser of humanity (see, e.g., Zech 3:1; 1 Chr 21:1; and Ps 109:6). This is most clearly observable in the first chapters of the book of Job (1 and 2). Descriptions of Satan as the mastermind of evil became much more pronounced towards the beginning of the intertestamental era. In the New Testament, Satan has become God's opponent, the powerful parasite who threatens and destroys God's work. Fortunately, his power is no match for the might of the all-powerful God.

Is the devil an impersonal force or a person? The way he is described in the Bible, under different images and with various names, inevitably leads to the conclusion that he is more than an impersonal influence. But does that make him a *person*? We referred in chapter 2 to the triune God in terms of three persons. I used the word *person* advisedly, because we have no better word in our language, and we must keep in mind that God represents more than the concept of person entails when we speak of ourselves and others around us in our human world as persons. And even if we were to grant Satan a personality, we must not forget that he is certainly not a person in the way that God is. He is everything that God is not! In their *Christian Dogmatics*, Gijsbert van den Brink and Cornelis van der Kooi use an innovative term that I had not come across before. They call Satan an *Unperson*.[1] In doing so, they may be saying more about what the devil is *not* than what he actually is, but perhaps it is a very good characterization after all. Nonetheless, the *un*personal Satan and his perverse activities remain indeed in many respects shrouded in mystery.

The Definition of Sin

As I mentioned earlier, the first eleven chapters of Genesis are often referred to as *protohistory* or *primeval history*. These chapters contain foundational stories about the origin of the world and of humanity. They also tell us about sin and a dramatic change in God's relationship with his creation. Many (probably most) theologians see these chapters as a theological explanation rather than a historical record in the modern

1. Van der Kooi and Van den Brink, *Christian Dogmatics*, 331–36.

sense. Several of these stories share elements with ancient Mesopotamian myths, which suggest that they belong to a common cultural heritage rather than representing strict historical reporting. Reading these stories we are therefore, I believe, not looking for historical detail but for meaning and divine purpose. The creation stories of Gen 1 and 2 are not intended to tell us that God, less than ten thousand years ago, created the world and the first human beings in six literal twenty-four-hour days. Genesis does not provide us with scientific information but affirms in beautiful mythical language that everything that exists had a perfect origin and owes its existence to the Almighty God. The Genesis account continues to inform us that God's creation did not remain perfect, but that somehow things went awfully wrong when the heavenly rebellion we referred to above resulted in the contamination of this planet and everything in it. This is the meaning of the story of the fall in Gen 3 and of the narrative of the subsequent expulsion of the first human beings from their paradisiacal environment.

Numerous controversies have arisen in the Christian world from attempts to make the creation stories align with modern science. In 1926 a split occurred in one of the major Reformed denominations in the Netherlands after a prominent theologian dared to suggest that we need not take it literally that there was a speaking snake in paradise. Although a few years ago the Seventh-day Adventist Church further tightened its fundamental belief about a "recent" creation in six literal days, and holds on firmly to a literal ("plain") reading of the story of the fall, many church members no longer accept this official view and look in these stories for theological truth rather than for historical and scientific information. I have also come to that conclusion.

A nonliteral reading of the story of the fall does not in any way obliterate its profound meaning. The narrative underscores the truth that sin is an awful reality that has not only affected humanity (personified by Adam and Eve) but has also dramatically impacted on the world around us. Perfect life and perfect relationships were marred by death and decay after sin made its entry into the world.

Sin

Sin is one of those common words that have undergone a constant devaluation. People use it in all kinds of settings and at times even attach the positive connotation of adventure and fun to it. It may be linked to exciting sexual behavior or to various forms of overindulgence, which may be unwise but are nonetheless painted as understandable or even enjoyable. However, sin is a reality with a totally different dimension, and before we focus on how God dealt with the sin problem, we must explore the true meaning of the term by determining how the Bible defines sin. In the original languages we find several words that are usually translated as "sin" but have different shades of meaning and express different aspects of sin.[2]

Four Hebrew words demand our attention. First, there is the word *pesha*, which means rebellion, revolt. Indeed, this is what sin is: rebellion, a rejection of God's demands, a "deliberate, premeditated, willful violation of a norm or standard."[3] The second word, *chata'ah*, is best translated as missing the mark, not reaching the goal, falling short. It suggests that sin not only includes wrongful actions but also covers the idea that we are not what we should have been. Sin is falling short of God's standard. In addition, we have the word *a'won*, which means something like crookedness, straying from the right track, and also the word *remiyyah*, which has the connotation of deception and self-deceit.

The New Testament likewise uses different words to refer to sin.[4] *Hamartia* occurs some 175 times; its literal meaning is missing the mark, as in target practice. In the New Testament it has the connotation of the deliberate failure to attain God's standard. *Parakoē* is best translated as unwillingness to hear, and the word *parabasis* as to pass beyond, to enter into forbidden territory. *Anomia*, a word that is used fewer times, is based on the Greek word for law (*nomos*) and suggests a violation of the law.

None of these various terms refer to sin as merely an unfortunate weakness for which humans cannot be held responsible. They all suggest in different ways that sin is mutiny against the Lordship of God—a refusal to accept his authority over our life and our destiny and a state of being less than we ought to be.

2. For a good summary of the use and meaning of the various Hebrew and Greek terms, see Fowler, "Sin," 237–39.

3. Fowler, "Sin," 238.

4. Fowler, "Sin," 238–39.

The Reality of Sin

Sin is defined in the Bible as opposition to the law of God (1 John 3:4). This makes it, at first sight, rather simple: we must consult the divine law and whatever is not in agreement with it is sin. But to what law does this statement of John refer? Is he speaking only of the Ten Commandment law? Or is there a broader application that includes other biblical laws and injunctions? Responding to that question requires a further discussion about the question of which categories of Old Testament law still apply to Christians who live in the twenty-first century. We will return to this matter in a later chapter. But even if, for now, we focus specifically on the Ten Commandments, things are not as straightforward as many tend to think. What, for instance, are the implications of Jesus's teachings? Did he not tell his disciples that the impact of this divine law extends far beyond an immediate literal application, and includes our inner motives as well?

In the Bible sin is not limited to wrong actions. Looking at the interpretation Jesus gave to several commandments, we discover that there can be sin even before we have actually done anything, for sin also has to do with what happens in our minds. Adultery, for instance, is not just having an affair or a one-night stand with someone we happen to meet during an after-office party. Jesus says, "I tell you that anyone who looks at a woman lustfully has already committed adultery with her in his heart" (Matt 5:27).

Other issues may be even more difficult to handle. We realize that theft is wrong, or "sinful," as a Christian would say. If I steal an expensive BMW, because I am not content with my modest Kia, I most definitely commit a sin. If I steal $100,000 by defrauding the company for which I work, I am a thief. But what if someone has absolutely no money (through no fault of his own) and grabs a loaf of bread, simply to stay alive? Does that act of desperation also qualify in the same way as "sin"? And what if someone is a kleptomaniac, who is mentally unable to resist the impulse of stealing? He is not stealing because he wants to have all kinds of luxury items; he takes small things, often of little value, forced by some strange, inner compulsion that is beyond his control. Does that make this person a thief, or is he rather a patient in need of therapy?

Murder is usually considered the worst possible type of sin. In our scale of values, we recognize a wide chasm between telling a white lie and willfully stabbing our neighbor after a confrontation about the number of decibels coming from his audio system. But is physical violence in principle more objectionable than verbal abuse? And is murdering two people intrinsically more evil than killing just one person? Is a serial killer a greater criminal than someone who killed just once or twice? Or could the mass murderer be actually less culpable if it is established that he suffers from some inner coercion that has starkly reduced his personal responsibility?

Again: *What is sin?* Whatever else it is, it is a rupture in relationships. The bottom line of the Genesis story of the fall is that sin caused an instantaneous sense of distrust between the first humans and their God. Adam and Eve hid from God (Gen 3:8) and Adam admitted, "I was afraid" (v. 10). Sin also brought an immediate physical estrangement between Adam and Eve, and even between the first couple and their environment. In a dramatic way sin tragically disturbed all originally perfect relationships. Moreover, the Genesis story about this first couple called Adam and Eve suggests that somehow human sin drastically affected the environment and even the animal world. This raises lots of difficult questions, but it is a clear warning against a too simplistic view of sin.

Original Sin

Other questions arise as soon as we begin to dissect the concept of sin. Is there something called "original sin," or "hereditary" or "ancestral" sin? These terms have found their way into the Christian vocabulary. They refer to the general condition of sinfulness into which all human beings are born, rather than to actual evil acts intentionally committed by individuals. One might compare original sin to a virus that has stealthily infected the world after the first human couple "fell" into sin. Church father Augustine, and others after him, made the (unbiblical) suggestion that infant baptism is required to deal with the lethal result of original sin. If an unbaptized child dies, Augustine maintained, it is destined for hell because of its inherited sinful condition.

But why do we have to start out in life with a serious disadvantage because of the mistake of our first parents? What justice is there in the fact that the sin of Adam and Eve not only resulted in their death but also that, as a result, death spread to everyone, everywhere? Adam's "one trespass resulted in condemnation for all people" (Rom 5:12, 18). How fair is this?

Several other questions could be added to those already posed in the previous paragraph. The above text quoted from Rom 5 suggests an element of causality. One thing is caused by the other, and thus a chain of events is set in motion. One sin tragically led to universal sin, and universal sin led to universal death. This seems the inescapable message of the biblical narrative. Yet, we must be careful not to speak only in terms of causality, as if every specific problem, and every specific case of human suffering, is caused by an identifiable sin on the part of a specific individual. We must remember the biblical story of the man who was born blind. Jesus's disciples, who were used to thinking in terms of cause and effect, asked, "Rabbi, who sinned, this man or his parents, that he was born blind?" (John 9:2). Jesus told them not to draw any rash conclusions. "Neither this man nor his parents sinned. . . . This happened so that the works of God might be displayed in him" (v. 3). This same point was also underlined when Jesus referred to an incident that had caused the death of eighteen men. The Tower of Siloam had caved in and had buried eighteen victims under its debris. "Do you think they were more guilty than all the others living in Jerusalem?" Jesus asked (Luke 13:4). Clearly Jesus did not want people to draw this conclusion and link the accidental death of these people with any specific sinful behavior.

And what to think of the ominous statement in the Ten Commandments that God will punish "the sin of the parents to the third and fourth generation" (Exod 20:5)? How does this harmonize with the reassuring words of the prophet Ezekiel, when he answered the question, "Why does the son not share the guilt of his father?" The prophet left those who came with that question in no doubt: "No!" he says. "The child will not share the guilt of the parent. . . . The righteousness of the righteous will be credited to them, and the wickedness of the wicked will be charged against them" (Ezek 18:19–20).

Things are complex indeed. Bad things do frequently happen to bad people, but they happen to good people as well. Bad things do not just happen occasionally but they are constant facts of life! That is the core issue with respect to the controversial concept of original sin. "Once [sin] entered the sphere of human existence, there is no escaping its influence. . . . No Christian belief has more practical evidence to support it than this one. . . . Sin affects human nature, not just behavior. It is a basic condition of our existence and has an influence on everything about us."[5]

5. Rice, *Reign of God*, 147–48.

In discussions about the sinful condition of man, we often hear the term *total depravity*. It emphasizes the devastating effect sin has on everything about us. There is nothing sin does not touch, defile, and eventually destroy. The Swiss Reformer John Calvin expressed it in these powerful words: "The whole man is overwhelmed—as by a deluge—from head to foot, so that no part is immune from sin and all that proceeds from him is to be imputed to sin."[6]

Romans 5:12–19 is a key passage in this connection. Paul goes back to the biblical creation story. He does not worry about questions of historicity but zooms in on the theological truth that sin is universal. The apostle reminds us that when Adam sinned, sin infected the entire human race. Adam's sin brought death, and death spread everywhere. Adam's one sin brought condemnation for all people. Paul does not explain *how* sin was transmitted from Adam to his posterity (as Augustine would later do). His main point is this: sin brings separation between God and humanity. "Because of Adam's sin, we have inherited this separation from God and more—a propensity to sin, wrongful tendencies, perverted appetites, debased morals, as well as physical degenerations."[7] We are not born morally neutral, but every person has an inborn "bent" towards evil.[8]

The church father Augustine was of the opinion that sexual intercourse was the *modus operandi* in the transmission of original sin. His negative view of sex was to have a disastrous influence on millions of Christians in the centuries to follow. There is, however, nothing in Rom 5, or in other texts, to support this unfortunate idea. The text wants to impress us with the fact that sin is utterly real, but the same passage also stresses the glorious fact that God is willing to accept us, nonetheless, as a result of the intervention through his Son.

Augustine is on safer ground when he tries to describe original sin with three terms that we find easier to understand. Sin, he says, is like a hereditary disease that is transmitted from one generation to the next. Sin is also like a power that holds us imprisoned, and we have no chance to free ourselves from it through our own power. And, third, sin is like a debt that is passed on from one generation to the next.[9]

6. Calvin, *Institutes*, 2.1.9, quoted in Rice, *Reign of God*, 147.

7. Fowler, "Sin," 237.

8. Knight, *Sin and Salvation*, 34.

9. McGrath, *Christelijke Theologie*, 384.

Personal and Corporate Sin

There is *personal* sin, and there is also *corporate* sin. Sin has infested the world and, as a result, the world has fallen victim to death and decay. The apostle Paul states that God's entire creation suffers from the effects of sin and that sin therefore has a *cosmic* dimension. "We know," the apostle Paul affirms, "that the whole creation has been groaning as in the pains of childbirth right up to the present time" (Rom 8:22).

There is a definite link between individual and corporate responsibility. Because all of us, as individuals, make wrong choices, countless events in the world take a disastrous turn and a kind of society develops in which man, rather than God, is the measure of all things. Because lots of men and women all around the world do not control their greediness and egoism, the world is polluted by gross materialism and by a debilitating self-centeredness. Tragically, the kind of selfish and violent environment mankind has created will inevitably affect all who now and in the future are born into the world. This lethal "cancer" of sin keeps on metastasizing and cannot be stopped.

We cannot merely blame our upbringing, the environment, our genes, or whatever else for what goes wrong in our lives. In the Bible sin is indeed described as an infection that has spread and now holds all of us captive. But that is not all that can be said. The primary biblical definition of sin refers to conscious sinful behavior. "All wrongdoing is sin," we read in 1 John 5:17. When we sin, we break the law of God (3:4). I repeat what I said earlier: sin is not disregarding some vague ideal or ignoring some general principle; it is nothing less than outright rebellion against the Ruler of the universe. This is what David recognized when he meditated upon his adulterous past: "Against you, you only, have I sinned" (Ps 51:4).

Note that sin has to do with an act of will. It is acting against an absolute norm: the law of God. This differs radically from what most postmodern people believe. For them no absolute rules exist. We are, they maintain, primarily dealing with individual preferences and with a consensus that has developed in society. We may not like certain things, but that does not make these things inherently evil. We may feel the need for personal growth and may regard some things in our own conduct as undesirable weaknesses that we would like to outgrow, but all this falls far short of the biblical view of sin as willful, active rebellion against an absolute norm given by a supreme divine Lawgiver. "Sin is the transgression of the law." Once again, I quote 1 John 3:4, but this time from the King

James Version. This translation most poignantly underlines how God has defined a boundary for mankind. God says that sin is transgressing his holy, spiritual law (Rom 7:12–14). Breaking that law—crossing that divine boundary, the limit God set for us—is sin.

The medieval Christian believed that seven sins were in a special category. These were the so-called deadly sins, also known as the cardinal sins. These seven sins required special sacramental action, if forgiveness and absolution were to be obtained. We meet these for the first time in a sixth-century list that originated with Pope Gregory the Great (ca. 540–604). The seven sins are lust, gluttony, greed, idleness, anger, envy, and pride. Each of these sins was thought to correspond with a particular virtue: chastity, abstinence, generosity, diligence, patience, kindness, and humility. There is, however, no biblical foundation for a distinction between cardinal and lesser sins, the so-called venial sins. This medieval list, and any other lists people might have compiled of sins that, supposedly, are more serious than other wrongdoings, may mislead us more than they can help us, because they may suggest that some sins are not very serious. It may also lead us to forget that attitude and motive play an important role. The truth is, sin is always an utterly serious business.

Sins of Omission

A description of the phenomenon of sin is not exhausted by stating that sin is an act of willful transgression of a holy law, which has been revealed to us for our guidance through life. And it also goes beyond the cultivation of a desire to commit such a transgression, if we only had the courage to do so. James 4:17 adds a significant aspect: "If anyone, then, knows the good they ought to do and doesn't do it, it is sin for them." So, in addition to the sins of *commission*, there are sins of *omission*. Jesus's parable of Lazarus and the rich man (Luke 16:19–31) provides a prime example of this kind of sin. The story tells us that the rich man bitterly complains to "father Abraham" about his fate in the hereafter, comparing his own agony to the bliss the poor beggar is experiencing. Abraham explains to the rich man that he could (and should) have done things in his earthly life that he failed to do. These omissions now come to haunt him. The parable of the sheep and the goats in Matt 25:31–46 teaches the same lesson. When Jesus returns with his reward, things we have failed to do may be the reason why we miss out on eternal life.

It takes but little thought to realize that all kinds of things happen because people fail to act. An observation attributed to Edmund Burke (an Irish statesman and philosopher, 1729–1797) remains very pertinent—namely, that evil will triumph when good people decide not to anything.[10] Yet, sin stretches even further. As we noted earlier, its meaning also covers the idea of missing the mark. This is the root meaning of one of the frequently used Greek words (*hamartia*) and its Hebrew equivalents that are usually translated as "sin." Jesus's words, "Be perfect, therefore, as your heavenly Father is perfect" (Matt 5:48), continue to worry and confuse many believers. If the goal is to reach perfection, we seem indeed doomed to miss the mark. But this text must never be isolated from another key Bible verse: all have sinned; all fall short of God's glorious standard. But, it is added, we are all "justified freely by his grace through the redemption that came by Christ Jesus" (Rom 3:23).

Our falling short, or missing the mark, is a tragic reality we constantly experience in our daily lives. There are so many ways in which we fall short of the ideals we profess to uphold. There are so many ways in which we disappoint others and ourselves, as we fail to keep promises that we should have kept and fail to attain goals that we should have reached. But when we feel frustrated because of our missing the mark and not reaching God's ultimate goal for us, we are put at ease by what we read elsewhere in God's word about our ultimate salvation through grace alone. "God saved you by his grace when you believed. And you can't take credit for this; it is a gift from God" (Eph 2:8 NLT).

The Solution for the Sin Problem

Evil has put its dark footprint on God's world and is an ugly reality in the lives of all of us. But evil does not have the final say. From the moment evil emerged, the triune God had a plan to deal with the sin problem. We find a first indication of this in the story of the fall. After the serpent misled Eve, and Adam had joined in his wife's disobedience, the treacherous snake is cursed. God announced that he would "put enmity" between the power who had assumed the appearance of a snake and the human family, and that in the end the head of the snake would be "crushed" (Gen 3:15).

10. Burke, *Thoughts*, 103.

In various places in the Old Testament a redeemer is promised. Many texts—certainly when regarded from a later perspective—point to the coming of Jesus. As time progressed, the pointers became clearer. When, shortly before his demise, patriarch Jacob blessed his sons, he had a special promise for Judah: "The scepter will not depart from Judah, nor the ruler's staff from between his feet, until he to whom it belongs shall come and the obedience of the nations shall be his" (Gen 49:10). This passage foretells that a ruler would come from Judah, which was fulfilled in Jesus, who was later referred to in Rev 5:5 as the Lion of the tribe of Judah. Deuteronomy 18:15–19 looks forward to a time when the Lord will "raise up" a prophet like Moses, whom the apostle Peter later recognized in Christ (Acts 3:22–23). The prophet Isaiah prophesies about a young woman who will give birth to a son and will call him Immanuel—God with us (Isa 7:14). He also predicts about a child who will be the Prince of Peace (Isa 9:6–7), and he speaks about a suffering servant, who "will be pierced for our transgressions" (Isa 53:5). Matthew links a prophecy of Micah about Bethlehem as the place of birth of a "ruler over Israel" (5:2) explicitly to Jesus (2:5–6). Other so-called messianic prophecies could be mentioned.

The plan of salvation was a reality long before the prophets I just cited spoke of the coming Savior. It was not an afterthought, for Christ was the Lamb "who was slain from the foundation of the world" (Rev 13:8).

"God so loved the world that he gave his one and only son, that whoever believes in him shall not perish but have eternal life" (John 3:16). God gave his Son as a *sacrifice*. John the Baptist pointed to Jesus as a sacrificial lamb: "Look, the Lamb of God, who takes away the sin of the world" (John 1:29). Jesus himself used sacrificial language when he instituted the Eucharist and told the disciples about his body that was to be given and his blood that was to be poured out as a sacrifice on their behalf (Matt 26:26–28). In Paul's letters the sacrifice of Christ is an oft-recurring theme. First Corinthians 5:7 is one of the texts that emphasize this: "For Christ, our Passover lamb, has been sacrificed."

The sacrificial ritual that we meet in the Old Testament and that received its most extensive form in the services in the tabernacle, and later in the Jerusalem temple, was an impressive symbolism intended to teach the people that sin is an extremely grave matter and that it would require a costly intervention to deal with its consequences. The organization of the Old Testament sanctuary service was not left to the imagination of Moses or the creativity of the tribe of Levi; God provided a model that was to be followed in every detail. Moses received comprehensive instructions with regard to the tabernacle and its furnishings: "See that you make them according to the pattern shown you on the mountain" (Exod 25:40). The book of Hebrews confirms that the earthly sacrificial system reflected a heavenly reality (Heb 8:5). Every sacrifice foreshadowed the sacrifice of the Son of God.

The sin problem was resolved through the sacrifice of Jesus Christ on Calvary. According to Peter we are not redeemed with "perishable things" but "with the precious blood of Christ" (1 Pet 1:18–19). Paul agrees: "In him we have redemption through his blood, the forgiveness of sins, in accordance with the riches of God's grace" (Eph 1:7).

Theories of the Atonement

The question has often been asked why God chose his particular method to save mankind. Why did Christ have to suffer so terribly and to die such a ghastly death? One of the classic answers to this question came from Anselm, the medieval Benedictine monk—abbot, philosopher, and theologian of the Catholic Church, who served as Archbishop of Canterbury from 1093 to 1109. In his book *Cur Deus Homo?* (Why Did God Become Man?) Anselm explored the necessity of the incarnation and of Christ's death on the cross.[11] Why did God have to become a human being in order to redeem humanity? Anselm argued that Christ's death was not merely an example of God's great love. Sin is a violation of divine honor, creating a debt humanity cannot repay. Only *God* can make adequate satisfaction for this offense, while only a *human* can justly pay for it. The solution must be a God-Man—Jesus Christ. Through his voluntary death, Christ satisfied divine justice and restored humanity to righteousness. A crucial element in this theory is that of *substitution*, "the idea that Jesus steps in and takes our place before God. He gets what we deserve, and we get what he deserves. He accepts the punishment that our sins incur, and we inherit the privileges that divine sonship involves."[12]

This theory, which is one of several theological explanations of the atonement, became highly influential in Western Christian thought and is usually referred to as the satisfaction theory. Key texts that are cited

11. Aulén, *Christus Victor*, 81–92.

12. Rice, *Reign of God*, 194.

in support of this view are Rom 3:25–26 ("God presented Christ as a sacrifice of atonement"); Heb 9:24 (the blood of Christ "cleanses" us); and 1 Pet 2:24 ("He himself bore our sins in his body on the cross").

Several other theories have also been proposed. The penal substitution theory is an extension of the satisfaction theory and emphasizes that Jesus bore the punishment that humanity deserved and thereby made sure that divine justice was served. This theory has found support in many Protestant denominations, in particular in churches of the Reformed branch. They point to texts like Isa 53:5–6, where it is said that the suffering servant "was pierced for our transgressions" and was "crushed for our iniquities," and 2 Cor 5:21, where Paul states that "God made him who had no sin to be sin for us."

The ransom theory was popular with some early church fathers and was later revived by Gustav Aulén, a Swedish Lutheran theologian. This theory, also referred to with the words *Christus Victor*, which highlight its major theme, teaches that the death of Christ was the ransom that was to be paid to free mankind from sin and death and deliver it from the devil. Christ's resurrection marks the victory over the evil powers. In Mark 10:45 the term *ransom* is actually used: "For even the Son of Man did not come to be served, but to serve, and to give his life as a ransom for many."

The governmental theory, which dates from the seventeenth century, was defended by the Dutch legal scholar and theologian Hugo Grotius (1586–1643). He suggested that Christ's death upholds God's moral order. It demonstrates the seriousness of sin, but it is not a direct substitution. Nowadays it is popular with some Methodist and Arminian theologians. "God as the Governor of a moral universe was bound to see to it that violation of the moral order of the universe would be treated with due punishment, that the debt incurred be paid. . . . The payment need not be in terms of an exact correspondence of offense and penalty. . . . The penalty could be set at the discretion of the Governor of the universe."[13]

There are two kinds of theories of the atonement: *objective* and *subjective* theories. The first category, to which the theories that were mentioned in the previous paragraphs belong, stress that the atonement is grounded in an external event. Something extraordinary happened on Calvary, and this solved the sin problem and brought salvation within the reach of all who want it. Subjective theories focus on what happens in human hearts

13. Vick, *Let Me Assure You*, 43.

as people contemplate the unparalleled love of Jesus Christ, who was willing to suffer and die as an ultimate demonstration of that love. The moral influence theory falls in this second category. The twelfth-century theologian Peter Abelard was among the early advocates of this subjective view. Friedrich Schleiermacher in the nineteenth century, and more recently several liberal theologians, followed him along these lines.

The moral influence theory holds that Jesus's sacrifice inspires moral transformation in believers rather than providing satisfaction for divine justice. It builds on such passages as Rom 5:8, "God demonstrates his own love for us in this: while we were still sinners, Christ died for us," and 1 John 4:10–11, "This is love: not that we loved God, but that he loved us and sent his Son."

None of these theories provides us with a complete and final explanation of what is involved in the atonement, and what it means that "God was reconciling the world to himself in Christ" (2 Cor 5:19). Different Christian traditions emphasize different aspects of the atonement. Evaluating these different theories has been compared to taking pictures of the Himalayas. The people who climb this "roof" of the world take pictures from various angles at different spots along their route. All these pictures show aspects of the mountain, but only an aerial view can give a complete picture. Likewise, only God has a complete, full panoramic view of the atonement, and the various theological theories are at best partial descriptions of the Himalayas of God's grace. We must, therefore, not take one of these theories as the "full" truth of the atonement and it would be wrong to play the various theories off against each other. We must not choose an objective approach and reject the subjective perspective, since these two approaches are intertwined. What happened at Calvary must resonate in our soul. But without the objective, historic, real event of the cross, our experience of salvation remains a hollow optimism that eventually things will turn out all right for us. At the same time, without a heartfelt gratitude and a response of love for what God did in Christ for us, our religion is no more than a formal theory.

"Traditionally, Adventist authors have understood Christ's atoning death as a penal substitutionary sacrifice. In recent times few have advocated a view reminiscent of Abelard's moral influence theory."[14] The influential theologian Graham Maxwell (1921–2010) has, rightly or wrongly, often been regarded as an Adventist proponent of this moral

14. Dederen, "Christ," 199.

influence view. Seventh-day Adventist believers have always run the risk of undervaluing the subjective aspect of the atonement and emphasizing doctrinal truth over the experiential aspect. I believe they must constantly guard against this spiritually debilitating imbalance.

Who Will Be Saved?

The Christian church has always regarded it as its mission to share the gospel with as many people worldwide as possible, knowing that God "has committed to us the message of reconciliation" (2 Cor 5:19). However, preaching the gospel only makes sense if it actually makes a difference whether we do it or not.[15] Will people be eternally lost because we have failed in our missionary task? But perhaps this is asking the wrong question for, when push comes to shove, it is not what *we* do but what *God* does that saves people. The gospel is about God's grace. God's greatest desire is to see people saved for eternity. God is "not wanting anyone to perish, but everyone to come to repentance" (2 Pet 3:9). This gives us reason to believe that, when the moment of Christ's second coming arrives, the number of those who are saved will be surprisingly large! For the gospel is good news. "It is not an announcement of terror, but news of God's boundless generosity."[16] The hymn written more than 150 years ago by Frederick W. Faber (1814–1863) states a truth never to be forgotten: "There's a wideness in God's mercy / like the wideness of the sea," and "The love of God is broader / than the measure of man's mind."[17]

From very early on in the history of the Christian church some have asserted that in the end all people will be saved. Origen (ca. 184–253) believed that even the devil will eventually be reconciled to God and be restored to his original celestial state. Through the centuries the so-called universalists have defended that in the end all people will be accepted by God and receive eternal life. The biblical data do not, however, support universalism—that is, the view that ultimately all people will be saved.

I had a very intense look at the universalist position when, in the late 1990s, I translated a book into English that was written by Jan

15. This section is a condensed version of what I wrote in *He Comes: Why, When and How Jesus Will Return*, 112–15.

16. Pinnock, *Wideness in God's Mercy*, 178.

17. Faber, "There's a Wideness."

Bonda, a Dutch Reformed minister.[18] In a very thorough review of all biblical passages that have a direct or indirect bearing on the topic, the author made a strong case for the theory of universalism. However, I concluded, at the end of the almost three hundred pages, that he did not quite succeed in his argumentation. The fact that Bonda needed many different Bible versions (some of them little known) to prove his points, made me rather skeptical. And I could not suppress the growing conviction that there simply are too many places in the Bible where we are told that there will be a judgment and that at least some, who have turned against God, will be lost.

I had a similar feeling when I recently read another book that also offers a robust defense of universalism: *That All Shall Be Saved: Heaven, Hell, and Universal Salvation* by David Bentley Hart, an American Eastern Orthodox theologian. The author contends that ultimately all people will be saved. To allow people to be lost, Hart says, is totally incompatible with the nature of a loving and omnipotent God. It is a very positive and agreeable book, but, in this case also, we must conclude that Hart ignores relevant data that do not allow for universalism.

The supporters of universalism tend to focus on a limited number of biblical passages that appear to stress the universal impact of divine grace. A favorite text of the universalists is 1 Cor 15:22–28. It refers to the sequence in which various groups will be saved, with the glorious end result that "God may be all in all" (v. 28). Other oft-quoted texts include 1 Tim 2:3–4; Rom 2:6–16; 1 John 2:2; Rom 5:12–19; and Phil 2:9–11. Those who defend the universalist view fail, however, to take into proper account those passages that emphasize other aspects of God's interactions with humanity. Texts that speak about eternal damnation are played down and are explained as hyperbolic figures of speech. Some universalists believe that those who have not made the right choice in this life will get another chance after they have died. Statements in 1 Pet 3:18–20 and 4:6 are cited in support of this idea. This is a striking example of how at times one or two problematic texts are used to give support to a certain theory, while other texts, which affirm the opposite position, are ignored!

Universalism clearly is a bridge too far, but the idea that only a small remnant will make it is a bridge that, I believe, is far too narrow. The gospel message is abundantly clear: it is difficult *not* to be saved. God does everything possible to reconcile as many people as possible to

18. Bonda, *One Purpose of God*.

himself. The vision of the apostle John in Rev 7:9 does not point to a small remnant: "After this I looked, and behold, a great multitude that no one could number, from every nation, from all tribes and peoples and languages, standing before the throne and before the Lamb, clothed in white robes, with palm branches in their hands." And Jesus clearly indicated that he is not thinking small: "When I am lifted up from the earth, [I] will draw all people to myself" (John 12:32). Paul echoed the same sentiment: "This is good, and it is pleasing in the sight of God our Savior, who desires all people to be saved and to come to the knowledge of the truth" (1 Tim 2:3–4).

A related question, that also is the topic of an ever-ongoing debate, is whether only Christians will be saved, or whether non-Christians (adherents of other religions and unbelievers) may also receive eternal life. Among Bible scholars three main positions have emerged.[19] One of them is the universalist view we just discussed. In addition, there are two other perspectives.

Some are of the opinion that God reveals himself in all religious traditions and that every religion provides a road to the beyond. These roads, they say, are all historically and culturally conditioned, but in essence lead to the same destination. This sounds like an attractive idea, and it certainly appeals to postmodern minds. It has, however, serious implications for the whole enterprise of preaching the gospel. For if this view is correct, why "go" out into the world and try to persuade adherents of non-Christian religions and unbelievers to become followers of Christ? Why should they listen? They will be saved anyway, as long as they are sincere in what they believe! This view is usually referred to as pluralism.

Another theory (exclusivism or restrictivism) defends the view that salvation is only available through Christ. It affirms that people need to hear the gospel and must have an opportunity to respond. There is no other name that brings salvation than the name of Christ (Acts 4:12), the supporters of this view contend. The most popular texts in support of this view include also John 14:6; Mark 16:16; and 1 Tim 2:5. If some "honest" people will be saved without having had the opportunity to hear the full gospel, their salvation will—whether they realize it or not—be through the merits of Jesus Christ.

19. See Fackre et al., *What About Those?* Also Newbigin, *Gospel in a Pluralist Society*; Netland, *Dissonant Voices*; Knitter, *No Other Name?*; Sanders, *No Other Name*; and Tiessen, *Who Can Be Saved?*

Adventists are among those who believe that when all the biblical data are fully considered and weighed, the only defensible view is the last one. They do not believe that non-Christians are beyond God's reach of grace, and they also believe that, *through Christ*, people may be saved even though they never had the opportunity to hear about him, and to consciously decide to follow him. Ellen White remarked on this connection in nineteenth-century language: "Even among the heathen there were men through whom Christ was working to uplift the people from their sin and degradation."[20] She adds that this continues to be the case in the present: "Among the heathen are those who worship God ignorantly, to whom the light is never brought by human instrumentality, yet they will not perish."[21] The Canadian emeritus professor in systematic theology Terrance Tiessen opines that God expects people to respond to what they know about him, "but he does not require a faith that would be impossible for anyone by virtue of their ignorance."[22]

As I predicted at the beginning of this chapter, some questions have remained unanswered. But we can be sure of two fundamental realities: (1) the *temporary reality* of evil, its supernatural origin, its ugly reign of death and decay, and its irrevocable demise, and (2) the *ultimate reality* of the triumph of the love of God, who in Christ devised a way to terminate the satanic sway of terror, to redeem us and accept us as his sons and daughters, for now and forever.

20. White, *Desire of Ages*, 35.

21. White, *Desire of Ages*, 35.

22. Tiessen, *Who Can Be Saved*, 478.

Chapter 6

What God Does *for* Us and *in* Us

God bridged the chasm of sin that estranged his creation from him. He reconciled the world unto himself through the sacrifice of his Son Jesus Christ. This ultimate act of love brought about what theologians call: atonement—*at-one-ment*. What had been ruptured was healed. The English word *atonement* can indeed be read as *at-one-ment*, meaning "to make two parties one again." The word *atonement* was first popularized in a theological sense by William Tyndale (d. 1536), who used it in his translation of the Bible to express the concept of reconciliation between God and humanity.

We saw in the previous chapter how theologians struggled to define the meaning of the atonement and how they developed different theories. We concluded that these theories all point to important aspects, but that none of them can fully express the reality of what happened on that Good Friday and on that Paschal Sunday some two thousand years ago. But whether or not we can satisfactorily define the atonement in human words, Christ's death on Calvary and his subsequent resurrection from death form the basis for our salvation and our eternal life. The bottom line is and remains, "He was pierced for our transgressions; he was crushed for our iniquities" (Isa 53:5).

Yet, more needs to be said. How does the Christ-event become effective *for* and *in* us? How did what happened *then* affect us *now*? Is there something we must say or do to ensure that, indeed, Christ's suffering and death changes our personal situation and enables us to embrace what happened so long ago in Jerusalem as a power that can transform our lives? And can it give us the assurance that *we* were included when God said he so loved the *world* he gave his one and only son so that *we* (that is also, you and I) would not "perish" but have eternal life (John 3:16)?

This chapter will attempt to explain what must "happen" in order that my (informed) belief—that the death of Jesus Christ and his emergence from the tomb were the definitive victory over sin and death—becomes a deep conviction that, because of this event, the consequences of my sin are taken care of; and that I can live in the certainty of being saved and of having a ticket for eternity. Other questions also demand our attention: How do justification and sanctification relate to each other? And what about an investigative judgment, which, according to traditional Adventist theology, is currently taking place? I hesitate to phrase the question as, *What steps must be taken*—by God and by me—if I want to be assured of my salvation? Or, *What phases should we distinguish*, such as conversion, baptism, and spiritual growth?

I am reluctant to speak about "steps" or "phases" for two reasons. As humans we feel most comfortable when things happen in a particular, predictable sequence. It makes things clear, orderly, and manageable. We tend to like it when things are systematic and transparent. This also applies to the "*plan* of salvation." Since the seventeenth century, Protestant theologians have used the term *ordo salutis* (the order of salvation) to systematize their theological discussions of salvation and explore the sequence in which aspects of our salvation take place. There is indeed a biblical basis for this, as long as we use the term *ordo* in a *descriptive* sense, describing what usually happens, and not in a *prescriptive* manner, with the idea that this is how it always *must* take place in anyone's individual spiritual life; and as long as we do not neglect the possibility that some of these aspects may well be simultaneous.

The second reason why I am hesitant to give too much emphasis to the idea of a definitive *ordo salutis* is that the eternal God does not experience time and sequence in the same way as we do. Salvation, and everything that is part of it, is a gracious divine gift that is beyond human comprehension and beyond our ability to dissect and order it into a process that in all respects will make sense to us. The truth is that salvation is such a mysterious miracle of God's grace that we may gratefully study it and marvel about it, but it will never be a topic that we fully understand. So, when we proceed on the following pages with a more or less sequential survey of the various aspects that are part of the reality of our salvation, and of our experience of it, it is with this caveat, but nevertheless with the hope that it does provide us with a glimpse of what God does *for* us and *in* us.

Faith

Our path of salvation begins and ends with faith, and every part of the journey is based on faith.[1] Our spiritual pilgrimage begins when we first become aware of the gospel message—when we hear about Jesus and about what he came to do for humanity. We may hear it in different ways and from different sources—from our parents, in school, in church, by reading in a Bible, or through a visit to a gospel concert. We may remember exactly when we first heard the essence of the gospel message, or we may not remember where or when it was that we were first consciously confronted with it. But whether or not we can pinpoint the exact moment, this is how it begins: with our response of faith (however weak or tentatively) to the good news of what Jesus Christ did for us. Faith comes, Paul says, from listening to the message of the gospel (Rom 10:17).

Faith is a term with different shades of meaning. We speak of the Christian faith, but also, more specifically, of the Catholic faith, the Methodist faith, the Baptist faith, et cetera. And we sometimes use the plural *faiths* for different religious systems. In the following paragraphs I will use the word *faith* mostly in the sense of *trust*, but we will need to further narrow it down, since trust can have many gradations. We can trust in things, or in the weather prognosis. I can have trust in the strength of the bridge I must cross, or in the engine and the brakes of my car. I can trust in certain skills and abilities that (I think) I have. I can have trust in the people around me, my family, and my friends.

When it concerns faith in a person the element of relationship enters the picture. *Faith in God* is relational trust at the highest level. It is not primarily believing things *about* God but believing *in* him. It

1. This section is adapted from parts of the chapter "Faith" in my book *Keywords of the Christian Faith*, 22–31.

is entering into an intimate relationship with him. Hebrews 11:1 offers this definition of faith: "Faith is confidence in what we hope and assurance about what we do not see." This kind of confidence can only be based on a close relationship; without a relationship such confidence would be very precarious indeed.

Having faith is quite natural. We have faith in all kinds of things, and, unless we are extremely suspicious and distrustful, we have trust in—at least some—people. Few of us would ever go to a doctor or a dentist if we did not have at least some trust in his medical skills. And we would not put a letter in a mailbox if we did not have a degree of faith in the postal service, even though that trust may at times have been severely put to the test. But when it comes to the most important relationship we can have—faith in God—many will say that they simply do not have this faith, and many will add that they wished they had it but have no idea how they can *get* it. *Get* is actually the right word, for faith is not the result of hard work or concentrated thinking. Faith is a free gift, for which we cannot take any credit ourselves.

Ephesians 2:8 states, "For it is by grace that you have been saved, through faith, and this is not from yourselves. It is the gift of God—not by works, so that no one can boast." This does not mean that reading and thinking (and praying, in particular) have no place in receiving the gift of faith. It is important to place yourself where you may expect this gift to be distributed. It is in a sense like learning another language. If you want to learn French, you do well to spend time in a Francophone country. To learn the language of faith you must go to places where that language is spoken. The Czech theologian Tomáš Halík emphasizes that faith as a divine gift is "intrinsically intertwined" with the human willingness to receive it.[2]

True faith has a childlike quality (Luke 10:21). Children do not begin to negotiate when a free gift is within their reach. They simply rush forward and grasp it with both hands. Being open to the gift is essential, but hanging on to it is also crucial. For we can lose our faith, as has happened to untold millions in today's secularized society.

The definition of faith in Heb 11 mentions *confidence*. This confidence is not based on the kind of evidence that many people are looking for to corroborate their faith. It affirms that faith is related to evidence of a special kind. The confidence of faith has to do with things that are as yet

2. Halík, *Afternoon of Christianity*, 124.

not seen—things that belong to another realm: spiritual things that are discerned in a spiritual way (1 Cor 2:14).

Some have argued that our faith in the Bible is confirmed by the results of biblical archeology, and that "the spade" has proven the trustworthiness of "the book." Biblical archeology certainly has much value, but it also leaves us with many questions and does not offer absolute and unshakable evidence for our faith in God. But let us face the fact that we also have no absolute evidence for the trustworthiness of the people we love. Trust in a person we love does not need verification by a detective bureau or a constant checking of his iPhone. Granted, the comparison is not perfect, but it does make the undeniable point that an intimate relationship is based on experience rather than on "hard" tangible evidence. The possibility of a faith relationship between God and us is, in fact, evidence of the divine love that ever continues to reach out to us.

Faith and Reason

The relationship between faith and reason has been a hotly debated topic, especially since the emergence of modern sciences and, more specifically, of the evolutionary thesis. For fundamentalist readers of the Bible, who believe in its inerrancy, the choice is clear: when modern science contradicts the Bible, the only option is to accept the words of the Bible and to reject the findings of science. This is the basis for such theories as young earth creationism, which supports a "recent" six-day creation and defends the historicity of a "recent" global flood. In many cases those who defend a literal reading of the biblical narrative, even when it conflicts with the consensus of current scholarship, argue that science has often been obliged to revise earlier theories and that many aspects of the scientific arguments are based on unproven assumptions. The young earth creationists and other scholars who are in this fundamentalist camp are mostly found in (ultra-)conservative denominations. Seventh-day Adventists have played a prominent role in this approach to the faith-science debate.[3] The Geoscience Research Institute on the campus of Loma Linda University (California) was established by the Adventist Church to serve as its scientific arm in matters of creationism, earth history, and the relationship between science and faith. Its main aim was to provide scientific

3. For a detailed history of scientific creationism, with extensive attention for the role of Seventh-day Adventist scientists and theologians, see Numbers, *Creationists.*

research and support for the Adventist understanding of creation and to find the weaknesses in evolutionary theories. On the more popular level Adventist author and editor Clifford Goldstein has been in the lead in attacking science, in particular with regard to issues related to evolution, with his constantly repeated contention that science is mostly based on suppositions rather than on incontrovertible evidence. In his book *Baptizing the Devil: Evolution and the Seduction of Christianity*, Goldstein questions the attempts to harmonize evolutionary theories with Genesis and challenges the notion that scientific assertions should automatically override religious beliefs. Christians, he says, need not compromise their faith to align their beliefs with prevailing scientific perspectives.

Most other Christians, however, have tried to find other ways of dealing with the faith-science dilemma. Many attempts have been made to reconcile the scientific findings with a nonfundamentalist reading of the Scriptures. Some of these attempts are more promising and credible than others. I feel comfortable in the camp of the many Christians scholars and theologians who believe that God is the Creator of everything that exists but are also convinced that the Bible does not provide us with scientific information about how and when God created. I want to be authentic in my beliefs and will not change my mind simply because my church teaches differently. When we decide to become part of a faith community, we do not leave our intellect at the door. Christ called us to "love the Lord your God with all your heart and with all your soul *and with all your mind* (Matt 22:37; italics added).

Through many centuries a war has been waged by the Christian church against new scientific discoveries. By and large, as time went by Christians have made peace with science, but in some quarters this war, unfortunately, continues. This is true for a significant part of Adventism. It has been very challenging for many educated members and has raised perplexing questions for many young people about how to reconcile what they learn in school with what they hear in church.

Faith and Works

Christians in many denominations have struggled to get the balance right between faith and works, but perhaps Seventh-day Adventists have often struggled more intensely with this challenge than the members of most other faith communities. Adventists certainly believe in grace. But when speakers or organizations emphasize this grace, church leaders often worry that there may be too much talk of grace and that the doctrines of the church are not receiving enough attention. I have often heard people say, "What we need is balance. Christian obedience and belief in divine grace must go together. If we fail to keep the two elements of faith and work in balance, we either end up with 'cheap grace' or with dry legalism." However, I believe, rather than insisting on *balance* we must intentionally opt for *imbalance*—individually and as a church—and unreservedly embrace God's grace as the overarching principle in our Christian Adventist experience.[4]

In discussions about faith and works, church members will usually acknowledge that our salvation is entirely dependent on God's grace. However, after having said that, there usually follows a "but . . ." We are saved by grace, *but* we must show our gratitude by keeping God's commandments! It is not by our works that we can earn salvation, of course, *but* doesn't the apostle James tell us that we must show our faith in our actions? (Jas 4:14–26). Few books have made such an enduring impression on me as Philip Yancey's *What's So Amazing About Grace*?[5] He makes it abundantly clear that there is no "but" when we really believe what Paul tells us in Eph 2:8–9: "For it is by grace you have been saved, through faith—and this is not from yourselves, it is the gift of God—not by works, so that no one can boast."

Many Adventist Christians struggle with legalism. They are convinced that obedience to God's law and doing good works is all-important, and that people may claim credit for what they are able to do or even be proud of what they have achieved. This, Paul writes to the Galatians, is a perversion of the gospel, which "is really no gospel at all" (Gal 1:6–7). Legalism is expecting "to be accepted by God or to be able to remain in him simply because of obedience. It is the foolish sin of self-righteousness and the tragic mistake of missing the righteousness freely given by God's grace in Christ."[6]

This does not mean that it does not matter what we do. Works still have an important role, but they must be embedded in faith. Edward Vick put it like this: "Faith is a work we must do, but we cannot do it except God grants us grace. . . . All the works that Christians do are works of faith. No others have any importance to Christians. There is

4. Bruinsma, "Grace vs. Works."

5. See Yancey, *What's So Amazing.*

6. Veloso, "Law of God," 483.

no work that can be done independently of God's grace. There is no work for which we can claim credit."[7]

Conversion

For some, their conversion has been a spectacular event, while for others becoming a believer has been a long and arduous journey. The American philosopher and theologian Nicholas Wolterstorff (b. 1932) is one of many who do not have an exciting conversion story to tell: "The grace that shaped my life," he says, "came not in the form of episodes culminating in a private experience of conversion, but first of all in the form of being inducted into a public tradition of the Christian church." He explains how his journey of faith began:

> My induction into the [Reformed] tradition, through words and silences, ritual, and architecture, implanted in me an interpretation of reality—a fundamental hermeneutic. Nobody offered "evidences" for the truth of the Christian gospel; nobody offered "proofs" for the inspiration of the Scriptures; nobody suggested that Christianity was the best explanation of one thing and another. Evidentialists were nowhere in sight! The gospel was report, not explanation.[8]

My personal story—and I am sure that of many others—about the early development of my faith very much resembles that of Wolterstorff. However, there have always been men and women who can pinpoint exactly what marked the moment of their conversion and what precisely sparked it. A dramatic example of this was the conversion of Paul on the Damascus Road (Acts 9:1–18).

Conversion is a mysterious concept. "Being converted" is often used interchangeably with "the new birth" or "being born again." A key text is found in John 3, in the context of Jesus's encounter with Nicodemus, the Pharisee, who came to Jesus "at night" and shared his conviction that Jesus was "a teacher who has come from God." His belief was based on the miracles Jesus was performing. Jesus replied that this perception was valuable, but it was not enough. He said, "Very truly I tell you, no one can see the kingdom of God unless they are born again" (v. 3). When

7. Vick, *Is Salvation Really Free?*, 72.

8. Wolterstorff, "Grace That Shaped," 259.

Nicodemus wondered what this might mean, Jesus expanded on this introductory statement: "Very truly I tell you, no one can enter the kingdom of God unless they are born of water and the Spirit. Flesh gives birth to flesh, but the Spirit gives birth to spirit. You should not be surprised at my saying, 'You must be born again.' The wind blows wherever it pleases. You hear its sound, but you cannot tell where it comes from or where it is going. So it is with everyone born of the Spirit" (vv. 5–8).

Conversion is in many cases linked to a (sudden or gradual) awareness that one is heading in the wrong direction and that a drastic change in one's orientation is needed. It presupposes the existence of a free will, the belief that it is possible to repent, to end a particular course of action, and to turn around (which is what conversion literally means). We are not predestined to move in a predetermined direction—either towards eternal life or eternal death. Christian traditions differ on what role human decision and response play in the new birth. We must, however, not expect to have final answers to all our questions, as Jesus's metaphor of the wind underlines: "You hear its sound, but you cannot tell where it comes from or where it is going." God's grace enables us to respond in faith and repentance, but the decision to do so is with us. This is clearly implied in the appeal that is found towards the end of Christ's message to the church in Laodicea: "Be earnest and repent. Here I am! I stand at the door and knock. If anyone hears my voice and opens the door, I will come in and eat with that person, and they with me" (Rev 3:20).

Conversion is the beginning of the Christian pilgrimage. It involves a change in worldview and priorities (Phil 3:7–8), and a transformation by "the renewal of your mind" (Rom 12:2). It is linked to a newfound identity, as Paul experienced: "I have been crucified in Christ and I no longer live, but Christ lives in me. The life I now live in the body, I live by faith in the Son of God, who loved me and gave himself for me" (Gal 2:20).

The beginning of our conversion "may be imperceptible, but it is still real; like the wind, it has perceptible consequences. Similarly, people who have been born again may not be able to pinpoint the moment the experience occurred, but their life will be the evidence that it has taken place."[9]

9. Rice, *Reign of God*, 267.

Justification

At what point in one's spiritual journey is a person assured of being accepted as a child of God and of being saved? Some Adventists would respond that one cannot have that certainty, because it depends on the outcome of the investigative phase of the judgment, which is now taking place in heaven. Since 1844—a moment that Adventists believe has been foretold in prophecy—"the books" are "opened"; our deeds our examined and it is determined whether we are eligible for the resurrection and thus for eternal life. This may indeed be traditional Adventist teaching, but for many it is a very scary thought. They wonder, Will I be okay when my case comes up? Most Adventist pastors will reassure their parishioners with a resounding "yes." We need not worry, they will say, since Christ is our heavenly Advocate, whose sacrifice guarantees a positive outcome for all who have placed their trust in what he did for mankind. However, we are not notified when our name has been cleared. Must we wait for the final total assurance of our salvation until the last judgment has taken place and we come back to life in the resurrection?

I believe we can have this certainty of salvation already now. We may have questions about the interpretation of the symbolism of heaven and the new earth, but in whatever way the imagery is understood, it refers to a glorious heavenly reality that awaits all those who have chosen to follow Christ. (We will return in an excursus at the end of this chapter to the concept of a pre-Advent investigative judgment.)

The reality of a divine judgment cannot be pushed aside. But for those who have made the choice to be Christ-followers, the sting has been removed. Paul assured us that "God did not appoint us to suffer wrath but to receive salvation through our Lord Jesus Christ" (1 Thess 5:9), and that "there is now no condemnation for those who are in Christ Jesus" (Rom 8:1). It is what Jesus himself told the Jewish leaders: "Very truly, I tell you, whoever hears my word and believes him who sent me has eternal life and will not be judged but has crossed over from death to life" (John 5:24).

The reason why we do not have to fear a coming judgment and can be sure of our acquittal is that our status as approved candidates for heaven is certified at the moment we commit ourselves to Christ. In theological language this moment is referred to as our *justification*; that is, our being declared righteous before God. This is not based on any good intentions we may have expressed and any good deeds we have attempted to do, but exclusively on our faith in Jesus Christ. The righteousness of Christ is *imputed* to us, or, in other words, credited to us, because of what Christ did for us. The apostle Paul is the absolute champion of this truth.

In Rom 3:28 we read, "For we maintain that a person is justified by faith apart from the works of the law." And in 2 Cor 5:21: "God made him who had no sin to be sin for us, so that in him we might become the righteousness of God." The wonderful result is that, "since we have been justified through faith, we have peace with God through our Lord Jesus Christ" (Rom 5:1).

Justification is being acquitted of sin and being "clothed in Christ's righteousness." We find a stunning illustration of this in the fourth vision of the prophet Zechariah concerning the restoration of the high priest Joshua. Zechariah 3:1–5 describes a vision where Joshua, the high priest, stands before the angel of the Lord, with Satan accusing him. The Lord rebukes Satan, emphasizing his mercy on Jerusalem and comparing Joshua with a "burning stick snatched from the fire." Joshua, dressed in filthy clothes, which symbolize his sins, has his iniquity removed, and is now being clothed in fine garments and a clean turban, representing purification and restoration. This is a wonderful symbol of the justification of the sinner. It is instantaneous and complete: it happens when a person has faith, and it is not a process that continues over time. *A person is either justified or he is not.* It is God's declaration that a believer is righteous because of Christ's intervention.

Sanctification

In contrast to justification, which is a for-once event, sanctification is an extended process. Theologians of various religious traditions have emphasized this. The great medieval theologian Thomas Aquinas defined sanctification in these words: "Sanctification is the effect of grace by which a person is made holy, transformed in soul, and drawn into deeper union with God."[10] Adventist pioneer Ellen G. White also stressed that sanctification is progressive and is a process that continues throughout life. It is "not the work of a moment, an hour, a day, but of a lifetime. It is not gained by a happy flight of feeling, but is the result of constantly

10. Aquinas, *Summa Theologica*, I–II, q. 113, art. 8.

dying to sin, and constantly living for Christ."[11] Karl Barth emphasized the divine initiative in our sanctification: "Sanctification is the act in which man is claimed by God as his own, is made and preserved as his own, is awakened and maintained in the freedom which is obedience."[12]

A key passage about sanctification is Phil 2:12–13, which links two fundamental elements in a way only an inspired apostle could do: "Continue to work out your salvation with fear and trembling, for it is God who works in you to will and to act in order to fulfill his good purpose." The text seems to begin with the suggestion that sanctification is hard work and that its success depends on what we ourselves can bring to the table. It mentions "work" and also "fear and trembling." But the idea that sanctification could result from human effort is immediately corrected: sanctification means that we have decided to align our life with that of Christ. Sanctification is the corollary of commitment. But the bottom line is grace: "It is God who works in you to will and to act in order to fulfill his good purpose."

Sanctification follows our conversion, and builds on our justification, as we are "being transformed into his image with ever-increasing glory" (2 Cor 3:18). Edward Vick states it succinctly: sanctification "is a state of acceptance with God, in which, despite our sin, we progress in the life of faith. It is the state of faith. So every Christian is a saint."[13] Sanctification is accompanied by growth, struggle, and, beyond everything else, cooperation with the Holy Spirit. We must "make every effort" to be holy (Heb 12:14). But the "fear and trembling" of Phil 2:13 is not an incessant anxiety whether our actions are good enough; it points to the sincerity of our living out the righteousness that justification has declared, in the power of the Spirit (Gal 5:16–25).

Justification is the *root*, while sanctification is the *fruit*. Sanctification does not bring our salvation about but flows from it. One might say—as is also expressed in the title of this chapter—justification is God's work *for* us and sanctification is God's work *in* us. Or, in theological terms, justification has to do with God's *imputed* righteousness, while sanctification is about his *imparted* righteousness. This latter term refers to the actual transformation of the believer's life through the work of the Holy Spirit. It is an internal change that enables a person to live righteously.

11. White, *Acts of the Apostles*, 560.

12. Barth, *Doctrine of Reconciliation*, 509.

13. Vick, *Is Salvation Really Free?*, 88.

Can We Be Perfect?[14]

I am returning to a statement made by Ellen White that has caused endless debate: "When the character of Christ shall be perfectly reproduced in his people, then he will come to claim them as his own."[15] As we saw earlier, this statement is a vital ingredient in LGT and has been a basic premise for the widespread belief that *sinless* perfection is possible.

The view that becoming perfect is an attainable goal is not an Adventist invention. Perfectionism is a phenomenon with a very long history. Even before Christianity came on the scene, we find clear traces of perfectionism among the Jewish sect of the Essenes, who lived in the Qumran community near the Dead Sea.[16] And throughout the early centuries of Christian history there have been individuals, groups, and even large movements within the church, or at the edges of the church, that promoted perfectionism. Closer to our times, perfectionism was an important element of Christian life in such movements as Pietism, Quakerism, and, in particular, Methodism. The Methodist influence on Adventism was, to put it mildly, significant, especially through Ellen G. White, who came from a Methodist background. The views of Ellen G. White regarding salvation and sanctification—and also with respect to perfection—resemble in many ways those of John Wesley, the founder of Methodism. It is therefore important to note that, for Wesley, perfection was not final or absolute. Perfect people, he said, are never so perfect that they are totally sinless. They can always grow further.[17]

Early Adventism continuously struggled with the tendency to place a one-sided emphasis on obedience to God's commands, the Sabbath commandment in particular. This was perhaps to be expected, as the Adventist believers were constantly forced to defend their Sabbath praxis. However, the sad reality was that, as a result, the basic Christian truth that salvation is by grace, through faith in Jesus Christ, was often obscured. The issue came to a climax during the 1888 General Conference in the American city of Minneapolis, where A. T. Jones and E. J. Waggoner (with the support of Ellen G. White) soon dominated the

14. In this section about perfection I rely on a chapter in my book *In All Humility*, 91–116.

15. White, *Christ's Object Lessons*, 69.

16. For a description of perfectionist movements, see LaRondelle, *Perfection and Perfectionism*, 246–324. Also Flew, *Idea of Perfection*.

17. Wesley, "Plain Account," 366–67.

proceedings with their powerful messages on righteousness by faith.[18] Their presentations met with stiff opposition during those historic meetings from (mostly older) church leaders. In retrospect we can see that the conference was a watershed moment in the Adventist struggle against a legalism that emphasizes human works, in favor of a gospel emphasis on Christ's work on our behalf. But even today Adventists all too often stray towards a legalistic concept of the Christian life.

In his Sermon on the Mount, Jesus challenged his audience: "Be ye therefore perfect, even as your Father which is in heaven is perfect" (Matt 5:48 KJV). Writing to the Ephesians about the unity and the diverse ministries in the church, the apostle Paul explained, "And he gave some, apostles; and some, prophets; and some, evangelists; and some, pastors and teachers; for the *perfecting* of the saints . . . till we all come in the unity of the faith, and of the knowledge of the Son of God, unto a *perfect* man, unto the measure of the stature of the fullness of Christ" (Eph 4:11–13 KJV; italics added). I quoted these few verses from the King James Version, since most recent Bible translations do not use the terms *perfect* or *perfection*, but speak of *being mature* and *maturity*. We find a similar use of perfection versus maturity in the King James Version and other translations of Heb 6:1. In the New International Version, the author admonishes the believers to "move beyond the elementary teachings" and progress "to maturity" (KJV: "unto perfection").

A number of times the Old Testament refers to persons who were "perfect." Noah is one of them. Here again, the word *perfect* is found in the King James Version, but is avoided by newer versions. We read in the King James Version that Noah "was a just man and perfect in his generations" (Gen 6:9). The New International Version describes Noah as "a righteous man, blameless among the people of his time." The King James Version rendering should immediately set some bells ringing. Was Noah a perfect man? What about the incident after the flood when we find this supposedly perfect man in a state of drunkenness in his tent? Or, to take another example, in Gen 17:1 God challenges Abraham to be "perfect" (KJV) or "blameless" (NIV). Anyone who has some knowledge of the Bible would not describe Abraham as a faultless person. Quite clearly, he did not reach a state of sinlessness! Job is characterized as "blameless

18. Many books have been written on the 1888 Minneapolis Conference, about its main players and the issues at stake, as well as about the aftermath. For a concise guide to the topic, see Knight, *User-Friendly Guide*.

and upright" (NIV). Here also the King James Version tells us that this patriarch was "perfect" (Job 1:1).

A number of biblical passages clearly underline that "perfection" is not some vague desire, or a beautiful but impossible ideal, but a requirement for all believers. *The issue is, therefore, not whether perfection is possible, but what is meant by perfection.*[19]

The Greek word for perfection (*teleios*) has the same basic connotation as the Hebrew words *tãmîn* and *salêm*. Language experts agree that these words do not refer to absolute sinlessness. The word *teleios*, we read in *The New International Dictionary of New Testament Theology*, is based on the word *telos*, meaning "end" or "goal." It may refer to the end of time—not as a sudden, abrupt end, but as the conclusion of a dynamic process. But *teleios* more often points to "that which has reached its goal and is thus completed and perfected." In the fullest sense it can only be applied to God (Matt 5:48) and to Jesus Christ (Heb 7:28). The concept of *teleios*, the author of the article in this prestigious dictionary insists, "does not carry the idea of ethical perfection that is to be gradually acquired. It refers to a state of maturity, of having come of age. It does not denote some endpoint of human conduct, but rather the "undivided wholeness of a person in his behavior."[20]

Let us take another look at Matt 5:48 and compare this verse with its parallel in the Gospel of Luke. Instead of echoing the very same words ("be perfect"), Luke reports Jesus's words as, "Be merciful, just as your Father is merciful" (Luke 6:36). Could it be that the essence of biblical perfection is found in receiving and giving love? When we read Matt 5:48 in its wider context, we notice how the word *love* is mentioned a number of times. That we are sons and daughters of God is demonstrated in our love for others, even for those who are our enemies. Loving others is the distinguishing mark of God's children. After all, did God not already love us before we loved him? "Therefore," Matt 5:48 says, we must be perfect in love and reflect the fatherly love of God.

Reading the first letter of John, we cannot escape the conclusion that love is the essence of our spiritual pilgrimage. According to Paul, it even surpasses faith and hope (1 Cor 13:13). Christ's ideal for us is that we shall be "perfect in love" (1 John 4:18).

19. Knight, *Sin and Salvation*, 138.

20. Schippers, "Goal," 59–65.

> This is love: not that we loved God, but that he loved us and sent his Son as an atoning sacrifice for our sins. Dear friends, since God so loved us, we also ought to love one another. No one has ever seen God; but if we love one another, God lives in us and his love is made complete in us. . . . God is love. Whoever lives in love, lives in God and God in them. In this way love is made complete in us so that we will have confidence on the day of judgment: In this world we are like Jesus (1 John 4:10–12, 16–17).

The apostle Paul stresses the same point: "The only thing that counts is faith expressing itself through love" (Gal 5:6). Being perfect is not a matter of outward compliance to a series of instructions—important though they may be—but requires a consistent attitude of love as the basis for reaching our spiritual goal (1 Thess 3:12–13).

Sinlessness

Can we live without sinning? Some biblical passages seem to suggest that this is possible. Says 1 John 3:6: "No one who lives in him [Christ] keeps on sinning. No one who continues to sin has either seen him or known him." And verse 9: "No one who is born of God will continue to sin, because God's seed remains in them; they cannot go on sinning, because they have been born of God." The same thought is repeated in 1 John 5:18: "We know that anyone born of God does not continue to sin."

However, in the same short letter from John we also read something that sounds very different. In fact, it seems to be the exact opposite of the verses just quoted. First John 1:8–10 states unequivocally, "If we claim to be without sin, we deceive ourselves and the truth is not in us. . . . If we claim we have not sinned, we make him [Christ] out to be a liar and his word is not in us."

How can we reconcile these seemingly contradictory statements? Romans 6 can help us here. Paul argues that those who have accepted Christ have "died to sin" (vv. 2, 11) and "have been set free from sin" (v. 22). This means, the apostle says, that sin no longer "reigns" in us and that we are no longer slaves to sin but slaves of God (vv. 12, 18, 22). Paul was a man of great faith but also a man who was painfully aware of his sinfulness. He never reached sinless perfection. In his "inner being" he delights in God's law, and he has "the desire to do what is good," but he finds that he continues to commit sins, however much he tries not to. "Although I want to do good, evil is right there with me." This realization brings him to the point of despair, and he cries out, "What a wretched man I am!" (Rom 7:18–24). In his letter to the Philippians Paul tells the addressees, whom he describes as "mature" ("perfect," KJV), about the dynamic process that continues to define his own life as a follower of Christ: "Not that I have already obtained all this, or have already been made perfect, but I press on to take hold of that for which Christ Jesus took hold of me. Brothers, I do not consider myself yet to have taken hold of it. But one thing I do: Forgetting what is behind and straining toward what is ahead, I press on toward the goal to win the prize for which God has called me heavenward in Christ Jesus" (Phil 3:15, 12–14).

"Mature" believers no longer have sin as the governing principle in their lives; they are *teleios* (perfect), because they have a clear *telos* (goal). It is one of the great paradoxes of faith that believers can be called perfect (mature) even though they must still grow further. They do still commit sins, for which they continue to need forgiveness, and they are still subject to sins of omission and subconscious wrongdoings. (Remember what we said about the nature of sin in chapter 5.) They are not sinless in any absolute sense of the word, but they have ceased to be slaves of sin! They were justified when they accepted Christ, and they are being sanctified as they live the life of a disciple of Christ. Let us, however, not forget that both justification and sanctification are 100 percent the work of God. "Genuine sanctification—let it be repeated—stands or falls with this continued orientation toward justification and the remission of sin."[21] "Now that you have been set free from sin and have become slaves of God, the benefit you reap leads to holiness, and the result is eternal life. For the wages of sin is death, but the gift of God is eternal life in Christ Jesus our Lord" (Rom 6:22–23).

Ivan Blazen (1934–2023), an Adventist New Testament scholar, has summarized what we have discussed in this section in these two crisp statements: "Paradoxically, perfection as present is sanctification; sanctification as future is perfection. This means that the two realities are part and parcel of the same reality—likeness to God." And, "Perfection is not so much something we reach, as something that reaches us, not so much as what we attain, as something which grasps our life from beyond."[22]

21. Berkouwer, *Faith and Sanctification*, 87.

22. Blazen, "Salvation," 299–300.

Excursus: The Investigative Judgment

The Sanctuary Truth

It is often claimed that the sanctuary doctrine is the only teaching that is truly unique to Adventism. (The Sabbath is not a fully unique feature, as some other small denominations also consider the seventh-day Sabbath as the genuine day of the Lord.) However, the sanctuary doctrine, and its accompanying belief in a pre-Advent (investigative) judgment, is not only *unique*, but also the most *controversial* Adventist teaching that has been attacked and criticized by many outside Adventism and has also been questioned or ignored by many church members.[1]

In Old Testament times God instituted the sanctuary service as a *tableau vivant* (dramatic representation) to impress upon the Israelite people that the rupture between him and mankind could only be breached by a gracious divine intervention. An elaborate system of sacrifices was given to the people to point them to the ultimate Sacrifice, the divine Lamb, who would restore the relationship between man and God. Christ was that Sacrifice, but his ministry was also symbolized by the priesthood, and in particular by the high priest, who prefigured Christ's role of the great

1. For a detailed defense of the traditional Adventist view of the investigative judgment, see Moore, *Case for Investigative Judgment*.

High Priest, as is described in the book of Hebrews. Thus, everything that happened in the Old Testament sanctuary service, all its different services—daily and annually—and all those who served in the sanctuary, were a collective symbol of Jesus Christ and his saving ministry.

On the basis of several prophetic statements in the Bible, the Baptist farmer-turned-preacher William Miller (1782–1849), who became the leader of a major revival movement, concluded that Christ's return was imminent and could be expected "around 1843." Later he was more specific and, finally, agreed with some of the other Millerite preachers that the second coming would take place on October 22, 1844. This fateful day, however, became the day of the "great disappointment" for the Millerite believers, when it passed without any sign of Christ's return.

In the days and weeks after this disheartening experience the disillusioned followers of Miller wondered what had gone wrong. Had they made a mistake in their calculations? Or had the arithmetic been correct, but had they been wrong regarding the event that would occur on that day? A small group of these Advent-believers (as they were called) soon concluded that this date—October 22, 1844—did not point to an event on earth, but to a heavenly occurrence—namely, that Christ had begun his service as the heavenly High Priest in the sanctuary in heaven.[2] This special work of Christ was prefigured by the elaborate ritual on the Day of Atonement in Israel's sanctuary service. It was further argued that Israel's annual Day of Atonement was, in fact, a judgment day. The sins the people had confessed during the past twelve months, and for which they had brought their sacrificial offerings throughout the year, were blotted out on Yom Kippur—the Day of Atonement. This annual service, it was believed, pointed forward to the work of Christ in heaven during the so-called investigative or pre-Advent phase of the judgment. During this investigation it becomes clear who will be saved and who will be lost. Christ has brought his sacrifice on the cross, but the benefits of this sacrifice are now, during this heavenly Day of Atonement, applied to those who accepted Christ and will thus be acquitted in the investigative judgment.

2. Many regard this as a classic case of *cognitive dissonance*; i.e., persevering in a belief after having been proven wrong. The seminal book about cognitive dissonance is Festinger, *Theory of Cognitive Dissonance*.

Doubts

Why do many Adventists today find it impossible to hold on to this traditional Adventist teaching? Doubts about the sanctuary doctrine are not new, but in the past they centered on two issues. First, it concerned the question whether the work of Christ was really finished on the cross or whether the atonement was incomplete until Christ had performed his high priestly work in the heavenly sanctuary. For many it was (and is) important to emphasize that Christ's sacrifice on the cross was final and that his atoning work should not be split into a first and a second phase, as the Adventist sanctuary doctrine implies.

And second, there was uneasiness about the role of Azazel (see Lev 16). At the end of the ceremonies of the Day of Atonement a male goat was sent into the desert, symbolically carrying away all the sins of the people (v. 16). According to the traditional Adventist explanation, every detail of the Old Testament ritual has a counterpart in the "antitypical" Day of Atonement, in which Christ officiates. The male goat, called Azazel, was traditionally understood as representing Satan. There have, however, been fierce protests against this view, since this seems to imply that Satan actually plays a role in our redemption from sin.

Of late, the objections against the sanctuary doctrine tend to be more general and seem to focus on other aspects. Many objectors find it difficult to accept that there is some sort of literal, material, edifice in heaven, complete with literal furniture and artifacts, and with two separate apartments, as many of their fellow Adventists claim. They find it quite challenging to believe that in October 1844, Jesus Christ moved from one section in this heavenly location to the next, where he has remained ever since, working hard to ensure that no mistakes will be made in the heavenly accounting of human sin. They wonder: Must we really believe in such a literal application of the Old Testament symbolism? And does the book of Hebrews (6:19, 20; 9:12; 10:19, 20) not tell us that Christ already entered the most holy place of the heavenly sanctuary (in whatever way we envisage it) upon his ascension, rather than in 1844? Is this also not clearly implied in Heb 1:3, where it is stated that Christ sat down (aorist tense, indicating a completed action) "at the right hand of the Majesty in heaven" after he had provided "purification for sins"?

The 1844 Date

For many the 1844 date, as the time when Christ began his ministry as our High Priest and when the pre-Advent judgment started, is a sacrosanct aspect of Adventist teaching, which they believe is solidly based on Dan 8 and Dan 9. In the past, many Adventist publications contained schematic representations of the "2300 evenings and mornings" (Dan 8:14), with the 457 BC date at one end and 1844 at the other end, with somewhere in the middle the symbol of the cross. Today, even most Adventists who still insist on the importance of the 1844 date would not be able to explain how this date of October 1844 is arrived at. And, indeed, it involves a rather complex reasoning process. Many doubters would say that it requires a series of assumptions that appear to be extremely shaky.

Traditional Adventist teaching maintains that the book of Daniel contains a time prophecy that brings us to the year 1844 as the moment when something significant would happen in heaven. To arrive at this conclusion, one must be willing to take several major steps. In the first place, one must accept that the book of Daniel was written by a prophet who lived and worked at the Babylonian court, and later at the Persian court, in the *sixth* century BC, and that he conveyed a number of prophetic messages that relate to the period from his days until the end of time. As already mentioned earlier in this book, today most experts on the book of Daniel believe that this section of the Bible was actually written in the *second* century BC, by an unknown author who used the name of the prophet Daniel to lend added authority to his document. Nowadays, such a procedure would be considered extremely deceitful, but in ancient times it was a rather common practice.

In the standard Adventist interpretation of the book of Daniel the evil power that plays a key role ("the little horn") is identified as the Roman Catholic Church. Most scholars today argue, however, that this "little horn" is a symbol for a Greek king, Antiochus IV Epiphanes, who persecuted the Jewish people and desecrated the Jerusalem temple in 168 BC.

To arrive at the traditional Adventist view regarding the time prophecy of the twenty-three hundred days ("evenings and mornings") as ending in 1844, one must go against the majority scholarly opinion and stick to the early (sixth century BC) date of the book and reject the alternative theory that many find far more convincing.

The next step to arrive at the 1844 date would be to accept that Dan 8, in which the time period of twenty-three hundred days is mentioned, is connected with Dan 9, where the starting point of this prophetic period is allegedly found. Daniel did not understand the vision of chapter 8 about the twenty-three hundred days and kept worrying about its possible meaning. In Dan 9, so the explanation runs, he is given the key. A new time period is mentioned: seventy weeks, that are "cut off" for a specific purpose. It is argued that the period of the seventy prophetic weeks (or 490 literal years) is, in fact, the first section of the twenty-three hundred prophetic days (or twenty-three hundred literal years). Therefore, if we know the starting point of the seventy-week period of Dan 9, we also know when the twenty-three hundred days of Dan 8 began. Many interpreters, however, see it as a problem that there is a considerable lapse of time (some twelve years) between Daniel's vision in chapter 8 and the one in Dan 9, which makes this connection not as probable, they say, as Adventists have traditionally argued.

But then there is the next hurdle. In Adventist teaching the starting point for the seventy weeks, and therefore presumably also for the twenty-three hundred days, is found in Dan 9:25. This text points to the moment when a ruler would issue a decree allowing the Judeans, who had been living as exiles in Babylon, to return to Palestine and to rebuild Jerusalem. The traditional interpretation tells us that this decree was issued by the Persian king Artaxerxes I in 457 BC. However, more than one of such decrees was issued, and not all scholars would agree that this particular decree of Artaxerxes is the one Dan 9:25 refers to, and that we can therefore safely settle on the 457 BC date as the beginning of the seventy weeks (and, therefore, of the twenty-three hundred days).

This does not exhaust the number of steps we must take to eventually get to 1844. A key assumption is that in biblical-time prophecies a *prophetic day* must be interpreted as a *literal year*. If this is true, and if the choice of the 457 BC date is correct, and if the periods in Dan 8 and 9 do run concurrently, then, indeed the twenty-three hundred prophetic days are twenty-three hundred literal years and reach as far as 1844. But is there a solid basis for this so-called day-year principle?

The day-year principle is not an Adventist invention but has been used by many expositors of prophecy in the past. However, this was in a time when the majority of these expositors saw the apocalyptic prophecies (especially in the Bible books of Daniel and the Revelation) as a description of the history of the world until the second coming of Christ. Today most Bible scholars prefer other approaches to these prophetic portions of the Bible, and few would still defend the day-year-principle. They point out that the two texts that are usually cited in defense of this principle (Num 14:34 and Ezek 4:5–6) are not very conclusive—certainly not when read in their contexts.[3]

Another question regarding the October 22, 1844 date that remains quite puzzling to many Adventists is that a little-known Jewish calendar is used to determine on what day the tenth day of the Jewish month Tishri (when the Jewish Day of Atonement was to be celebrated) fell in the year 1844. The Adventist pioneers who developed the sanctuary doctrine opted for the calendar of the Jewish Karaite movement.[4] For most church members who try to understand the basis for the sanctuary doctrine, it remains a mystery why they preferred this particular calendar.

Yet other issues emerge. In the King James Version, Dan 8:14 reads as follows: "Unto two thousand and three hundred days; then shall the sanctuary be *cleansed*." Other versions indicate that the sanctuary was to be *restored*, or "to be *restored in its rightful state*." The entire doctrine stands or falls with the identification of this sanctuary and the interpretation of the term *cleansing* or *restoring*. For traditional Adventism, which places Daniel in the sixth century BC, and builds on a twenty-three-hundred-*year* period, it is clear that the sanctuary that is to be "cleansed" must refer to the heavenly sanctuary, as the Jerusalem temple no longer existed at the end of the twenty-three hundred *years*. And Adventists are supposed to believe that the word *cleansed* points to the ritual of the annual day of atonement, which includes an element of judgment. The antitypical day of atonement that is believed to have begun in 1844 thus refers to a phase of God's judgment.

3. Raymond F. Cottrell, one of the editors of the seven-volume *Seventh-day Adventist Bible Commentary* (1953–1958) wrote the article "The Untold Story of the Bible Commentary," published in the August 1985 issue of *Spectrum*, in which he provided details of the history of this project. He indicated that those who were working on this project were convinced that the day-year principle could not be defended, but was maintained "for pastoral reasons."

4. The Karaites are a Jewish sect that emerged in the eighth to ninth centuries, primarily in the Middle East. The Karaites reject the oral Torah (Talmud) and rely solely on the Hebrew Bible (Tanakh) for religious guidance. They emphasize personal interpretation of Scripture and follow a literal reading of the text. Small Karaite communities still exist today, notably in Israel, Lithuania, and Egypt.

There seems more than enough reason to wonder how anything so complicated as the traditional Adventist sanctuary doctrine can be crucial to people's faith. Many Adventists believe that Christ is their Mediator and that therefore they can feel secure. The idea of a literal sanctuary in heaven, where Christ entered in 1844 for a final phase in his redemptive work, does not sound very convincing to them. Besides, how relevant can it be to tell others about something that supposedly has been ongoing since 1844? Is it not far more important to worry about the significance of the gospel message for people in the first part of the twenty-first century?

It should be added that doubt about the traditional sanctuary doctrine is not limited to "believers on the margins" of the Adventist Church.[5] Both anecdotal evidence and some firmer data suggest that many church members have serious misgivings about the traditional sanctuary views, and especially about the interpretation of Dan 8:14 and the computation that is based on this text.[6] There is evidence to indicate that a significant percentage of Adventist pastors no longer supports the traditional view.[7]

The Australian theologian Desmond Ford[8] (1929–2019), who was accused by the leadership of the Adventist Church of teaching heresy, and as a result lost his ministerial credentials, has remained very influential. His views about aspects of the sanctuary doctrine, and most notably his rejection of the investigative judgment, have been adopted by many pastors and members in the pews, even though they often find it prudent not to side with Ford too openly.

5. See Verrecchia, *God of No Fixed Address*. Verrecchia pleads for a frank reappraisal of the traditional Adventist view of this doctrine, after stressing the widespread unease among many Adventist believers about the traditional interpretation. For a historical survey of how Adventism has related to the sanctuary doctrine, see Timm, "Doctrine of the Sanctuary," 331–59.

6. Dr. David Trim, director of the Office of Archives and Statistics of the worldwide Seventh-day Adventist Church, reported to the Annual Council in 2013 the outcome of a research project in which over four thousand church members around the world participated. Thirty-eight percent indicated that they do not (or do not fully) accept the doctrine of the sanctuary and the investigative judgment. Trim, *Global Data Picture*, 34.

7. A survey of over two hundred pastors in 2000 in the Los Angeles (US) region indicated that 41 percent of them did not accept the traditional version of the Adventist sanctuary doctrine. See Ozolins, "Doctrinal Dissonance."

8. For a biography of Desmond Ford see Hook, *Desmond Ford*.

Chapter 7

"There Remains a Rest"

Years ago I was on a United Airlines flight and did what I rarely do, which is read an in-flight magazine. Towards the back of the journal was a column titled "Ancient Wisdom." A blurb beneath the piece triggered my attention: "If you and your family are drowning in a sea of to-do lists, try doing nothing—for one day a week." In the article Nan Chase—at that time a frequent contributor to *The Washington Post* and since then to many other prominent publications—shared with her readers how she and her husband decided to start keeping the Sabbath in an attempt to get their busy lives back in order. It worked beyond their dreams. The author ended her article with these words: "I look forward to my weekly holiday. As the sun goes down each Friday evening, I take off my wristwatch, and for a night and a day time stands still."[1]

What Nan Chase describes about herself and her husband is totally different from how most people in the Western world experience their weekend. For many the weekend is by far the most important part of the week. Whereas former generations had a six-day work week, with only one day of rest in between stretches of fifty or more hours of hard work, today in many countries the work week has been shortened to less than forty hours, with a free Saturday and a free Sunday. However, this does not mean that the life of most people is more relaxed than that of their parents

1. Chase, "Ancient Wisdom," 118.

and grandparents. For many in Western countries their weekend is filled with sports, household chores, gardening, and shopping. Leisure activities include sleeping a few extra hours, hobbies, visits to aging parents and activities with friends, eating out, day trips with or without children, et cetera. Many parents have an extra weekend job or maintain a busy schedule of taking their children to their clubs and other activities.

For a steadily decreasing percentage of the population a part of the weekend is devoted to religious activities. Some Catholics avail themselves of the opportunity to attend mass on Saturday evenings, while others go to church on Sunday morning. Statistics differ greatly for individual countries. In Nigeria 94 percent of Catholics attend their church at least once a week. In the United States the percentage is 17, while in France and in the Netherlands, the percentage of regular Roman Catholic church attendees is 8 and 7 percent, respectively.[2] The statistics for Protestants vary widely, not only depending on geography but also on one's denomination. In the United States about 44 percent of Protestant Christians attend church services regularly.[3] A survey of church attendance in fifteen European countries revealed that nowadays on average only 22 percent of Protestant adults goes to church at least once a month.[4] In some countries the number is much lower.

After we discussed in the previous two chapters aspects of faith and salvation, particularly how God's grace works *for* us and *in* us, we now proceed to an important part of our faith experience—namely, to the day God has given to mankind to fortify the closeness with him that is available to us. In our focus on the Sabbath it is important to first look at the time element. Seventh-day Adventists practice Sabbath keeping on the seventh day of the week, usually referred to as the Saturday. Most Christians worship and "rest" on the first day of the week, the Sunday. Is there a decisive reason why Adventist should differ in this respect from almost all other Christians? Related are questions about the role Adventists attach to Sabbath keeping in the final phase of earth's history (we will return to that in a later chapter). However, concerns about the *timing* of the weekly Sabbath should not get in the way of our attempts to discover the *meaning* of the Sabbath.

2. McKeown, "Where Is Mass Attendance."
3. OSV News, "Gallup: Just 3 in 10."
4. Pew Research Center, "Religious Practice and Belief."

Sabbath Keepers

Adventists regard the observance of the Sabbath on the seventh day of the week as a central aspect of their theology and praxis. It is one of the core beliefs and practices that binds the twenty-five million Seventh-day Adventists worldwide together. Of course, the Sabbath is also a key characteristic of the Jewish religion, although the degree of strictness in current Jewish Sabbath keeping varies greatly.

Besides the Adventist faith community there are a few other Sabbatarian denominations. The oldest among these is the Seventh Day Baptist Church,[5] which traces its roots back to the end of sixteenth-century England. The first Seventh Day Baptist congregation was established in 1650 in London. Just twenty-one years later Stephen Mumford organized the first Seventh Day Baptist church in the US, in Newport, Rhode Island.[6] Today there are approximately thirty thousand Seventh Day Baptists worldwide. Another Sabbath-keeping group, which dates back to the 1800s, is the Church of God (Seventh Day). It has a global membership in excess of sixty thousand members.[7] In addition to numerous other small Sabbath-keeping groups, there are groups of so-called Messianic Jews who observe the Sabbath. They may number as many as 350,000 worldwide.[8]

There is a direct link between the Sabbath keeping of the Seventh-day Adventists and of the Seventh Day Baptists. Shortly before the great disappointment of 1844, when Christ did not return as the Advent movement of William Miller had predicted, Rachel Oakes-Preston (1809–1868), who had a Seventh Day Baptist background, introduced the Sabbath doctrine to the Adventists in Washington, New Hampshire. She was able to convince a few fellow believers of the Christian obligation to keep the Sabbath, with church founder Joseph Bates as one of the early adopters.[9]

5. Note the difference in the official spelling of the names: Seventh-day Adventists and Seventh Day Baptists.

6. For a history of the Seventh Day Baptists see Sanford, *Choosing People*.

7. Mead, *Handbook of Denominations*, 112–13.

8. Jews for Judaism, "How Many Messianic Jews."

9. Schwarz and Greenleaf, *Light Bearers*, 56–57.

From Sabbath to Sunday

Many Seventh-day Adventists, when asked about the origin of Christian Sunday observance, are clear about their answer. The Sabbath was exchanged for the Sunday by the Roman Catholic Church! According to the traditional Adventist interpretation of the book of Daniel, prophecy foretold a series of world empires—Babylon, Medo-Persia, Greece, and Rome. After the fall of the Roman Empire ten powers would fill the vacuum that the Roman Empire had left. Among these political entities a different kind of power was to arise and would play an ever-more sinister role in the affairs of the world. In ages past this power (the "little horn" of Dan 7) was identified by many, and, not surprisingly also by Seventh-day Adventists, as Roman Catholicism. One of the malicious characteristics of this religiopolitical body was that it would "speak against the Most High and oppress his holy people and try to change the set times and the laws" (Dan 7:25). This attempt to change "set times and the law" was seen as an irrefutable reference to the role of the Roman Church in substituting Sunday as the day of worship for the biblical Sabbath.

While it is undoubtedly true that the Catholic Church has played a decisive role in the process whereby Sabbath observance was largely replaced by Sunday keeping, and also that this church has frequently asserted it had the authority to choose Sunday over the Sabbath as the day of worship and rest,[10] the historical details are not as clear-cut as it often suggested.[11] In the New Testament we find a few texts that mention the first day of the week, which have often been seen as the earliest references to Sunday observance (Acts 20:7; 1 Cor 16:2; Rev 1:10). We will return to these texts later in this chapter. In reality, early Christians continued for a considerable time to observe the Sabbath from Friday evening to Saturday evening. But after some time, Christians began to gather for the ritual of their communal meal, first on Saturday evening and then on Sunday morning. From the writings of Ignatius of Antioch (ca. AD 107) and Justin Martyr (ca. AD 150) we learn that these Sunday meetings were seen as honoring the resurrection of Christ, which, according to the Scriptures, took place on the first day of the week.[12]

10. Bruinsma, *Adventists and Catholics*, 85–87.

11. For a recent, succinct, historical survey of the transition from Sabbath to Sunday, see González, *Brief History of Sunday*.

12. Rordorf, *Sunday*, 238–73; Strand, "Lord's Day," 346–51.

There is clear evidence that the transition of the day of worship from Sabbath to Sunday did not occur everywhere at the same time. Adventist theologian and church historian Samuel Bacchiocchi (1938–2008) did seminal research into the origin of Sunday worship. The results of his studies pointed to a key role of the church in Rome in the early promotion of Sunday worship.[13] He agreed with many other scholars who maintain that anti-Jewish sentiments, and the determination of (Gentile) Christians to put a distance between themselves and the Jews, were among the main factors in this process.[14] But other influences, such as the worship of the sun in parts of the Roman Empire, also played a role.[15] A few historians have, however, recorded that in some geographical areas, for a long time, both Sabbath and Sunday were kept side by side. Socrates (385–445), a church historian who lived in Constantinople, wrote, "Almost all the churches throughout the world celebrate the mysteries on the Sabbath of every week." Another historian, Sozomen (early fifth century), makes the same observation.[16]

Sunday worship developed organically in a large part of the early Christian world. However, an important new development took place in the time of Emperor Constantine. He issued a civil decree in 321 making Sunday a day of rest in the Roman Empire. Later in the fourth century, the Council of Laodicea (363–364) reinforced Sunday observance, while discouraging continued worship on the Sabbath. From this point onward, the element of Sunday *rest* was emphasized besides the aspect of *worship*. The Catholic Church and the Christian tradition affirmed Sunday as the primary day of worship and rest, but it was a gradual process rather than a sudden change. Sigve Tonstad notes, "As the Church increasingly embraces Sunday, the Sabbath sinks into oblivion almost unnoticed."[17]

The further history of Sabbath and Sunday observance makes fascinating reading, but the details are beyond the scope of this chapter.[18] We must limit ourselves to a few significant facets. In medieval Christianity,

13. Bacchiocchi, *From Sabbath to Sunday*.

14. Tonstad, *Lost Meaning*, 302–9.

15. González, *Brief History of Sunday*, 12–24.

16. Bruinsma, *Day God Created*, 80.

17. Tonstad, *Lost Meaning*, 301.

18. Recommended reading: González, *Brief History of Sunday*; Strand, *Sabbath in Scripture and History*; Tonstad, *Lost Meaning*; Bacchiocchi, *From Sabbath to Sunday*; Carson, *From Sabbath to Lord's Day*.

Sunday was both a day for worship and for "play."[19] Strict Sunday observance, inspired by Old Testament Sabbath laws, emerged among Protestants, in particular among the Puritans, who also had an important part in importing strict Sunday keeping into the American colonies.

While Sunday observance became the norm, Sabbatarian tendencies persisted through the centuries. Historical evidence indicates that some early Celtic Christian communities in Ireland and Scotland observed the seventh-day Sabbath (Saturday) as a day of rest.[20] We also hear of Sabbath observance in Egypt until the sixth century, and of periods of extensive Sabbath keeping in Ethiopia.[21] Sabbath observance was also found among some Waldensian groups in Northern Italy.[22]

Luther strongly resisted the Sabbatarian ideas of Andreas Karlstad, his former colleague and fellow reformer, arguing that Karlstad's focus on the Sabbath was based on a misunderstanding of Christian liberty and might lead to embracing a legalistic religion. In the Anabaptist branch of the Reformation we not only see a return to a more biblical form of baptism, but, in some quarters, also a reevaluation of the Sabbath. The Sabbath keepers among the Anabaptists were certainly a minority but they were found in several countries. Evidence points to Sabbath observance in Romania, Scandinavia, France, Russia, and possibly also the Netherlands.[23]

Bryan W. Ball (1935–2025), a Seventh-day Adventist church leader and historian, wrote an important study on Sabbatarianism in England and Wales in the seventeenth to nineteenth centuries.[24] He concluded that it represented a movement that was "diffused widely across the country" and was "resilient enough to survive by a century or more the rigors of an extended period of repression and harassment."[25]

19. González, *Brief History of Sunday*, 86–89.

20. Augsburger, "Sabbath and the Lord's Day," 194–95.

21. Vyhmeister, "Sabbath in Egypt and Ethiopia," 185.

22. Augsburger, "Sabbath and the Lord's Day," 208–9.

23. Bruinsma, *Day God Created*, 88.

24. Ball, *Seventh Day Men*.

25. Ball, *Seventh Day Men*, 310.

Creation Time

The creation story in Gen 1 tells us that God decided to make "heaven and earth." He began by creating light and was pleased with the result. He "saw that the light was good" (Gen 1:4). After each subsequent stage of his creative activity God affirmed that his work "was good." Then, "pleased with himself, God ceased his work on the seventh day, blessing this day and declaring it holy."[26] "This final day . . . forms the apex and goal of God's creative activity."[27]

For many Seventh-day Adventists it is important that we accept the creation story as a literal report of the beginning of our solar system and of life on our planet. The most recent version of the fundamental beliefs underlines that the creation week consisted of seven literal twenty-four-hour days. Belief number six reads as follows: "God has revealed in Scripture the authentic and historical account of his creative activity. He created the universe, and in a recent six-day creation the Lord made 'the heavens and the earth, the sea, and all that is in them' and rested on the seventh day. Thus he established the Sabbath as a perpetual memorial of the work he performed and completed during six literal days that together with the Sabbath constituted the same unit of time that we call a week today."[28]

This insistence on a literal reading of the creation story has much to do with the fear that the basis for observing the Sabbath on the seventh day of the week is fatally weakened (if not destroyed) if we no longer believe in a literal creation week, with the Sabbath as the God-given rest at the end of that week. This line of reasoning is, however, very problematic. It is misguided to stubbornly cling to a particular teaching or interpretation out of fear that otherwise our doctrinal edifice might come tumbling down. Fear that the Sabbath doctrine will be in trouble cannot be a valid reason to revert to a literal reading of a story that demands a theological understanding rather than a scientific approach.

The authors of the creation stories in Gen 1 and 2 want to impress us with the fact that God is the Maker of everything and that humans have a special status among all living creatures. Humankind is made in God's image and has the task of caring for God's creation. As creatures

26. Brams, "Creation,"13.

27. Turner, *Genesis*, 25.

28. General Conference, "What Do Adventists Believe?," no. 6.

they must know their place—their privileges and responsibilities—before their Maker. The story of Gen 1 refers to the Sabbath as the climax of God's creation. It is God's sublime gift to mankind. This emphasis on the Sabbath is intentionally embedded in the creation narrative. Rather than posing a problem for Sabbath keepers, a nonliteral, theological reading of the creation story strengthens the theology of the Sabbath. The structured, intentional, and climatic way in which the creation story is told underscores that the Sabbath is a crucial part of God's original design for humanity. Claus Westermann (1909–2000), a German Protestant Old Testament scholar, comments, "The seventh day is completely different from the previous six. It is not marked by the words 'and there was evening and there was morning'; it does not mention any creative activity. . . . Instead, it is a day of blessing and sanctification. This is not a continuation of the six days but their goal and culmination."[29]

An important aspect of the message of Gen 1 is that God created time for us in units of six-plus-one. Our divisions of time (days, months, years) are based on movements of celestial bodies, or are the result of human consensus (centuries, hours, minutes, seconds, etc.), except the week. Many theories have been proposed about the origin of the week, but none is truly convincing.[30] J. H. Meesters (1883–1955), a Dutch theologian who wrote his doctoral dissertation about the origin of the Sabbath and of the week, concludes, "The week of seven days is a time unit that was [in antiquity] only known in Israel. . . . The origin of the seven-day week cannot be determined, unless we can point to the origin of the Sabbath, which became an inalienable part of the week."[31] Seventh-day Adventists do not need to worry: the Sabbath on the seventh day of the week is solidly anchored in the theology of the creation story. Tonstad underlines the profound theological significance of the Sabbath in the creation narrative with the following statement: "Therefore, right from its debut, the seventh day is not a peripheral afterthought. God ceases from working in order to enjoy the company of the person God has created, suggesting that the seventh day speaks as much of the value of human beings to God as of God's valuation of human life. What lies in the foreground of the seventh day's mention in the Bible is God's gift, not human obligation."[32]

29. Westermann, *Genesis 1–11*, 115.

30. Meesters, *Op Zoek naar de Oorsprong*, 4–83.

31. Meesters, *Op Zoek naar de Oorsprong*, 81; my translation.

32. Tonstad, *Lost Meaning*, 34.

The Sabbath in the Old Testament

The longest commandment among the Ten Words is the fourth that instructs humankind to regard the seventh day of the week as "holy" time. The principles embedded in this law were not new when Moses brought the two stone tablets with him down from Mount Sinai, after his encounter with Yahweh. Killing unlawfully, committing adultery, telling lies, and the other principles enshrined in the Ten Commandments had been part of the moral compass of mankind long before the days of Moses. Significantly, the Sabbath commandment in Exod 20:8–11 begins with the word *remember*! Clearly, Sabbath observance was something already well-known. In fact, just a few chapters earlier in the Exodus account we find the story about the manna, in which the Sabbath plays a major role.

About six weeks after their deliverance from Egyptian bondage, the people of Israel "came to the Desert of Sin, which is between Elim and Sinai" (Exod 16:1). Not surprisingly feeding a large group of people in an uninhabitable wilderness became a critical problem, which God solved in a unique way. He arranged for the "raining" of food from heaven. Each morning during their forty-year sojourn in the desert, the Israelites could collect enough "manna" for the day. However, on every sixth day it would "rain" twice as much, so that they would also have enough food for the "Sabbath day of rest, a holy Sabbath to the Lord" (Exod 16:23). The gift of "manna" had a deeper meaning than simply the provision of enough calories for survival in a desert environment. God said, "In this way I will test them and see whether they will follow my instructions" (Exod 16:4).

The structure of the Ten Commandments in Exod 20 closely parallels ancient Hittite suzerainty treaties, particularly those from the second millennium BC.[33] These treaties between a dominant ruler (the suzerain) and a vassal people typically included a preamble identifying the ruler, a historical prologue with details of past acts of deliverance, stipulations for loyalty and conduct, and instructions for preserving and a regular reading of the treaty. Similarly, the Decalogue begins with God's self-identification ("I am the Lord your God") and a historical prologue ("who brought you out of Egypt"), followed by stipulations for loyalty (the Ten Commandments). These parallels suggest that the Ten Commandments

33. This suggests that the eternal principles of the Ten Commandments must in each new era be "translated" anew to reflect the changed circumstances. The versions of Exodus and Deuteronomy condone slavery in the fourth and in the ninth commandment; in a society without slavery these laws must apply to new social relationships.

were given in a form that Israel would recognize as covenantal language. They understood that, if they followed these principles, they could be totally sure of Yahweh's absolute protection![34]

The text of the Ten Commandments in Exod 20 has a parallel in Deut 5. One major difference is the motivation given for the Sabbath commandment. Whereas the Exodus version points back to God's status as the Creator as the basis for human loyalty to him and to his instructions, the Deuteronomy version mentions God's mighty acts in the delivery of Israel from Egyptian slavery. This raises the question about the precise wording on the stone tablets Moses received from God. Which of the two versions of the Sabbath commandment was the original? Old Testament scholar Jon Dybdahl suggested that this is not something we should worry about. Both versions of the rationale for Sabbath observance were, and remain, relevant. The only way we can respond to God's Sabbath gift is "by resting on the day God commanded as a memorial to both creation and redemption."[35]

Sabbath keeping was a serious business for ancient Israel, as we deduce from Num 15:32–36, where a Sabbath breaker ("a man who was found gathering wood on the Sabbath day") was brought to Moses, who told the Israelites to execute him. "The assembly took him [the offender] outside the camp and stoned him to death, as the Lord commanded Moses" (v. 36). It has been commented that this person was guilty of "an open, defiant act against God's law"[36] and was therefore to be punished in this manner. Stoning was the prescribed mode of execution for major transgressions (see Lev 20:2; 24:14; Exod 31:14; 35:2). "Hallowing the Sabbath was so important that one's very life was at stake."[37] While accepting that keeping the Sabbath "holy" is an important aspect of Christian living, passages such as these remain challenging for many present-day Christians. It seems that we must regard it as part of the larger biblical narrative that finds fulfilment in Christ's mercy and his interpretation of the law.

The book of Exodus contains several other statements about Sabbath observance. Exodus 23:12 emphasizes the social aspects of the Sabbath—others than the person's own household were included in the benefits of

34. See Kline, *Treaty of the Great King*.

35. Dybdahl, *Exodus*, 185.

36. Rodríguez, *Andrews Bible Commentary*, 297.

37. Maarsingh, *Numbers*, 55.

the Sabbath day. Exodus 34:21 addresses a realistic scenario in an agricultural society: the people were to refrain from work even in the time of ploughing and harvesting. A key passage about the Sabbath is found in Exod 31:13, 17: "You must observe my Sabbaths. This will be a sign between you and me for the generations to come, so you may know that I am the Lord, who makes you holy." And: "It will be a sign between me and the Israelites forever, for in six days the Lord made the heavens and the earth, and on the seventh day he rested and was refreshed."

An echo of these verses is found in Ezek 20:12, where the prophet transmits "the word of the Lord" to "some of the elders of Israel," who wondered whether there was a divine message for them. Surveying some of the deeds of God in the past, the message of the Lord continues: "Also I gave them my Sabbaths as a sign between us, so that they would know that I the Lord made them holy." And we read in verse 20, "Keep my Sabbaths holy, so that they may be a sign between us. Then you will know that I am the Lord your God." Old Testament scholar Gerhard F. Hasel (1935–1994) commented on this "sign" character of the Sabbath as follows: "Just as the rainbow is the perpetual sign of guarantee between God and the earth (Gen 9:13) that 'the waters shall never again become a flood to destroy all flesh' (v. 15), so the Sabbath is a 'sign of guarantee' whereby God assures his sanctifying purposes for his people. It is a sign of efficacious grace, a powerful sign of salvation. The Giver of the sign guarantees his pledge of making his people holy."[38]

The Sabbath was so much taken for granted in Israelite society that it can hardly surprise us to find only a few Sabbath passages in the remainder of the Old Testament. Second Kings 4:23 seems to indicate that in the ninth century BC the Sabbath was regarded as a suitable day to consult a prophet. Several prophetic books spoke out against the frequent desecration of the Sabbath. Amos criticized the traders who looked at the Sabbath purely from a commercial standpoint and resented the fact that they could not earn money on that day (Amos 8:4–5). The prophet Hosea told the people that God would bring their Sabbath and feasts to an end if they continued with their ungodly practices. Evidently, the Sabbath was deeply entrenched in the life of the Israelites. They did not give it up, even at times when they were heavily involved with various forms of idolatry. The prophet Jeremiah writes at some length about

38. Hasel, "Sabbath in the Pentateuch," 35.

the correct way to keep the Sabbath (17:19–27). As soon as the people would return to proper Sabbath observance, God would pour out in full measure the blessings he had connected to keeping his day holy. If they failed to do so, his judgments would surely follow.

Some more positive statements about Sabbath observance are found in the book of Isaiah. In chapter 56 non-Israelites (even eunuchs) are expressly included in God's covenant with Israel, and they may, therefore, also enjoy the blessings of the Sabbath (vv. 2–7). In chapter 58 Isaiah promises the people that they will "find joy in the Lord" if they keep their feet "from breaking the Sabbath" and honor it by not going their own way. He underlines that the Sabbath must be "a delight," rather than a burden (vv. 13–14). In the final chapters (65–66) the prophet Isaiah assures the people that God will create "new heavens and a new earth." In that new environment "all mankind" will "come and bow down" before the Lord, "from one New Moon to another and from one Sabbath to another." In Adventist literature this passage is often quoted as a prediction that the Sabbath will also be kept in the hereafter. (However, when this text is cited, the reference to the "new moon" is usually omitted.) John the Revelator used language that he derived from the prophet Isaiah, when he described the new world and the new city that he had been shown in a vision, but we must not forget that Isaiah was thinking of what would eventually happen to Israel and its neighbors *on this present earth* if they would live in total commitment to the Lord.

The last references to the Sabbath in Old Testament times are found in Neh 13:15–22. When, after the exile, Nehemiah returned to Jerusalem with a plan to rebuild the city, he found considerable indifference with regard to the Sabbath. He decided on a series of corrective measures. Clearly, the ideal situation the prophet Isaiah had anticipated, in which universal regard for God's holy day would have become a reality, had not yet materialized in the days of Nehemiah.

The Sabbath in the New Testament

During the period between the Old and the New Testament, attitudes towards Sabbath observance became increasingly strict and formalized. Jewish groups, particularly the Pharisees, stressed meticulous Sabbath regulations as a marker of identity and piety. The Essenes followed even stricter Sabbath rules, avoiding all sorts of "work," including assisting animals or people. The book of Jubilees and other apocryphal writings reflect this trend, emphasizing the Sabbath as a covenant sign. Overall, Sabbath observance shifted from a communal rest day to a symbol of religious purity and national distinction.[39] Traditions (until the creation of the Mishnah around AD 200 still mainly oral) specified an increasing number of "works" that were not permitted on the Sabbath. Final redemption was said to hinge upon correct observance of the Sabbath. Rabbi Johanan said in the name of Simeon ben Yohai, "If Israel were to keep two Sabbaths according to the laws thereof, they would be redeemed immediately."[40]

An awareness of this background helps to place the New Testament references to Sabbath observance in their proper context. Our focus, naturally, is on Jesus's attitude towards the Sabbath. As expected, Jesus (being a Jew) frequented the synagogue[41] on Sabbath (Luke 4:16). It should be noted, however, that Jesus did not comply with all customary Jewish rituals; see Mark 2:18–22; Matt 9:14–17; Luke 5:33–39; Matt 15:2; and Mark 7:1–7. We have every reason to think that the way in which Jesus observed the Sabbath was highly intentional and served as a model for his disciples to follow.

Mark 2:23–28 is a key passage about Jesus's relationship with the Sabbath:

> One Sabbath Jesus was going through the grainfields, and as his disciples walked along, they began to pick some heads of grain. The Pharisees said to him, "Look, why are they doing what is unlawful on the Sabbath?" He answered, "Have you never read what David did when he and his companions were hungry and in need? In the days of Abiathar the high priest, he entered the house of God and ate the consecrated bread, which is lawful only for priests to eat. And he also gave some to his companions." Then he said to them, "The Sabbath was made for man, not man for the Sabbath. So the Son of Man is Lord even of the Sabbath."

The dispute with the Pharisees was not about the eating of the grain, since the law made provision that hungry people could satisfy their

39. Cohen, *Maccabees to the Mishnah*, 114–20.

40. Johnston, "Rabbinic Sabbath," 72.

41. The synagogue emerged during the Babylonian exile (sixth century BC) after the temple in Jerusalem was destroyed (586 BC), and Jews needed a place to gather for worship, study, and community life. Synagogues became also the central places for worship, and maintaining Jewish identity, in diaspora communities.

hunger from a neighbor's field (Lev 19:9–10; 23:22; Deut 23:25). The question revolved around the definition of work. The Pharisees regarded what the disciples were doing, as they walked through the grainfields, as harvesting, and thus as a work that was considered taboo on the Sabbath.[42] Jesus defended his disciples by putting things in the right order of priority and by stating the ultimate purpose of the Sabbath. *The Sabbath was made for man, not man for the Sabbath* (v. 27).

In his commentary on Mark, American New Testament scholar James R. Edwards (b. 1945), opines, "Jesus reorients the Sabbath from a legalistic system to its original intent: a blessing for human well-being and rest."[43] Pope Benedict XVI (Joseph Ratzinger) stated, "Jesus does not abolish the Sabbath but interprets it correctly: as a day for man, a day of freedom and healing, not of bondage to rules."[44] By telling the Pharisees that the Sabbath was made for man, Jesus "made a strong statement in favor of the universality of the Sabbath as a gift of God. It is clearly intended against those who would restrict its benefits exclusively to the Jews."[45]

Jesus performed many miracles and did so, presumably, on all days of the week (Matt 9:35). However, all four Gospels record healing miracles on the Sabbath, often in the context of controversies with the Jewish leaders. One of the most striking passages about a healing on the Sabbath is found in John 5:2–9.[46] It concerns an invalid man at the Pool of Bethesda, who had been waiting for thirty-eight years for a chance to be miraculously healed. One day Jesus came to this place near the Sheep Gate in Jerusalem and asked the sick man whether he wanted to get well. After the man explained his predicament, Jesus told him, "Get up! Pick up your mat and walk." After stating that the man was "cured at once" and was able to walk, it is mentioned, almost in passing, "The day on which this took place was a Sabbath" (v. 9). When the Jewish leaders heard about the incident, they were greatly upset. Their main objection was the carrying of a mat on the Sabbath. Jesus was, of course, aware of the rule that forbade carrying an object on the Sabbath, and he could have told the man to pick up his mat after sundown. But Jesus demonstrated that he is the Lord of the Sabbath

42. Rodríguez, *Andrews Bible Commentary*, 1295.

43. Edwards, *Gospel According to Mark*, 97.

44. Ratzinger, *Jesus of Nazareth*, 121.

45. Weiss, *Day of Gladness*, 95.

46. For a profound commentary on this and other Sabbath healing passages, see Tonstad, *Lost Meaning*, 181–203.

and used a different definition of work. "In his defense, Jesus said to them [the Jewish leaders]: My Father is always at his work to this very day, and I too am working" (John 5:17). As could be expected, Jesus's claim to intimacy with God created an additional aggravation.[47]

The Sabbath healings "are so numerous as to make them a characteristic feature of Jesus's ministry."[48] Jesus is not caught unawares by the controversies that erupted because of his Sabbath activities. Mark recorded the healing of the man "with a shriveled hand" in a synagogue (3:1–6), and mentioned how some "were looking for a reason to accuse Jesus, so they watched him closely to see if he would heal him on Sabbath." The story goes on to tell the reader that the man was indeed healed and adds, "Then the Pharisees went out and began to plot with the Herodians how they might kill Jesus."

For Jesus the Sabbath healings were deliberate actions and a matter of principle. The Sabbath was a day for doing good, and the Sabbath controversies were a means of persuading Jesus's opponents "to see him for who he truly is."[49] When defending his Sabbath healing miracles, Jesus never admitted that he was breaking the Sabbath commandment or that the Sabbath had in some way lost its validity. To celebrate the Sabbath was one of his holy customs. But he insisted on celebrating it on his own terms, not in the manner set down by the rules and restrictions of the Jewish teachers of his time.[50]

Professor Herold Weiss (b. 1934) makes an important point with regard to Jesus's Sabbath healings. The Sabbath healing controversies, he says, "do not show Christians, who have declared the Sabbath an obsolete Jewish feast, arguing against Jews who insist on the validity of the Sabbath legislation." Rather, Weiss concludes, "these controversies show that, for some time after the death of Jesus [when the Gospels were written], the Sabbath commandment retained its validity within the Christian communities, even if the manner of its observance was a disputed matter."[51]

In his eschatological discourse (Matt 24; Luke 21) Jesus foretold the destruction of Jerusalem and counseled "those who are in Judea" (Matt 24:16) and who would experience this disaster, to pray that their "flight will not take place in winter or on the Sabbath" (v. 20). Cold and rainy

47. Tonstad, *Lost Meaning*, 190.

48. Tonstad, *Lost Meaning*, 187.

49. Tonstad, *Lost Meaning*, 189.

50. Bruinsma, *Day God Created*, 36.

51. Weiss, *Day of Gladness*, 100.

weather in the winter could result in extra suffering at that fateful time. But why would Jesus suggest that their flight would not be on a Sabbath? It seems unlikely that Jesus worried that the people might have to travel further than the limited distance of a "Sabbath journey" (about 1.2 kilometers). Some commentators indicate that Jesus was "merely recognizing the conscientious scruples of Jewish Christians about fleeing on the Sabbath." Others "see in Matthew 24:20 an indication that the Christian community for which Matthew writes was still observing the Sabbath."[52]

The New Testament expressly mentioned that it was Jesus's custom to worship on Sabbath in a synagogue, and also that the apostle Paul shared in this practice (Acts 13:5, 14–15; 17:1–2, 10; 18:4; 19:8). It seems to have been part of the missionary strategy of Paul and his associates to choose synagogues as places where they could meet an audience that might be interested in their message. For Paul, as a Christian with a Jewish background, it was natural to visit a synagogue on the Sabbath, wherever his missionary journeys took him. But if he had felt any resistance against continued Sabbath observance, especially among Christians with a non-Jewish background, he almost certainly would have put more distance between himself and the synagogue.

In Heb 4:9–10 we read, "There remains, then, a Sabbath rest for the people of God; for anyone who enters God's rest also rests from their works, just as God did from his."

The author of this passage refers to God's resting on the seventh day (Gen 2:2) and Israel's failure to enter the promised rest due to their unbelief. The term *Sabbath rest* (Greek: *sabbatismos*) in verse 9 is unique and suggests a spiritual rest that parallels God's own rest. The "rest from works" in verse 10 suggests ceasing from self-effort and legalism, resting instead in the completed work of Christ. Hebrews 4:9–10 primarily points to the deep, spiritual rest that is available to believers. It assumes the continued validity of the Sabbath but reorients its meaning towards fulfillment in Christ. Both the author and his audience were Sabbath keepers and "were not debating the merits of Sabbath versus Sunday."[53] The weekly day of worship and rest in the here and now is a foretaste of the eternal rest that "remains" for God's people. Tonstad remarks,

52. Specht, "Sabbath," 103.

53. Rodríguez, *Andrews Bible Commentary*, 1832.

"The Sabbat of the past reaches across the ages to clasp hands with the Sabbath of the future."[54]

A few New Testament texts are frequently quoted that, at first sight, appear to suggest that the Sabbath was a Jewish institution that was abrogated by Christ. However, when read in their context they do not provide convincing evidence for that view. In Rom 14:1–12 the apostle Paul differentiates between those who are "weak" and those who are "strong" in the faith and indicates how these groups might quarrel about "disputable matters." These controversial issues concerned matters of diet and of giving significance to particular days. "One person considers one day more sacred than another, another considers every day alike" (v. 5). Although many commentators believe that these particular days would include the weekly Sabbath, others believe it is extremely unlikely that the issue was over the day of worship. "It is more likely that Paul had in mind days of fasting—an important matter for Jews and Christians in the first century."[55]

Many opponents of continued Sabbath observance believe that the letter to the church in Colossae contains a definitive statement that supports their position. Paul wrote, "Therefore do not let anyone judge you by what you eat or drink, or with regard to a religious festival, a New Moon celebration or a Sabbath day. These are a shadow of the things that were to come; the reality, however, is found in Christ." Like in the text in Rom 14, it is very likely that the apostle is speaking of other feast days and not of the weekly Sabbath. In any case, a definitive interpretation of Paul's words is impeded by the fact that the apostle is reacting to a heresy in the Colossian church with features that remain obscure. Clinton Arnold (b. 1958), a professor of New Testament at the University of Aberdeen, wrote a book about the Colossian heresy, which he gave the subtitle *The Interface Between Christianity and Folk Belief at Colossae.*[56] Arnold argues that Paul is not merely concerned about specific days, but rather about a syncretistic system of religious observance that blended Jewish, pagan, and local folk religious elements with ascetic and mystical practices.

Another oft-mentioned argument in favor of an early transition from Sabbath to Sunday is the statement by John the Revelator (1:10) that he was "in the Spirit" on "the Lord's Day." Since in some early Christian documents the Sunday is referred to with that term, many

54. Tonstad, *Lost Meaning*, 291.

55. Rodríguez, *Andrews Bible Commentary*, 1604.

56. Arnold, *Colossian Syncretism.*

have assumed that it also has that meaning in this text in Revelation. This would, however, be a rash conclusion, to say the least. The term more likely points to the Sabbath[57] (considering that Jesus calls himself the Lord of the Sabbath; Mark 2:28), or to the eschatological day of the Lord at the end of time.[58]

Why the Seventh Day?

Most Christians no longer view the Sabbath as a special, sacred day but are Sunday keepers. Asked why they celebrate the Sunday, most of them will answer that this day is different from the other days of the week because Jesus was resurrected on a Sunday. And, indeed, after dying on a Friday afternoon, and resting in the tomb on the Sabbath, Jesus rose from death early on Sunday morning. The Gospels also tell us about several subsequent appearances of the risen Christ on the first day of the week (see John 20:1–23; Matt 28:1–10; Luke 24:13–49). Moreover, Pentecost (Acts 2) occurred on a Sunday (see Lev 23:15–16). In addition to the frequent references to Paul's synagogue visits on the Sabbath, there is mention of a church gathering that took place on the first day of the week (Acts 20:7–12). This was a farewell evening meeting in Troas that, in fact (by our present reckoning), took place on a Saturday evening rather than on the Sunday. Citing this meeting as an early example of Sunday observance—supposedly already in ca. AD 56—does not fit with the other historical evidence about the Sabbath-Sunday transition.

However, many have asked—and are still asking—what difference does it make whether we observe the Sabbath or the Sunday? Why do Seventh-day Adventists and a few other small groups of Christians stubbornly stick to the *seventh* day of the week, while almost the entire world considers the *first* day of the week as a special day? Why does the Seventh-day Adventist Church make life so difficult for its members by requiring them to go against the tide? Quitting work on Friday before the arrival of the Sabbath at sundown, and refraining from work on the Saturday, poses serious problems for many church members in our 24/7 economy. And, while for the people in Bible times it may not have been very problematic to celebrate their Sabbath from sundown Friday to sundown Saturday, it

57. Doukhan, *Secrets of Revelation*, 21.

58. Stefanovic, *Revelation of Jesus Christ*, 93.

poses a major challenge for those who live in Arctic regions. Besides, we now realize that the Sabbath goes around the world[59] and that since 1884 the international date line allows us to deal with this by either "losing" or "gaining" a day. This has a major impact on Sabbath keeping when traveling and for those who live in the islands states near the date line.

Common sense might be on the side of those who favor the Sunday above the Saturday as their day of worship and rest (whatever content is given to the word *rest*). Many believers cannot imagine that God would be unduly worried about this matter, as long as we keep one in seven days "holy." But this is more than a matter of common sense or about any random twenty-four-hour period. We must go back to a core element of the Genesis story: "By the seventh day God had finished the work he had been doing; so on the seventh day he rested from all his work. Then *God blessed the seventh day and made it holy*, because on it he rested from all the work of creating that he had done" (Gen 2:2–3; italics added). There is something very special about the seventh day *because God blessed it and made it holy*. The seventh day of the week is not special because of anything we do, or do not do, on that day. It is special because of the added value God gave this day.

Thus, when we decide to obey the fourth commandment and "remember" to keep it holy, it is because God made that day holy and never gave any indication that he removed this holiness from the seventh day and transferred it to another day. That is a good enough reason to remain with the Sabbath as our weekly day of rest. As we saw above, the Sabbath was a sign of loyalty for the Israelites in their covenant relationship with God, and it still is a sign of our loyalty to our Lord. We may not understand why it has to be the seventh day rather than the first, or any other day, but we must trust that God knows best. Says Adventist theologian Ángel Manuel Rodríguez, "The Sabbath is not merely about resting; it is about recognizing God as Creator and Redeemer. To change the Sabbath is to alter a sign of God's authority and covenant with his people."[60]

Keeping God's Day Holy

God attached a special blessing to the seventh-day Sabbath and made it a holy day—that is, a day set apart for a specific purpose. Because of this,

59. See Odom, *Lord's Day*.

60. Rodríguez, "Sabbath," 34.

observing the *seventh* day of the week as the Sabbath is nonnegotiable. However, in urging their fellow men to join them in observing the Sabbath, Adventists have too often mainly emphasized the *time* of the Sabbath and not paid enough attention to the *meaning* of the Sabbath. What is involved in keeping the Sabbath "holy"? For many Sabbath observers "keeping the Sabbath" is mostly a matter of not doing certain things. The list of activities Adventists have frowned upon, or strongly condemned, varies greatly from country to country or even between regions within in country.[61] Much may depend on culture or on the traditions of the majority religion in a given environment. Growing up in the only Adventist family in a Dutch village with a large percentage of relatively strict Sunday keepers, our way of spending the Sabbath resembled in many ways their Sunday observance. Because of the many rules and traditions about the observance of the weekly day of rest, for many—in particular for children and young people—the Sabbath was certainly not always the "delight" that the prophet Isaiah envisaged (58:13). Even though Seventh-day Adventists observe their Sabbath on the correct day of the week, there may well be Sunday observers who are more successful in keeping their day of rest "holy" than their Sabbath-keeping fellow Christians.

The holiness of the Sabbath—that is, the special character of the day that sets it apart from the other six days—is related to several important aspects.

1. *The Sabbath is a day of worship.* This means that, first of all, the Sabbath is a day on which we have extra time to connect with God. The Lord of the Sabbath gave us an example by worshipping on "his" day in the synagogue. Although there are no direct instructions in the New Testament about attending regular worship services, it seems that from the start church members assembled regularly. As the missionary work of the apostles resulted in the creation of local churches, the members met for communal worship in private homes that were large enough to hold a group of people (see, e.g., Acts 12:12; Rom 16:5; 1 Cor 16:19). When some church members suggest that they can also worship alone in their own home or by going into nature, they may be reminded of the fact that Christ wanted to have a church, a community of believers who could gather for communal worship. On the Sabbath the church gathers "to praise

61. Colón, "Sabbath-Keeping Practices."

him in word, prayer, and hymn for his mighty acts. . . . The central focus on every worship service must be what God has done for us through Jesus Christ. The Sabbath celebrates redemption."[62]

2. *The Sabbath is a day of rest.* The Sabbath commandment stresses that keeping the Sabbath means ceasing from our daily work. Lynne M. Baab, the author of several devotional books, gave her delightful book on Sabbath keeping the subtitle *Finding Freedom in the Rhythms of Rest.* She writes, "We need to learn how to rest and the Sabbath provides a practical, helpful framework in which to do just that. The Sabbath invites us to rest for a long enough period that we can let down from our rapid pace and our undone tasks."[63] The rest of the Sabbath has both physical and spiritual aspects. It includes much more than sleeping a bit longer in the morning and enjoying a nap after lunch. It is more than just "doing nothing." Lynne Baab's emphasis on "freedom" is very appropriate. Determining what constitutes "work" and must be left undone can easily lead to a burdensome legalism that destroys the Christian freedom that Christ has blessed us with, as we find true Sabbath rest (Gal 5:1).
3. *The Sabbath is a time to spend with others.* Because we are freed from our daily work we have special time for God, but also for those around us: our family and friends and meaningful others. Jesus consistently demonstrated that the Sabbath is a day to do good and to care for people rather than for strictly adhering to ritualistic practices.

Ángel Manuel Rodríguez, whom I quoted earlier, brings those three aspects together in these words: "In a world where the boundaries between work and rest are increasingly blurred, the Sabbath calls us to stop, reflect, and reconnect—with our Creator, with others, and with ourselves. It is not a relic of the past but a radical invitation to live in God's rhythm today."[64]

But with all this, the *social aspects* of justice and equality that were attached to the Sabbath must never be forgotten. The Sabbath commandment included not only the immediate family members ("your son or daughter") but also the slaves ("your male and female servant") and

62. Kubo, *God Meets Man*, 60.

63. Baab, *Sabbath Keeping*, 122.

64. Rodríguez, "Sabbath," 34.

even the animals that "worked" on the fields or carried heavy loads ("your animals"). And it also provided rest to "any foreigner residing in your town." These social aspects of the seventh day are echoed in two institutions that were closely connected with the rest of the Sabbath—namely, the Sabbath Year and the Jubilee.

During every seventh year—the so-called Sabbath Year—the Israelites were to refrain from agricultural work and to let the land rest (Lev 25:1–7). Debts were to be forgiven, and Hebrew slaves were to be set free (Deut 15:1–2, 12–15). This reflected God's care for the land and for the vulnerable members of society, while reminding the people that the land ultimately belongs to God (Lev 25:23). The Jubilee occurred every fiftieth year, following seven cycles of seven years (Lev 25:8–12). It marked a time of liberation and restoration: land that had been sold was to be returned to its original family, and debts were to be canceled. Had the Jubilee been carried out in accordance with the divine instructions, poverty could not have become a permanent condition.

Much of the prophetic criticism regarding the Sabbath observance of the Israelites centered on their failures to practice justice and solidarity. Sigve Tonstad comments, "To some of the most distinguished prophets in the Old Testament, the relationship between the seventh day and the cause of social justice is so organic, that they repudiate any version of the Sabbath that does not reflect that reality."[65] It is something twenty-first-century Sabbath keepers should never lose sight of.

A Divine Remedy for a Burned-Out Generation

The Bible is positive about work but does not encourage us to become workaholics. "There is a time for everything and a season for every activity under the heavens" (Eccl 3:1–2). Untold millions in today's world ignore these wise words that stress the need for balance in all we do. There is a time for work—but the maximum is six days per week. And there is a time for rest: the seventh-day Sabbath. If we ignore this God-given rhythm, we run the risk of becoming "burned-out" or falling victim to other work-related illnesses. If there is any Seventh-day Adventist teaching that has an immediate relevance for people today it is the Sabbath. It is God's gift to people of all ages, but also a very concrete remedy for our restless world and its ever-busy population.

65. Tonstad, *Lost Meaning*, 131.

Some twenty years ago American journalist A. J. Jacobs decided to follow all biblical rules during one entire year—both the well-known and the more obscure laws. He wrote a humorous, yet profound, reflection on the complexities of a literal biblical interpretation: *The Year of Living Biblically: One Man's Humble Quest to Follow the Bible as Literally as Possible.* When the experiment had ended and the book was ready, he was asked about his experiences. He told the interviewer that enough was enough, and that he would no longer pay attention to these, mostly cumbersome, biblical rules. But there was one thing he (and his wife) did not want to give up. He said he had fallen in love with the Sabbath. It had become an essential part of his life.[66] Millions still need to make that same discovery!

66. Almendrala, "*Year of Living Biblically.*"

Chapter 8
Christian Living

In most books on Seventh-day Adventist theology the topic of stewardship does not have a prominent place and does not merit a full chapter. In the taxonomy of doctrines stewardship usually tends to rank towards the lower end of the scale. Most Adventists will probably say that doctrines such as the Trinity, the atonement, the Sabbath, and life after death are more important than the traditional teachings about tithing and about not eating unclean meat. They undoubtedly have a point when things are stated in that way. But perhaps it is precisely in the area of stewardship where the doctrinal rubber hits the road of Christian discipleship.

In this treatment of authentic Adventist theology the theme of stewardship has an important place. Its weight depends on its practical nature. If we plead for significance of our religious convictions in our everyday life, this is where we must focus a great deal of our attention. Stewardship has to do with how we *live* our faith. It is a much broader concept than many church members may realize. Many contemporary Christians want to discover how the Christian faith connects with the world in which they live today. They believe that their faith can respond positively to the findings of modern science, and that it must interact in a credible and constructive manner with developments in today's world. This may mean that their faith inspires them to become activists in the pursuit of certain social and political causes. It may also mean that they will appear "woke" to some who want a total separation of their faith from politics or to those who have opted for an approach to society that is contrary the fundamentals of Christ's Sermon on the Mount. Calling for the kind of faith that gets involved with the issues of real life may scare many traditional Adventists and make them wonder, Does this approach not compromise our Adventist message? Should we not stay away from politics and from an emphasis on social issues, as this will easily interfere with the proclamation of the "three angels' messages"? But could it be, in fact, that preaching the traditional doctrinal message without a clear application to real life situations no longer works—in particular for the younger generations who ask, What difference does it make in my life and in how I relate to others, to my work and to other aspects of my world, that I believe in the twenty-eight fundamental beliefs? Could it be that the stewardship principle actually belongs to the core of genuine Adventism?

Many Seventh-day Adventists who constantly urge their coreligionists to return to what the pioneers of their movement believed tend to forget that the faith of these early Adventist leaders was often much more activist than theirs! Several of these pioneers in nineteenth-century North America were active in assisting fugitive slaves.[1] Remember that slavery was a hot topic in the years preceding and during the Civil War (1861–1865). John Byington (1798–1887), the first president of the General Conference of the Adventist Church, was a strong opponent of slavery. His home served as a station for the Underground Railroad, which helped slaves to escape and find refuge, notably in Canada. Joseph Bates, one of the cofounders of the church, and other early leaders, were also outspoken abolitionists. Ellen White repeatedly protested against slavery and called it "a sin of the darkest dye."[2]

Anyone who has only a cursory knowledge of early Adventist history knows that the church originated in an environment of multiple reform movements and that many Adventists intensely participated in these movements and adapted the goals and methods of these movements to align them with their gradually emerging theology. Ellen G. White became heavily involved with health reform and became a staunch advocate of temperance and vegetarianism.[3] As the movement grew, campaigning for religious liberty became a prominent aspect of

1. Schwarz and Greenleaf, *Light Bearers*, 95.
2. White, *Testimonies for the Church*, 359.
3. See Knight, *Ellen White's World.*

the public presence of Adventism. All this was regarded as a vital part of "present truth." As time moved on, these characteristics of Adventism receded to a large extent into the background. We must remember this aspect of our corporate past and consider how these stewardship activities can once more become "present truth."

God Owns Us

Christians must live in constant awareness that God is the owner of everything. Psalm 50 reminds us that "every animal of the forest" is his, and that he owns "the cattle on a thousand hills" (v. 10). Psalm 24:1 emphasizes the same key principle: "The earth is the Lord's and everything in it, the world, and all who live in it." In his first letter to the Corinthian believers the apostle Paul reminds them (and us) of this basic truth: "Do you not know that your bodies are temples of the Holy Spirit, who is in you, whom you have received from God? *You are not your own*, you were bought at a price" (6:19–20; italics added). This means that everything we tend to claim as our own is in fact lent to us—it is given to us to be used to God's honor and glory. The biblical term for our status as the curators of what has been lent to us is *steward*. Baptist theologian R. Scott Rodin comments, "We do not have any terms in our modern vocabulary that carry the richness of this term. *Caretaker* fails to capture the responsibility laid on the steward. *Manager* seems inadequate to describe the relationship between the owner and the steward. *Custodian* is too passive a term. *Ambassador* is too political, and it lacks the servant aspect. *Warden* is too administrative and loses the sense of the personal. *Guardian* is too closely tied to parental responsibilities."[4]

Jesus's parable in Matt 14:1–29 sets the parameters for what we will discuss in this chapter. As Jesus was leaving this world, he is portrayed as "a man going on a journey" who entrusts his possessions to his "servants." According to the New International Version rendering, they receive different amounts of "gold," each "according to his ability." Each of the servants puts what was entrusted to him to work and was able to show a significant profit when the owner finally returned. They were handsomely rewarded for their loyalty and industriousness. But one servant had not tried to make a gain on what he had received, out of fear that his

4. Rodin, *Stewards in the Kingdom*, 27.

project might backfire, and he would lose his master's money. Instead of being rewarded he was severely disciplined.

The parable of the ten minas (a mina amounted to roughly three month's wages) conveys the same message: "A man of noble birth went to a distant country to have himself appointed king and then to return." He called ten of his servants and gave them ten minas," with the instruction: "Put this money to work . . . until I come back" (Luke 19:13).

So, while Jesus Christ is no longer with us—in the interim between his first and second coming—he expects us to be diligent in the custody of what he has given into our keep. Work "as long as it is day," Jesus exhorted his disciples, before the night comes "when no one can work" (John 9:4). Matthew 24:46 makes the same point: before leaving on a journey "the master" told his "faithful and wise servant" to take care of his household. He ends his instructions with the statement, "It will be good for that servant whose master finds him doing so when he returns" (Matt 24:42–46).

This is the basis for what follows in this chapter. Followers of Christ must realize that whatever they do with their "gold," "minas," or "talents" must be to the honor of God. "*Whatever you do, whether in word or deed, do it all in the name of the Lord Jesus, giving thanks to God the Father through him*" (Col 1:17; italics added). To some this may sound like a prescription for a difficult and dull life, void of all the things that are interesting and fun. Many may find it difficult to believe that this is the life "to the full" that Christ promised his disciples (John 10:10). But taking good care of what the Owner of everything has entrusted to us does not mean that we cannot have a "good" and "full" life while we are good stewards of God's possessions. On the contrary. It means, however, that we should never forget that, if we want to have a really happy and fulfilling life, we must not place ourselves at the center of the universe, and that our own interests cannot be our primary concern. Everything we do must be anchored in our relationship with God, embedded in service and loyalty to him.

We all have talents and skills. Some of our talents may have been upgraded as spiritual gifts. Some of us are more talented than others. My talents in some areas may exceed those of some of my colleagues, and vice versa. I know many people who have more technical skills than I have, or are better preachers than I am. It is important to realize our own limitations and there is always the temptation to use our abilities and giftedness in ways that are totally self-centered, focused on our own status, financial gain and reputation. Christians should know that God expects them to use their talents not only to increase their own happiness, but also for the benefit of others, far and near, in the church and in the society of which they are part. As long as we live in this world, Christ says to us, "Do that until I come" (Luke 19:11–13).

Which Laws Are Still Valid?

Before continuing our discussion about stewardship, we must touch on an important preliminary issue. Besides the Ten Commandments there are many other laws in the Bible. How many of these rules are still applicable today?[5] Most Christians will agree that the Ten Commandments, or in any case the principles behind them, have a timeless and universal validity. And most will also agree that some categories of Old Testament laws, such as those that governed the sacrificial offerings (Lev 1–7) and the duties of the priests and the Levites (Lev 8–10) are no longer relevant, since at the cross all rituals that anticipated Christ's sublime sacrifice came to an end (Heb 10).

Other Old Testament laws governed the social, economic, and judicial aspects of Israelite life. We find examples of these in the regulations in Exod 21–23 that deal with property rights, personal injuries, social responsibilities, the treatment of orphans and widows, and justice and mercy. It would seem that these laws do not apply one-to-one to our present world, but that the principles behind these laws may still be applicable today. Some of these laws may continue to inform present-day Christian ethics. The same is true for laws concerning ritual cleanliness, as for instance rules about sanitation (Lev 12–15).

For Adventists the discussion about the Old Testament laws have tended to center on the rules for the giving of tithes and on the distinction between clean and unclean meat. As they defined their doctrinal package, Seventh-day Adventists adopted after a few decades the tithing system as the biblically informed financial support system for the denomination. The refusal to eat unclean meat was a gradual development that was not final until early in the twentieth century. In the paragraphs that follow we will analyze different aspects of stewardship and consider how some of these Old Testament laws—notably those that

5. For a comprehensive study of the significance of Old Testament laws for today by an Adventist scholar, see Gane, *Old Testament Laws*.

deal with food and with finances—are still relevant for good stewardship in the twenty-first century.

Stewards of Our Bodies

The third letter of John is addressed to a church elder with the name Gaius. He was a friend of the author, who was not only interested in his friend's spiritual well-being, as is clear from his statement in 1 John 3:2: "Dear friend, I pray that you may enjoy good health and that all may go well with you, even as your soul is getting along well." The text underlines the basic biblical view of the holistic nature of humankind. Soul and body cannot be separated; they belong together and form one indivisible entity. (We will return to this when, in the next chapter, we will discuss what happens to us when we die, but first we want to focus on how this impacts on our present life.)

Our faith is of vital importance for our spiritual well-being, but also for the physical aspects of our life. As already noted, our body is a temple of the Holy Spirit, and we are, therefore, not our own (1 Cor 6:19–20). Being a steward has far-reaching implications for how we care for the body that has been entrusted to us. Although Christians are fully aware of the fact that sin has had damaging consequences for human health and physical strength, they still appreciate that they are "wonderfully made" (Ps 139:14). Protecting our health does not only make sense but is a practical aspect of being a Christian.

The definition of health of the World Health Organization[6] accords fully with the holistic view of health that, from its beginning has been one of the hallmarks of Seventh-day Adventism. Health goes beyond the absence of disease and is a holistic state of wellbeing, including physical, social, mental, and spiritual dimensions. Adventists have consistently emphasized that their theological package includes a "health message." As a result of their emphasis on health, Adventists tend on average to live longer than most other people. Studies in several countries have confirmed this. The most extensive study, conducted over a long period, compared Californian Adventists with the general population. It found that Adventist men live 7.3 years longer than their Californian male counterparts. The extra lifetime for women is 4.4 years.[7] The area around

6. World Health Organization, "Constitution."

7. Loma Linda University, "Findings for Longevity."

Loma Linda in southern California—a major Adventist center—is one of the so-called blue zones in the world, with a population with exceptional longevity.[8] Although for most of us a *long* life seems highly desirable, the *quality* of our life is at least as important as its *length*.

What We Eat

Our health depends on many factors, a balanced, nutritious diet being one of them. Many people look for external guidelines to help them in their dietary choices. Of course, staying informed about the value (or the harmful elements) of various foods is highly advisable, but depending too much on detailed lists or regulations can lead to obsessions or to a legalistic approach, especially when some foods are considered "sinful."[9] The realization that we are stewards of our body will certainly impact our dietary practices. A daily intake of fast food from the various popular chains that have spread around the world, and overindulgence in unhealthy kinds of food, are definitely not part of a Christian lifestyle. However, it must be stressed that our dietary choices are primarily a personal responsibility, and judging and reprimanding others for what they eat is not okay. Paul criticized the believers in Rome about "quarreling over disputable matters." Some of these quarrels concerned their eating habits. It was not about vitamins or proteins, but over an issue that no longer concerns us—namely, whether Christians could in good conscience eat meat that had been part of sacrificial rituals for pagan idols.[10] In that context the apostle commented, "One person's faith allows them to eat anything, but another, whose faith is weak, eats only vegetables. The one who eats everything must not treat with contempt the one who does not, and the one who does not eat everything must not judge the one who does, for God has accepted them" (Rom 14:2–3; see also 1 Cor 8:1–13; 10:25–26). This principle still applies today with regard to controversies over what we should and should not eat and drink.

8. Buettner, "Secrets of Longevity."

9. A new edition of the compilation *Counsels on Diet and Food* by Ellen G. White was published in March 2024. It contains the same text as the original edition of 1938. Statements by Ellen White about health, diet and nutrition were posthumously assembled from letters, manuscripts, periodical articles, and other published sources. When people regard this as a divinely inspired set of rules, which are to be meticulously followed, it can easily lead to an unbalanced and legalistic approach to one's dietary habits.

10. Boa and Kruidenier, *Romans*, 419–22.

Adventists have long promoted a vegetarian lifestyle and in more recent times many have adopted a vegan diet. There is no doubt that a balanced vegetarian or flexitarian diet has definite health benefits when compared to regularly consuming substantial amounts of meat. The fact that the Genesis story informs us that the original diet of the first humans was vegetarian, and that certain categories of meat were only added for human consumption after the flood, is for some a convincing reason for being a vegetarian. Moreover, in today's world, in which over eight billion people must be fed, it is problematic (to put it mildly) to produce enormous quantities of animal feed, rather than using the land for the production of food for the people. In addition, one could cite ethical reasons for the vegetarian option. But Paul's advice, that we should refrain from judging others with regard to what they eat is still valid, also for modern Seventh-day Adventists.

For those who eat meat the question remains whether the distinction between "clean" and "unclean" meat is still relevant. This distinction is already found in the flood story (Gen 6–7), but received its most detailed expression in the Mosaic code that is found in Lev 11 (and see also Deut 14:3–8). Land animals must have a split hoof and chew the cud. That excludes pigs and horses but allows for cows and sheep. Seafood must have fins and scales, which excludes shell food and eels. Predatory and scavenger birds are generally considered unclean, as are most insects, except certain types of locusts, crickets, and grasshoppers. Reptiles and other creeping animals are also not considered fit for human consumption.

Opinions differ as to whether these regulations must be seen as purity laws, or primarily as health laws.[11] The Adventist position on clean and unclean meat underwent a long development and was not incorporated into the fundamental beliefs until 1980. In recent decades a few studies have underlined the theological rationale for accepting the regulations regarding clean and unclean meat as also valid for today's Christians. Some have stressed the health benefit of leaving unclean food aside, in particular pointing to the risk of parasitic infections resulting from the eating of pork.

11. Moskala, "Clean and Unclean." See its bibliography for an overview of relevant Adventist literature. The most complete treatment of the topic by an Adventist scholar is Moskala, *Laws*. For the gradual development of Adventist thinking about clean and unclean meat, see Graybill, "Development."

The statement of Jesus in Mark 7:18–19 has often been cited as proof that the Lord revoked the Old Testament rules regarding clean and unclean meat. It is clear from the context that Jesus's concern was primarily about the things people *say* rather than about what they *eat*. But he added: "Don't you see that nothing that enters a person from the outside can defile them? For it doesn't go into their heart but into their stomach, and then out of the body. (In saying this, Jesus declared all foods clean.)" Although the last bracketed sentence in this passage is a comment of the evangelist rather than a direct quote from Jesus, it does suggest that in the mind of the Gospel writer Jesus's words did also apply to food.[12]

The story of Acts 10 is also often interpreted as a signal that the "Jewish" food laws are no longer in force for Christians. Before he felt free to go to the home of a (pagan) Roman officer, the apostle Peter had a vision in which he was commanded three times to eat both clean and unclean food. This incident is usually seen as a clear indication that the Old Testament food laws no longer apply to Christian believers. However, the deeper meaning of the vision is subsequently expressed by Peter in these words: "God has shown me that I should not call anyone impure or unclean" (v. 28), and "I now realize that God does not show favoritism but accepts from every nation the one who fears him and does what is right" (vv. 34–35). The renowned evangelical theologian F. F. Bruce comments, Peter's "vision on the housetop in Joppa taught him to call no food common or unclean, if God pronounced it clean; but he was quick to grasp the analogy between ceremonial food laws and the regulations affecting intercourse with non-Jews."[13] Adventist theologians emphasize that this passage in Acts is not about food but about the full inclusion of all people into the Christian community. This explanation does, of course, leave us with the question why God would choose such an easily misunderstood method to teach the apostle about the intrinsic equality of people with a Jewish and with a Gentile background.

The decision of the apostolic council that is reported in Acts 15 is probably the most challenging for the traditional Adventist view. The leaders of the emerging Christian church came to a compromise solution about the restrictions that Christians from the Gentiles should adhere to: "It seemed good to the Holy Spirit and to us not to burden you with anything beyond the following requirements: You are to abstain from

12. Moule, *Gospel According to St. Mark*, 242. See also Eike Müller's 2015 doctoral dissertation "Cleansing the Common."

13. Bruce, *Book of Acts*, 222.

food sacrificed to idols, from blood, from the meat of strangled animals and from sexual immorality. You will do well to avoid these things" (vv. 28–29). Significantly, there is no mention of classes of unclean animals in this declaration, but Adventist commentators assume that this distinction was understood and was not a point of discussion.[14] It seems that Paul, as time went by, became somewhat less strict about some of these rules, in particular regarding food offered to idols (1 Cor 8–10; Rom 14).

Whatever decision one reaches regarding the abstention from certain kinds of food, it is a personal responsibility. I have never felt there was a good reason to give up my Adventist tradition regarding unclean meat. However, when all is said and done, we must take care not to reduce the principle of healthful living and of responsible eating habits to a list of dos and don'ts, as has all too often been done. It is much wider than the issue of clean and unclean food, and must be approached from a positive angle, rather than with a narrow, legalistic attitude.

Harmful Substances and Addictions

A consensus developed among Adventists, and was later incorporated into the statement of beliefs, that the stewardship principle requires Christians to abstain from tobacco and other harmful substances.[15] The 1863 "health vision" of Ellen G. White played a crucial role in this development. It became foundational for Adventist health principles and led to strong opposition to tobacco, alcohol, caffeine, and meat consumption. Ellen White explicitly condemned tobacco use as "a slow, insidious, but most malignant poison."[16] By the early twentieth century, abstinence from tobacco was not only taught but became an expectation for church members. Later, Adventists became known for their anti-smoking campaigns, often in cooperation with government entities and NGOs.

Number twenty-two of the fundamental beliefs of Seventh-day Adventists deals with a healthy lifestyle and includes this statement: "Since alcoholic beverages, tobacco, and the irresponsible use of drugs and narcotics are harmful to our bodies, we are to abstain from them as well."[17]

14. Rodríguez, *Andrews Bible Commentary*, 1510–11.

15. For the historical background, see Numbers, *Prophetess of Health*. Also, Schwarz and Greenleaf, *Light Bearers*, 488–94.

16. White, *Spiritual Gifts*, 128.

17. General Conference, "What Do Adventists Believe?," no. 22.

Of course, the Bible does not present us with any clear-cut instructions about the use of tobacco products, drugs, and other harmful substances. But Adventists believe that the principle of being stewards of our body implies that Christians should abstain from habits that are not only demonstratively very unhealthy but also addictive and have other seriously negative effects. Smoking and the use of drugs simply does not accord with the concept of our bodies as a temple of the Holy Spirit and with the instruction to "honor God" with our body (1 Cor 6:19–20). And any form of addiction is contrary to possessing the "fruit of the Spirit," which includes "self-control" (Gal 5:22–23).

The Adventist praxis varies substantially. Many Adventists around the world drink tea and coffee and other caffeine-containing drinks, but a significant percentage do not. In some countries, consuming low-alcoholic beverages or a modest quantity of wine is not uncommon. However, not smoking and refraining from recreational drugs and addictive substances is still very generally adhered to and people are supposed to quit such habits before being baptized and being officially admitted as church members. Opinions differ whether this should actually be a condition for baptism and church membership. It is rare, at least in the Western world, to see church discipline applied to members who continue or relapse in their smoking or other harmful habits.

Romans 12:1 sets the tone for a responsible and clean lifestyle, in which harmful substances have no place: "I urge you, brothers and sisters, in view of God's mercy, to offer your bodies as a living sacrifice, holy and pleasing to God—this is your true and proper worship." We should note that this "offering" of our bodies is not something we can take credit for; we can only do so in an authentic ("true and proper") way, through "God's mercy."

Alcohol—Use and Abuse

It is impossible to prove from the Bible that a modest use of alcohol is taboo for Christians. The theory that, when Jesus changed water into wine at the wedding in Cana (John 2:1–11), he must have produced non-fermented grape juice is rather improbable.[18] The Greek word *oinos* refers in most biblical contexts to "normal" fermented wine. Paul's advice to Timothy, "Stop drinking only water and use a little wine because of your

18. Keener, *IVP Bible Background Commentary*, 268–69.

stomach" (1 Tim 5:23), indicates that in Bible times drinking wine was considered acceptable. In Jesus's day, without refrigeration, unfermented grape juice (though probably not completely unknown) was difficult to preserve. There is no suggestion in the story that Jesus's miracle was associated with overindulgence, with its related negative effects.

However, the Bible does clearly condemn drunkenness and excessive drinking. According to Prov 20:1, "whoever is led astray" by beer and wine "is not wise." A little further on in the book of Proverbs a rather realistic description is given of the misery that is caused by an excessive use of alcohol (Prov 23:29–32). In Eph 5:18 Paul paints the stark contrast between drunkenness and being filled with the Spirit, and in 1 Cor 6:10 the apostle lists drunkards among the people who will not "inherit the kingdom of God."

Alcohol abuse was taking on disastrous proportions in early nineteenth-century North America, in particular in the frontier regions. "Alcohol consumption cut across social class, age, sex and race." Although there were other nations that consumed much alcohol, the United States was, in the words of historian W. H. Rorabaugh, an "alcoholic republic." "Americans," Rorabaugh comments, "drank on all occasions. Every social event demanded a drink. . . . Guests at urban dances and balls were often intoxicated; so were spectators at frontier horse races," et cetera.[19] To a large degree, this pattern of heavy drinking inspired the temperance movement,[20] which began gaining strength by the mid-1800s, especially among the Baptists and the Methodists. The Adventist Church soon had a close tie with the temperance movement,[21] with Ellen G. White as the outstanding spokesperson on the topic.[22]

By the 1870s, abstention was widely practiced by Seventh-day Adventists. However, it was not until 1980, when the church formally adopted a set of (then twenty-seven) fundamental beliefs, that abstinence from alcohol was explicitly included. One of the baptismal vows of candidates for baptism includes a promise to abstain from alcohol: "Do you believe that your body is the temple of the Holy Spirit and will you honor God by caring for it, avoiding the use of that which is harmful, abstaining from all unclean foods, from the use of alcoholic

19. Rorabaugh, *Alcoholic Republic*, 19.

20. Clark, "Crusade Against Alcohol," 131.

21. Reid, *Sound of Trumpets*, 22–48.

22. See Robinson, *Story*.

beverages, tobacco in any of its forms, and from the misuse of or trafficking in narcotics or other drugs?"[23]

Adventists cannot defend their stand on the total abstention from alcoholic drinks on purely biblical grounds, but I believe there is good reason to uphold this tradition, considering the enormous problems alcohol abuse still causes in our society, and the danger that modest drinking in many cases leads to addiction, with all its terrible consequences. So, for Christians who want to be an example for others, and who believe their body is a temple of the Spirit, of which they are stewards, abstention from alcohol still makes good sense. Whether this is enough reason for making teetotaling a criterion for church membership is a different matter, on which we will touch in the chapter on the doctrine of the church.

Stewards of Our "Wealth"

Proverbs 3:9 admonishes the reader to "honor God with your wealth." The term *wealth* will, of course, mean different things to different people, but for the author of these proverbs it included all one's possessions. For people in our day and age it includes the money we have in our bank accounts, the investment portfolio that we may have built up, the home we own, the car(s) in our garage, and any luxury items we enjoy. The text teaches us "that God, as the giver of all our benefits, has a claim upon them all; that his claim should be the first consideration, and that a special blessing will attend to all who honor this claim."[24] A first fundamental principle of financial stewardship is that God always comes first (Matt 6:25–34). A second fundamental principle in Bible times was the returning of 10 percent of one's wealth to God. The Israelites, who lived in an agricultural setting, received this instruction: "A tithe of everything from the land, whether grain from the soil, or fruit from the trees, belongs to the Lord; it is holy to the Lord" (Lev 27:30). This 10 percent was intended for the support of the clergy (priests and Levites). Another tithe was annually set aside in connection with festival visits in Jerusalem (Deut 14:22–27), while there was also a third tithe, given once every three years, in support of orphans and widows and other needy people (Deut 14:28–29).

23. See Kidder and Weakley, "Baptismal Vows," para. 50.

24. Tasker, "Proverbs," 738.

Adventists, together with many other (mostly evangelical) Christians, believe that the first kind of tithe, from which the sanctuary system, with all who served in it, was financed, is an arrangement God wants to see continued today for the support of the church. Often a passage from Mal 3 is cited, which defines a failure to give a tithe as "robbing" God (7–12). This passage has frequently been used (and at times abused) to pressure people to give tithes. It must, however, be noted that this statement is found in the context of a community that was drifting spiritually, with a breakdown of temple support and social justice. It was not a blanket accusation for people who might have been in such economic distress that giving tithes had, perhaps temporarily, become impossible.

The New Testament is almost totally silent on the topic of tithing. The only text in which the giving of tithes is directly mentioned is Matt 23:23. Jesus uttered a series of woes directed at the religious leaders, who focused on minute details, while ignoring the core values of justice, mercy, and faithfulness. He said, "Woe to you, teachers of the law and Pharisees, you hypocrites! You give a tenth of your spices—mint, dill and cumin. But you have neglected the more important matters of the law—justice, mercy and faithfulness. You should have practiced the latter, without neglecting the former."

The New Testament encourages the believers to be systematic in their giving by referring to the example of the financial support for the church in Jerusalem. Paul writes to the church in Corinth, "On the first day of every week, each one of you should set aside a sum of money in keeping with your income, saving it up, so that when I come no collections will have to be made" (1 Cor 16:2). Besides stressing this aspect of regularity, the aspect of generosity is paramount in the New Testament. The story of the widow who gave generously from the little she possessed makes this point in a stirring manner: "Jesus sat down opposite the place where the offerings were put and watched the crowd putting their money into the temple treasury. Many rich people threw in large amounts. But a poor widow came and put in two very small copper coins, worth only a few cents. Calling his disciples to him, Jesus said, 'Truly I tell you, this poor widow has put more into the treasury than all the others. They all gave out of their wealth; but she, out of her poverty, put in everything—all she had to live on'" (Mark 12:41–44).

The New Living Translation of 2 Cor 9:7 summarizes the New Testament approach to Christian giving in these beautiful words: "You must each decide in your heart how much to give. And don't give reluctantly or in response to pressure. 'For God loves a person who gives cheerfully.'"

The early Adventist leaders were faced with the constant challenge how to finance their fledgling movement and to ensure that the ministers were recompensed in a way that would enable them to support their families. In 1859 the system of systematic benevolence (nicknamed "Sister Betsy") was officially adopted. Members were encouraged to pledge weekly offerings that were based on their income and property holdings. Towards the end of the 1870s this arrangement for the support of the church and its workers was gradually replaced by tithing.[25] In fundamental belief number twenty-one it is stated, "We acknowledge God's ownership by faithful service to him and our fellow human beings, and by returning tithe and giving offerings for the proclamation of his gospel and the support and growth of his church."[26]

Whether or not the giving of tithes is specifically mandated for New Testament Christians, it is, no doubt, a good arrangement to ensure that the church can function and carry out its mission. It is in harmony with the principles of regularity and generosity. However, how a "tenth" of our income is calculated, where it is to be sent, and for what purposes it may be used, is not based on biblical instructions but is an arrangement decided by the denominational leadership.

Unfortunately, many Seventh-day Adventists have equated the giving of tithes with financial stewardship, not realizing that the stewardship concept has a much broader application. Giving 10 percent of our income to the church or to other charitable causes does not mean that stewardship has nothing to do with the remaining 90 percent of our income. On the contrary. Christian values such as honesty, solidarity, modesty, and prudent planning for the future will guide us in all our financial decisions. However, once again, it must be stressed that this is a domain of personal responsibility rather than of external rules and being subject to the judgment of other believers and church authorities.

25. Schwarz and Greenleaf, *Light Bearers*, 171, 172.

26. General Conference, "What Do Adventists Believe?," no. 21.

Caring for Our Planet

The commission of being stewards of our planet is rooted in the creation stories in Genesis. God made "mankind" in his "likeness," with the intention that these human beings should "rule over the fish in the sea and the birds in the sky, over the livestock and all the wild animals, and over all the creatures that move along the ground" (Gen 1:26). The first human beings, so the story tells us, were told to "be fruitful and increase in number; till the earth and subdue it" (v. 28). The rendering of the King James Version, which says that God told the first couple to "have dominion" over the earth, has often been misunderstood to mean that human beings have the right to do with our planet as they wish. However, the divine instruction does not allow for irresponsible exploitation and for causing circumstances that let plants and animals go extinct. Human beings are called by God to care as his representatives for all that he created.[27]

In this facet of stewardship Seventh-day Adventists, unfortunately, have not assumed any leadership role. In many countries a major segment of church membership has tended to be politically quite conservative and to vote for parties that are not noted for "green" sympathies or concerns about climate change and other ecological issues. However, those who want to take the concept of stewardship seriously will be concerned about the transition to a more durable lifestyle. Being a steward of what God has given us does not only affect what we eat and drink, and how we spend our money, but it also has to do with how we travel, how we insulate and heat our home, and how we do our shopping. The Christian charge to care for our planet as God's stewards must inform our political choices. It will stimulate us to support measures that limit (or even stop) large-scale factory farming and industrial fishing, and initiatives that strive to limit the use of pesticides and other harmful products.

This is where the stewardship principle must make a major difference in how we choose to live. Could it be that younger generations of Adventists are waiting to see their denomination discover what it truly means to be disciples of Christ in our twenty-first-century world?

27. Jagersma, *Verklaring van de Hebreeuwse Bijbel*, 31.

Stewards of Our Time

A final aspect of our stewardship that should be mentioned concerns the use of our time. It is easy to forget that time is a costly commodity that has been graciously given to us and is something that must not be wasted. That is not to say that every minute of our life must be devoted to some useful project. The crucial element remains: balance. God created time for his creatures in units of six days plus the seventh-day Sabbath. Work and rest were to be in a healthy balance.

The author of Ecclesiastes reminds us that there is time for the various aspects of our life (chapter 3). Besides time for work and household chores, there is time for hobbies, recreation, and sports. But there must also be time for family and friends, and for social activities. For Christians it is natural to devote time for church activities, both in a passive and active capacity. Moreover, we must have time for the nurturing of our own soul.

Through and beyond all of this, a Christian is called to *enjoy* life and all the good things he has been given. Those who think that Christian stewardship is mostly dull and onerous, with more burdens than blessings, have not understood what Christ meant when he said that he wants us to have "life to the full" (John 10:10).

Chapter 9
Endings and New Beginnings

MUCH OF THEOLOGY AND ethics are about the beginning and the end of life—of our own life and of everything around us.[1] I touched earlier in this book on the origin of all that exists and concluded that, in faith, we trust that the triune God is the Creator and Upholder of all that is. But I also suggested that neither science nor religion has given us all the answers as to when and how this creation took place. We have some information about our own individual start in life, but much about the beginning of life in general remains shrouded in mystery. The same is true when we think about the end of life. We do know that we are mortal and that we must live with the undeniable fact that one day our life will end. We may not know when and how our end will come but denying that it will come would be foolish.

Many elements of what exactly happens at death and after death remain shrouded in mystery. I believe the Bible lifts a corner of the veil, but does not answer all our questions. The Scriptures give enough information for us to know that the end is actually the beginning of something new, and that a Christian may live in hope rather than in despair. But

1. In this chapter I will make use of two recent books that I wrote on eschatology: *I Have a Future: Christ's Resurrection and Mine* and *He Comes: Why, When and How Jesus Will Return.*

right at the beginning of this chapter we must be aware that, as long as we are this side of death we "only know in part," since "we see only a reflection as in a mirror" (1 Cor 13:12).

In theology the doctrines that deal with the end belong to the domain of eschatology: the teachings about the last things. That is what this chapter will be about. It has two distinct aspects. We want to discuss the last things that pertain to our life as human beings, such as the arrival of death, the state in death, and the hope of returning to life. But also the last things for this planet (and beyond), such as the time of the end, the events surrounding the return of Jesus Christ, the millennium, and eternal life on a new earth. We will begin with *personal* eschatology and then move on to *corporate* eschatology.

Life and Death

We know life in many different forms. We share our *human* life on planet Earth with some eight billion people. Every day worldwide about 150,000 people die, but this is more than compensated for by the 385,000 births per day.[2] People differ in many ways with respect to culture, gender, age, skin color, sexual orientation, and many other characteristics, but whether we are white Americans or Asians, Africans or Inuits, and whether we belong to the category of elderly women or are male adolescents, et cetera, we all belong to the same species of *Homo sapiens*.

Human beings are surrounded by an amazing variety of other forms of life. There are about 5,500 different species of mammals on our planet and over 9,000 species of birds and some 33,000 species of fish. And this does not exhaust the rich diversity of life. Just think of the one-million-plus different kinds of insects. Add to this the 300,000 species of trees and plants.

The kind of life that humans possess is, however, unique. This is underlined by the creation stories at the beginning of the Bible. We are living beings who not only can reproduce and respond to various stimuli, but we can love and hate, use language, understand symbols, and are capable of aesthetic experiences and religious feelings. Human life is much more than an assemblage of chemical and biological processes; in addition to physical characteristics there is also an intellectual and spiritual dimension.

2. World Counts, "How Many Babies?"

It is crucial to note that a human being is not a composite of a material elements (the physical body of flesh and blood) and something non-material (a soul), whereby the body is usually defined as temporal and the soul as eternal. Biblical anthropology underlines that the whole person *is* a living soul and not that a person *has* a soul as some separate entity.

We live and we die! Dictionaries largely agree on the definition of death: namely, the permanent cessation of all vital functions. This may seem very clear, but dying can be a slow process and a person can be "brain dead" before all functions have completely ceased. Is a person who is in a vegetative state still alive in a meaningful sense of the word? Of course, the question of the nature of *death* is not just a matter of biology, just as *life* is not something limited to the realm of chemistry and biology. What is death from a philosophical or religious point of view? What happens when life ends? Is death the absolute and definitive end of who and what we are now? Or is it the gateway to a new kind of existence? *To be or not to be*[3]—that is the very existential question we all face in one way or another.

Conditional Immortality

From the earliest days of the Christian church until the present there have always been supporters of "conditional immortality"—that is, of the conviction that human beings do not simply possess an immortal soul, but that immortality is a gift that may be acquired on condition of loyalty to the Creator. Seventh-day Adventist church historian LeRoy E. Froom (1890–1974) has chronicled the history of the view of conditional immortality. A mere glance at his momentous work will suffice to realize that the rejection of the idea of an inherent immortal soul is not just found with a few people at the fringes of Christianity.[4]

The Swiss Lutheran theologian Oscar Cullmann (1902–1999) was one of the prominent scholars who during the last century opposed the idea of an immortal soul that can exist independently from the body. His treatise *Immortality of the Soul or Resurrection of the Dead? The Witness of the New Testament*, first published in 1955, was basically the text of a lecture in the famous Ingersoll Lectures series.[5] Cullmann underlined that

3. Shakespeare, *Hamlet*, 3.1.64.

4. Froom, *Conditionalist Faith of Our Fathers*.

5. The Ingersoll Lecture Series on Human Immortality was instituted through a bequest of Caroline Haskell Ingersoll in 1893, to be held at Harvard University. It is

the very concept of an immortal soul does not have its basis in the Bible but rather in ancient Greek philosophy, and that the Greek way of looking at death is in stark contrast with the biblical perspective. This, Cullmann said, becomes crystal clear when we compare Plato's description of the death of Socrates with the Gospel accounts of Jesus's death. Socrates's death is in conformity with the Greek ideas about death and dying. Death was seen as something normal, as part of nature. Socrates drinks his cup of poison in complete peace and composure. As long as a person is alive his soul is imprisoned in his body, which is only an outer garment that inhibits the freedom of the soul. Death is the great liberator. *How different is Jesus's death!* Jesus shares in the natural human fear of death. For him death is not a divine deliverance, but something utterly dreadful. While Socrates drinks the hemlock with absolute serenity, Jesus cries out in unspeakable anguish, "My God, my God, why have you forsaken me?" (Mark 15:34). For Jesus, death does not come as a welcome friend, but death is "the last enemy that is to be conquered" (1 Cor 15:26).

Man *Became* a Living Soul

For a long time the notion that humans consist of a material substance (body) and a nonmaterial something (soul) was dominant in most segments of the Christian church. In recent decades science has told us, however, that a human being is a psychosomatic unit and that there is little, if any, room for the concept of an immaterial soul.

This holistic concept of man that has gradually been gaining ground accords fully with what we can distill from the first pages of the Bible. In the creation story we read that "the Lord God formed the man [Adam] from the dust of the ground and breathed into his nostrils the breath of life, and the man became a living being" (Gen 2:7). In the King James Version we find a different rendering, with which many Christians are still more familiar: "Man became a living soul." The text in Genesis does not say that the first human being *received* a soul, but that he *became* a soul—that is, a living being. The Hebrew word *nephesh*, which is translated as "soul" (in the KJV) or, more correctly, as "living being" (in most more recent Bible translations), can have a number of

still held annually. Among other noted theologians who agree with Cullmann are Emil Brunner, Reinhold Niebuhr, John R. Scott, and Clark H. Pinnock.

different meanings, but it never refers to an immortal entity that can be separated from the body.[6]

The word *nephesh* appears no fewer than 755 times in the Old Testament. It may mean "breath" as, for instance, in Job 41:21, or "life" as in 1 Kgs 17:21 and other places. It may also refer to the "heart" as the seat of emotions (e.g., Gen 34:3). On the other hand, *nephesh* may in some cases simply emphasize the personal pronoun (e.g., in Ps 3:2), or denote a living being (as in Gen 12:5), or function as a synonym for blood (Deut 12:23). Leviticus 11:46 is an example where *nephesh* refers to animal life.

The word *nephesh* has all kinds of characteristics that we would not ascribe to an immaterial soul that can be separated from the body. The *nephesh* can hunger and thirst (e.g., Deut 12:15, 20), and it can desire all kinds of physical objects or even long for the presence of another person (e.g., 1 Sam 18:1, 3) or for a sexual relationship (Song 3:1–4). These and a multitude of other Old Testament passages make it abundantly clear that nowhere in the first part of the Bible does the soul "exist and function as a distinct, immaterial essence apart from the body."[7]

Turning to the New Testament, we soon discover that the same can be said for the word *psyche*, the Greek equivalent of *nephesh*. The Septuagint, the Greek translation of the Old Testament—which, as we noted earlier, was in use in the days of Jesus—employs *psyche* in a wide range of meanings.[8] The word occurs 101 times in the New Testament. It may have the meaning of the seat of life, or life itself (for instance in Mark 8:35). *Psyche* may also refer to "the inner life of man, equivalent to the ego, person or personality." In 1 Thess 2:8, for instance, Paul states that he and his colleagues "have given their 'souls,' i.e., their living powers of energy, themselves with all the powers of their personality, working day and night, in the care of the churches." But *psyche* may "also embrace the whole natural being and life of man for which he concerns himself and of which he takes constant care" (e.g., Matt 6:25).[9] In Luke 12:19 the rich man addresses his own *psyche*; in other words, he speaks to himself. In John 10:11 we read about Jesus as the Shepherd who is willing to lay down his life (his *psyche*) for his sheep. Acts 15:26 is another example of this particular usage. There

6. See comments on Gen 2:7 in Nichol et al., *Seventh-day Adventist Bible Commentary*, 1:223. Also Wheeler, *Beyond Death's Door*, 51–61.

7. Bacchiocchi, *Immortality or Resurrection*, 65.

8. See Brown, *New International Dictionary*, 3:682–85.

9. Brown, *New International Dictionary*, 3:683.

we are told that Paul and Barnabas risked their *psyche* for the name of their Lord Jesus Christ. In addition, the New Testament uses this word to indicate numbers of people, as in Acts 7:14 and 1 Pet 3:20. "Every soul" may simply mean "everyone" (Acts 2:43).

Nowhere does the usage of *psyche* in the New Testament "even remotely imply a conscious entity" that can survive death.[10] In fact, the New Testament specifically teaches that the *psyche* can be destroyed, together with the body, when God's final judgment is executed (Matt 10:28).[11]

Another important word is *spirit*. The Hebrew word *ruach* and the Greek word *pneuma*, which are usually translated as "spirit," show a similar wide range of meanings as we found for the Hebrew word *nephesh* and the Greek word *psyche*.[12] In many cases *ruach* and *pneuma* are used in connection with the Spirit of God. But when related to the human person, *ruach* and *pneuma* may, depending on the context, be translated as "breath," "wind," or "spirit," or be connected with a person's mood or attitude. It denotes "the energy, or life principle, that animates human beings"; it is "the energizing spark of life essential to individual existence."[13] The words *ruach* and *pneuma* underline that man is a spiritual being; he "belongs to the spiritual realm and interacts with the spiritual realm." The spirit is "that aspect of man through which God most immediately encounters him."[14]

What Then Happens at Death?

In death man "gives up" his spirit (e.g., Matt 27:50; Acts 7:59). When we die "the dust returns to the ground it came from, and the spirit returns to God who gave it" (Eccl 12:7). It is the reverse of what happened when God created man and "breathed into his nostrils the breath of life." This moment when the spirit of life leaves the body must not "be interpreted . . . as the release of the ghost from the machine, but in terms of the physical body ceasing to be the embodiment of the whole

10. Bacchiocchi, *Immortality or Resurrection*, 95.
11. Horn, *Seventh-day Adventist Bible Dictionary*, 1037.
12. Brown, *New International Dictionary*, 3:693–95.
13. Horn, *Seventh-day Adventist Bible Dictionary*, 1040.
14. Brown, *New International Dictionary*, 3:693.

man. At death man ceases to exist, both in the realm of the physical and in the realm of the spiritual."[15]

So, if there is no immortal soul that leaves the body and goes straight to heaven (or to hell), what happens when we die? To find an answer, we must once again turn to the story we find at the very beginning of the Scriptures. Genesis 3 tells us in story-form of the tragedy that has dramatically impacted all of humankind. The first human pair was disobedient and "fell" into sin (vv. 1–7). In this sad story of the entrance of sin into a perfect world we meet, for the first time, the deceiver, who is later in the Scriptures referred to as the devil. He, apparently, has access to the garden of Eden, creeps up on Eve in the disguise of a crafty serpent and says to her, "Did God really say: 'You must not eat from any tree in the garden?'" Eve immediately counters the devil's suggestion by stating that she and Adam were allowed to eat from all trees except from one particular tree. This tree "of the knowledge of good and evil" was created to test their commitment to their Creator. God had said, "You must not touch it, or you will die" (v. 3). The Hebrew text literally reads, "Dying you will die!" Note that humans were not destined to die, but that they could enjoy their uninterrupted, never-ending life on the condition of obedience. If they stood the simple test of not eating from that tree, they would live; if they failed, they would die. But the devil comes with a nasty lie that has been constantly repeated through the centuries in many different shapes and forms: "You will not surely die!" Instead of facing death, the devil says, humans have the unique potential to become like the immortal God.

"You will not surely die!" It was the greatest possible deception. According to the Genesis account the first ten generations or so lived very long lives, when compared to our present life expectancies, but (with the exception of Enoch; Gen 5:24) they all did die. The idea that the essence of man does not cease to exist at death but lives on in a different mode of existence perpetuates that first devious satanic lie, and it must be unmasked for what it is!

Like the account of the creation, the story of the fall and its consequences may not be a historical record in the modern sense of the word, but it reveals the existential truth of what happened to humankind.

15. Brown, *New International Dictionary*, 3:694.

In the Old Testament death is not spoken of as a transition to a new kind of life but as the absence of any form of consciousness. God said to David, "When your days are over . . . you will rest with your fathers" (2 Sam 7:12). That, apparently, is all there is to it. In his profound misery Job replied to his "friend" Eliphaz, "My life is but a breath . . . you will look for me and I will be no more." He added in more general terms, "As a cloud vanishes and is gone, so he who goes down to the grave does not return . . . his place will know him no more" (Job 7:7–10). And Job ended his speech with the words, "I will lie down in the dust; you will search for me, but I will be no more" (v. 21). A similar thought is expressed in Job 21:25. One man "dies in full vigor," while another man "dies in bitterness of soul, never having enjoyed anything good." But "side by side they lie in the dust, and worms cover them both." Psalm 146:4 further confirms this, when referring to the fate of "mortal men": "When their spirit departs, they return to the ground, on that very day their plans come to nothing."

Several biblical passages compare death to a state of *sleep*. David prays to God to be with him lest he will "sleep in death" (Ps 13:3). Psalm 115:17 tells us that it is not "the dead who praise the Lord, those who go down to silence." This text is especially meaningful in the context of our present discussion. One of the things that the defenders of the idea of an immortal soul will usually emphasize is that those who have "passed" are now in heaven, jubilantly singing God's praises. Not so, says this Psalm. The dead do not praise God, "they go down into silence." Their state may be compared, for lack of a better word, with a deep sleep.

Sleep is, in fact, the word Jesus Christ used when he was called by Jairus, the administrator of the synagogue, with an urgent plea to come and heal his daughter. When Jesus was late in arriving at the home of Jairus, the girl had already died, and Jesus was confronted with the loud sound of "wailing and mourning" as he entered the house. He told the people to stop their weeping, for, he said, "she is not dead but asleep." Then, as Jesus took the little girl by her hand and raised her up, "her spirit returned" (Luke 8:49–56).

Likewise, when Jesus was told that his friend Lazarus was seriously ill, he sent word to Lazarus's sisters Mary and Martha that there was no reason to unduly worry: "This sickness will not end in death." When the reply came that Lazarus had died and had already been buried, Jesus commented, "Our friend Lazarus has fallen asleep, but I am going to wake him up." The disciples, who accompanied Jesus on his journey to Bethany, did not understand the meaning of Jesus's words and said, "Lord, if he sleeps, he will get better." The Gospel writer then adds this short explanatory comment: "Jesus had been speaking of his death, but his disciples thought he meant natural sleep" (John 11:1–44).

When the apostle Paul wants to explain to the Thessalonians what will happen to the people who are alive at the moment that Christ returns—those who are "left till the coming of the Lord"—he tells them that they will not precede the believers who have already gone to their rest. He does not talk about those who have died in terms of souls that are already in heaven, but refers to them as people "who have fallen asleep" (1 Thess 4:13). The two groups, those believers who have died prior to Christ's return and those who are alive at the time of that momentous event, "will be caught up together . . . to meet the Lord in the air." And from that moment on, and not before, they "will be with the Lord forever" (v. 17).

At a given moment Jesus wanted to leave the crowds that surrounded him in no uncertainty about the purpose of his heavenly Father. God wants nothing more fervently than that "everyone who looks to the Son and believes in him shall have eternal life" (John 6:40). But when is this going to happen?

Jesus promises every person who wants to follow him, "I will raise him up at the last day" (John 6:44). This is what we may look forward to: "A time is coming, when all who are in their graves will hear his [Christ's] voice and come out—those who have done good will rise to live, and those who have done evil will rise to be condemned" (John 5:28–29). The prophet Daniel (or the person who used that pseudonym) was one of the few people in Old Testament times to whom it was clearly revealed what would happen when his life had come to an end: "As for you, go your way till the end. You will rest, and then at the end of the days you will rise to receive your allotted inheritance" (Dan 12:13).

Perhaps nowhere in the New Testament do we find a clearer picture of what awaits us, who are followers of Jesus Christ, than in 1 Cor 15. In this chapter Paul discusses at length the topic of the resurrection. He declares that the resurrection of Jesus is the guarantee that death has been overcome and that we can be sure that we will be woken up from our interim state, which is best compared with sleep. Listen to what the apostle says: "For as in Adam all die, so in Christ all will be made alive.

But each in his own turn: Christ, the first fruits; then, when the end comes, those who belong to him" (vv. 20–23).

I fully concur with these words of Professor Richard Rice: "The Biblical view of death sees death as a void, an emptiness, the absence of all experience. The future beyond death is the restoration of life."[16] It seems best not to spend too much time on any further speculation about the period between our death and our resurrection. After all, the concept of time is something that belongs to this world and time has no meaning once we are no longer part of this present world.[17]

A Few "Problem Texts"

We must, in all fairness, look at a few texts that, taken in isolation and seen from a particular viewpoint, appear to contradict the position we have put forward above.

Luke 23:39–43

Jesus was crucified between two criminals. One of these two individuals, who were executed together with Jesus, taunted him saying, "Aren't you the Christ? Save yourself and us!" The other criminal, however, had understood, at least to some extent, who Jesus was. He told the man who had mocked Jesus to be quiet, and said, "We are punished justly, for we are getting what our deeds deserve. But this man has done nothing wrong." Then he said, "Jesus, remember me when you come into your kingdom." Jesus answered him, "I tell you the truth, today you will be with me in paradise."

This text has often been quoted as the ultimate proof that, upon his death, a believer has an immediate entry into heaven. For is this not what Jesus unequivocally promised to this repentant criminal? It is important to know that the original Greek text contains only letters and no punctuation marks, such as full stops or commas. When reading the Greek text, the reader must determine which words belong together, and the lack of punctuations marks may sometimes cause confusion. Thus, the words of Jesus may be understood as they have been read by most people (and printed in most Bible translations): "I tell you the truth, today you will

16. Rice, *Reign of God*, 151.

17. Schwarz, *Eschatology*, 291.

be with me in paradise." But the text may just as legitimately be read as: "Today [this very day] I tell you the truth: You will be with me in paradise." Both renderings are grammatically correct. We must therefore look a little further to discover what Jesus could, in fact, have meant.

The crucial question is, Did Jesus go to paradise that very same day on which he was crucified, and did he meet the criminal there that same day? Note that no more than about twenty-four hours earlier Jesus had told the twelve disciples, "In my Father's house are many rooms . . . I am going there to prepare a place for you, and . . . I will come back and take you to be with me that you may also be where I am" (John 14:1–3). The disciples were not told that they would go straight to the heavenly rooms ("paradise") immediately upon their death. That would happen when Jesus would return, and he would come for them to take them with him. It is logical to assume that this is also when the criminal next to Jesus will arrive in the heavenly abode.

There are other clear indications that Christ did not go to paradise on that very same day. On the resurrection morning he told Mary, "Do not hold on to me, for I have not yet returned to the Father" (John 20:17). Acts 1:1–11 informs us about the exact moment when Jesus did, in fact, return to his Father. It was not until forty days after his resurrection that he ascended to heaven. All this is indisputable evidence that the commonly held idea that the criminal arrived in paradise the very moment he died is not correct. It does not necessarily follow from the original wording in the Greek text, and it would be at odds with many other passages, and with the general teaching of the Bible about the nature of death.

Luke 16:19–31

But what about the parable of the rich man and the poor Lazarus? Does this not clearly tell us that the dead live on, immediately after their death? The story is well-known. A rich man, who remains unnamed, lives in luxury without taking any notice of someone called Lazarus, a poor man who sits begging at his gates. After some time both men die. Angels come and carry Lazarus "to Abraham's side." But the rich man ends up in hell, "where he was in torment." Part of the rich man's misery is that he can see "Abraham far away and Lazarus at his side." Then follows an exchange between the rich man and Father Abraham. The rich man asks Abraham to send Lazarus to him, so that he may bring him some solace while he is in terrible agony. But his request is not honored. The rich man has received what he deserves, and the geography of the hereafter does not allow for any traffic between the department of bliss and the department of torment. When the rich man then asks that Lazarus be dispatched to warn his five brothers, who are still on this earth, he is told in no uncertain terms that they have enough information in the sacred writings. If those writings do not convince them what they should do, some supernatural event will not do so either!

In telling this parable Jesus may have adapted a popular story that is found in the Palestinian Talmud (a collection of Jewish laws). This story is about a rich tax collector who dies and, after a lavish funeral, finds himself in Hades, while a poor scholar, who departed from life with hardly anyone noticing, is surrounded by the blessings of paradise. The scholar enjoys happiness, while the rich man in vain seeks to quench his thirst.[18] This was not the only story with this motif that was known in the Mediterranean world. From which particular source Jesus drew cannot be established, but it was in all likelihood from one of these stories about the reversal of fortunes of the rich and the poor after death.[19] Listening to this parable, the audience around Jesus would immediately have recognized the similarity with this type of story. And, in addition, they would most definitely also have been acquainted with the nature of parables. Many religious teachers in Christ's day used the literary device of the parable, but Jesus "perfected and used it so extensively and so effectively that is has become identified with his teaching method."[20]

A parable is best defined as a short narrative, which can either be true or fictitious, that is told to illustrate a spiritual or moral truth. Jesus's specific purpose with this parable is to make his listeners understand that the decision regarding their eternal destiny is in the present. After death there is no second chance. It is impossible to distill a coherent eschatology from this parable. "The purpose of the parable cannot be to reveal the afterlife in detail; instead its importance lies elsewhere."[21] The parable of Lazarus and the rich man remains a powerful warning that we must be utterly serious about our eternal future and not postpone our decision to follow Christ and begin living a Christian life.

18. Andreasen, "Death," 324.

19. Papaioannou, *Geography of Hell*, 119.

20. Horn, *Seventh-day Adventist Bible Dictionary*, 810.

21. Papaioannou, *Geography of Hell*, 127.

Hebrews 12:22–24

This passage in Hebrews may seem somewhat puzzling, but it is, in fact, not very difficult to catch its meaning. The unknown author of this Bible book repeatedly contrasts the spiritual experience of ancient Israel with the experience of those who have come to know Christ and have decided to put their faith in him. The Christian believers, we read, have not come to the mountain in the Sinai wilderness, which they are forbidden to touch and that made even Moses tremble with fear (vv. 18–21), but they have come to "Mount Zion, the heavenly Jerusalem."

Those who listened to the reading of this essay were reminded of what lay ahead of them: "You have come to thousands upon thousands of angels in joyful assembly . . . you have come to God, the judge of all men, to the spirits of righteous men made perfect . . . to Jesus, the Mediator of a new covenant" (vv. 22–24). The expression "the spirits of the righteous men" is sometimes quoted by people who believe that reference is made to the bodiless entities from Old Testament times that now supposedly enjoy the presence of the Lord. But to make these "spirits of righteous men" refer to supposedly disembodied "spirits" would be to set the writer of Hebrews at variance with the many clear statements of the Holy Scriptures concerning the state of man in death.[22]

In figurative language the author describes the reality of the new covenant. The salvation is achieved and can already now be rejoiced in, but it remains to be consummated, when all the redeemed from Old and New Testament times will be assembled, together with the angels before God and the Lamb.[23] It may have seemed to these Hebrew Christians that they were but a desperate and despised group, but they are assured that this will not be the case in the New Jerusalem. There they will be part of an enormous multitude that includes millions of angels and the saved from all ages.[24]

Revelation 6:9

In Rev 6 John sees in a vision how the Lamb opens a scroll with seven seals. While he opens the fifth seal, "souls" under the altar cry out to

22. Nichol et al., *Seventh-day Adventist Bible Commentary*, 6:487.

23. Hagner, *Encountering Hebrews*, 164–65.

24. Knight, *Exploring Hebrews*, 235.

God, desperate to know how long God will still delay before he will judge those villains who had shed their blood in martyrdom. It is clear that this is symbolic language in a context that is full of figurative expressions. If we understand *souls* as eternal sparks that survive death, detached from their bodies, we should be consistent and also take the other elements of this description literally. A literal reading would force us to conclude that John saw the souls of these followers of Christ, not enjoying eternity, but in utter anguish. They are not pictured as inhabitants of a heavenly paradise but as hiding under an altar—a strange place indeed, if this is to be taken in any literal sense. The message of this, at first sight, somewhat obscure text is really one of hope. God has not forgotten what his people have suffered! "In this symbolic presentation of the resurrection hope, held by those who died long ago, the dead play no active role but must patiently wait for the time established by God. This confirms the biblical understanding that the dead rest in their graves until called forth at the time of the resurrection."[25]

2 Corinthians 5:1–10

In this text Paul speaks about our heavenly dwelling place. We know, he writes, that when our "earthly tent" is destroyed, we have "a building from God, an eternal house, not built be human hands." The apostle realizes that being at home with God has not yet become a reality for him. He wishes that he could transition in one single moment from being in his "earthly tent" to reaching his final God-given destination. In this connection he states, "I would prefer to be away from the body and be at home with the Lord." Does this mean what it suggests to some readers—namely, that Paul wished his soul would leave his body, and that he expects to be "away from his body" (v. 6) so that he can be with the Lord? A careful reading of the entire passage does not support that interpretation. Moreover, it would not be consistent with many other Pauline statements about death and resurrection. In this passage Paul expresses his wish that he could skip the period of death, which he here refers to as "being unclothed," and that he would be "clothed with our heavenly dwelling" (v. 4). This was indeed going to happen, but only after an interim period in which he would be "asleep" in death. At the end of this passage Paul moves on "to his final and dynamic conclusion." He "tells the Corinthians that regardless of where

25. Andreasen, "Death," 328.

we are in the stream of time, either in this life or when we are in heaven, it should always be our goal to please the Lord."[26]

Why It Matters

What happens with us when we die is not just an interesting academic question, but a truly existential issue for all of us. We are stewards of the life that God gives us, with the responsibility to deal with it conscientiously as long as we are alive. Our view of life and death is the basis for how we deal with various ethical matters surrounding the beginning of life and the approach of death.[27] It will prompt us to be quite restrained with regard to abortion as well as euthanasia. But on the other hand, I believe it reinforces our faith in a merciful and understanding God who will also help us to know when ending a life, which is either developing in a womb or in its final phase, is a deed of mercy, and when helping a person to "trans" into the "right" gender may be a gift of love.

Our view of life and death also impacts on a number of important theological issues. If all people (Enoch, Moses, Elia, and perhaps a few others excepted) rest in their graves, there are no saints in heaven who intervene for us. It means that Jesus Christ is the only Mediator and that access to God is only through him and not through a range of men and women who went through a process of canonization and who, supposedly, now are in heaven to help us on our pilgrimage to eternal life. And, although Christians will hold Mary in high esteem, the biblical evidence leads us to conclude that she does not hear any supplications to her, but that she awaits the resurrection, together with the "great multitude that no one could count" (Rev 7:9).

I am willing to take a leap of faith and believe that both *life* and *death* have to do with a dimension that is beyond our human comprehension. Life has its origin in the divine source of life, and death is ultimately caused by a fatal separation from it. Both life and death have unearthly dimensions. Somehow—in a way only known to our Creator—our "life is now hidden with Christ in God" (Col 3:3). In Christ's death and resurrection, life conquered death and the identity of all who have died (and whose bones or ashes may long have been absorbed by nature) are

26. Richards, *2 Corinthians*, 113.
27. See my book *Matters of Life and Death.*

safe in God's inexhaustible memory, waiting for the moment that they will receive a totally new lease on life.

Corporate Eschatology

Seventh-day Adventists have included the expectation of Jesus's return in their denominational name. When in 1860 the small group of Sabbatarian believers discussed the name they wanted to adopt, they decided to link their corporate identity with their belief in the seventh-day Sabbath and with their conviction that Jesus's second coming would occur in the near future. They had been wrong in calculating the time of Jesus's return, but the lesson of the 1844 debacle did not stop some of them (even until today) to keep suggesting new dates when to expect the *Parousia* (the Greek word for "coming" or "presence"), in spite of Jesus's assertion that no one, except God himself, knows the date of his return (Matt 24:36).

Standard Adventist exegesis has been that the *time of the end* refers to a relatively short period of calamitous events just before the sky opens for the Lord to appear; 1798 (the date given for the end of the 1260 year/day period; Rev 12:6) or 1844, are often cited as the moment when the time of the end began. This term does, however, have a wider connotation. Several New Testament authors emphasize the immediacy of the second coming (Rom 13:11–12; Jas 5:8–9; 1 Cor 10:11) and refer to the time after Christ's ascension as the "last days." At the very beginning of Hebrews we read, "In the past God spoke to our ancestors through the prophets at many times and in various ways, but *in these last days* he has spoken to us by his Son" (1:1–2; italics added). And on Pentecost, Peter applied the prophecy of Joel 2:28–32 to "the last days," suggesting that these were already underway (Acts 2:17). The same Peter places the incarnation of Christ in the context of the "last times" (1 Pet 1:20). In 1 John 2:18 the author stresses that his contemporaries are living "in the last hour."

Saying that the time of the end is the entire interim period between the first and the second coming of Christ does not rob the proclamation of the Parousia of its importance or urgency, but allows us to be more relaxed about the fact that the Lord has not yet come. We must realize that God's schedule may not coincide with ours, and that for God "soon" does not imply the same kind of rush as it does for us. Jesus promised the readers of the Revelation, "I am coming soon" (Rev 22:20). He also told the church of Philadelphia, one of the churches to which the book of Revelation was sent (Rev 1:11), "I am coming soon" (Rev 3:11). We realize, of course, that *soon* is a somewhat imprecise and relative term. The Greek word *tachu*, which is usually translated as "soon," has, in fact, a meaning that is a little more nuanced. According to several academic dictionaries *tachu* does not have "immediately" as its primary meaning, but rather "without necessary delay, once the appointed time arrives." The word *tachu* has, most of all, to do with the speed that is appropriate to a particular situation. In fact, some translators of Revelation have chosen the word "quickly" rather than "soon." The things that are described in the Revelation "must" take place "soon"—that is, without unnecessary delay, as specified by God's timetable.[28]

En Route to the End of Time

In trying to make sense of the apocalyptic messages, theologians sought for a system of interpretation that would "work." Many Bible scholars believe that these prophecies deal almost exclusively with things that are already in the past. They apply the prophecies of Daniel to events in the second century BC and the message of Revelation to events in the first century AD, with the imperial Roman power as the great villain that is featured in these prophecies. Other scholars disagree and are of the opinion that most of what we find in the book of Revelation will be fulfilled just before the very end of time. Others again do not want to make that choice but see patterns that have occurred in every age since the church was established. Seventh-day Adventists (and many evangelical groups) are among those who belong to the so-called *historicist* school. They see the fulfilment of most of the elements of Daniel and the Revelation in the course of the past twenty centuries.

The debate about this issue will continue and it may well be that there is truth in all of these approaches.[29] Adventist theologian Jon K. Paulien, a Revelation specialist, defends historicism: "The *historicist* view remains the best approach to apocalyptic prophecy,"[30] because "it

28. Bible Hub, "5035." Other Bible verses where the word *tachu* refers to speed rather than to immediacy are Luke 18:8; Acts 12:7; and Acts 22:18. See Bible Hub, "5034."

29. Bruinsma, "Adventist Hermeneutical," 5–24.

30. Paulien, "Hermeneutic of Biblical Apocalyptic," 268.

takes all the evidence of the Bible seriously."[31] Paulien echoes a long-established Adventist position: only the historicist approach unlocks the meaning of Daniel and Revelation. Adventists inherited the historicist approach from their Millerite forbears.[32]

Zdravko Stefanovic, a theology professor at Adventist Health University (Orlando, Florida), does not deny the important historical applications of Daniel. But he is also adamant that we must pay attention to the meaning the apocalyptic portions had for the original readers and to contemporary applications.[33] His brother Ranko Stefanovic, who teaches theology at Andrews University (Berrien Springs, Michigan), expresses himself in rather similar ways when he deals with the book of Revelation. He finds the historicist approach "sometimes problematic" because of the difficulty to fit every detail of the text into a historical fulfillment. On the other hand, he says, the other approaches can only have some validity "if the prophetic elements are taken into consideration and applied to the time that extends beyond John's days."[34] Ranko Stefanovic calls for making case-by-case judgments.

However, this is not all we must be aware of. If we follow a traditional historicist path (which I am nowadays rather hesitant to do), we must be extremely careful in linking passages in Daniel and the Revelation to specific historic events, persons, organizations, and dates. Even in our relatively short Adventist history several viewpoints we once were very sure about had to be revised, because what we proclaimed as present truth turned out to be simply wrong.

I should also add that prophetic interpretations do not develop in a vacuum. They have their roots in particular movements or intellectual developments in the past, and they develop in a specific historical, cultural, and religious milieu. It has often been noted that the Adventist interpretation of apocalyptic prophecy is very much centered on Europe and also, to a lesser extent, on the United States. The other parts of the world do not play any significant role. And it is hard to deny that the nineteenth-century Protestant aversion to Roman Catholics—in particular in the United States—left its imprint on Adventist prophetic interpretation and various end-time expectations.

31. Paulien, *Seven Keys*, 17.

32. Davidson, "Biblical Interpretation," 96.

33. Stefanovic, *Daniel*, 9.

34. Stefanovic, *Revelation of Jesus Christ*, 11.

I believe it is best to focus on the cosmic conflict as we try to unlock what often appear to be riddles in the apocalyptic writings, as, for instance, Sigve Tonstad does in his commentary on the book of Revelation.[35] He interprets Revelation as a portrayal of a universal struggle between good and evil, focusing on the vindication of God's character and governance. Elsewhere he observes, "The book of Revelation is not primarily about predicting the future but about revealing the character of God in the context of a cosmic conflict."[36]

Many are prone to forget that the Apocalypse is not *John's* Revelation, but the Revelation of *Jesus Christ*. The first chapters paint the comforting picture of Christ in the midst of his church, symbolized by seven candles, while keeping the leaders of his church in his hands. In the final chapters (21 and 22) we meet the Lord again amid his people when the heavenly city has become a reality. The chapters in between tell us about the trials of the people of God, the attacks of the evil one, the final combat between good and evil, the persistence of faith, and the victory of the Lamb of God. The central message is God's people are safe. Amid serious challenges the future is theirs.

Signals Along the Road

When the disciples asked at what time Jesus's predictions about the destruction of Jerusalem and about his coming at "the end of the age" would be fulfilled, and whether there would be any signs to help them understand, Jesus told them about the "signs of the times" that would occur. He spoke of wars and rumors of wars, of famines and pestilences, earthquakes, atmospheric phenomena, and spiritual deceit (Matt 24, Luke 21, Mark 13). These signs, he told them, would precede both the destruction of Jerusalem and the end of history, and would eventually culminate in the "sign of the Son of Man," when the people on earth "will see the Son of Man coming on the clouds, with power and great glory" (Matt 24:30).

The signs of the times may be of a natural or supernatural nature. The question is under what circumstances particular (often quite ordinary) events become signs. G. C. Berkouwer (1903–1996), a prominent Dutch systematic theologian in the Reformed tradition, made this important observation: "Only when signs are seen through the eyes of faith

35. Tonstad, *Revelation*.

36. Tonstad, *Saving God's Reputation*, 12.

can they display their meaning and significance."[37] Richard Rice agrees: "The signs are not just signs to anyone. One has to see them from the proper perspective in order to grasp their true meaning. We need faith to see that the end is near . . . the signs . . . corroborate and strengthen faith as well as bolster confidence that the end will come soon."[38]

The signs of the times are not given to us as a tool for calculating the date of the second coming. We are also on the wrong track if we try to systematize them and put them in a particular order, so that we may measure the time that is left before Christ comes back. Berkouwer warns us against that kind of "reportorial eschatology."[39] Ordinary and extraordinary—and sometimes spectacular—events may break into the normal course of history and impress us in a special way. They make us aware of what is going on in the world and tell us that history moves forward towards its climax.

The signs of the time remind us of what we read in 1 Chr 12:23–40 about the men from the different Israelite tribes who came to enlist in David's army, when it had become clear that David's power had been solidly established. Among them was also a contingent from the tribe of Issachar. We are told about the soldiers who came from various other tribes, that they were "brave" or "experienced" in warfare, but that the men who belonged to the tribe of Issachar had a different quality. They "understood the times and knew what Israel should do" (1 Chr 12:32). There is a parallel between the men of Issachar and us, who live in the twenty-first century. Understanding the times and being able to interpret the meaning of the signs for the time in which we live, and being able to analyze the trends in our society, is essential if we want to live our faith in a relevant manner and to communicate the message of Jesus Christ effectively.

"You understand the present time," Paul says (Rom 13:11). The apostle is not crediting his readers with theoretical insight into the philosophy of history. His point is clear: "The hour has come for you to wake up from your slumber."[40] Speaking of "the present time," Paul uses the word *kairos*, rather than *chronos*, which is another Greek word for time. *Chronos* has to do with the stream of time, while *kairos* refers to

37. Berkouwer, *Return of Christ*, 237.

38. Rice, *Reign of God*, 359.

39. Berkouwer, *Return of Christ*, 249.

40. Berkouwer, *Return of Christ*, 252.

a moment or period when the time is ripe for something.[41] Thus, Paul tells us, time is not simply flowing by in a constant stream, but it has a distinct significance—it is moving towards a divinely appointed destiny. The signs help us to discern this *kairos*, which moves forward towards the glorious second coming of our Lord.

Hope Versus Fear

For many Christians the topic of the signs of the times has an alarming character. They are inclined to focus on the dark side of the signs. When the signs appear, the "nations will be in anguish and perplexity. . . . Men will faint from terror, apprehensive of what is coming on the world" (Luke 21:25–26). Jesus warned us, however, against a one-sided emphasis on the dark side of things. He encourages us with these memorable words: "When these things begin to take place, stand up and lift up your heads, for your redemption is drawing near!" (v. 28).

Hope must triumph over fear—every day of our life. Richard Rice comments, "Hope never views the future with calm detachment. The hoped-for future is never something that has not happened yet. Hope makes a personal investment in the future; it views that future in distinctly personal terms. When I hope, I see *the* future as *my* future."[42] Berkouwer underlines another important aspect: "The signs are not pertinent to only a remote end-time. No, for believers they are a summons to constant watchfulness."[43]

Although the signs indicate that Christ's return is near, they do not pinpoint the exact time of his arrival. Since we never know just when he will come, we need to be ready at all times (Matt 24:36, 44). This lends a note of urgency to our preparation for the future. "The Christian's attitude toward the future, then, includes a confidence that does not harden into smugness or presumption and a sense of urgency that does not deteriorate into frenzy. It manifests itself in the faithful fulfilment of present responsibilities."[44]

I repeat: the signs of the times do not enable us to compute the time when Christ will come. The biblical message is clear "that no

41. Kittel and Friedrich, *Theological Dictionary*, s.vv. "chronos" and "kairos."

42. Rice, *Reign of God*, 358.

43. Berkouwer, *Return of Christ*, 48.

44. Rice, *Reign of God*, 359–60.

matter how carefully we interpret history, the coming of the end will be a total surprise."[45]

The signs of the times have accompanied the believers ever since the first advent of Christ, and they will continue to occur until his second coming. Paul saw clear signals that the kingdom of God was at hand. The church fathers saw the signs of the times; so did the Reformers of the sixteenth and seventeenth centuries, and the students of prophecy of the nineteenth century. So did our grandparents and our parents. And so do we, if we look for them! In all ages Christians have been able to base their hope on these signposts along their road of pilgrimage. They helped the believers to stay alert, to ever remember that the interim period between Christ's first and second advent has been irrevocably moving forward. All this, however, does not mean there cannot, now or in the near future, be a marked progression in these signs of the times. As time moves towards its climax, several of the signs may well increase in intensity. That is, for those of us who want to see it. The unbeliever often sees nothing remarkable in phenomena or events that for the believer are full of meaning.

When Christ became incarnate almost two thousand years ago, he was only recognized by a small group of people. Likewise, today it is very possible that we fail to see the clear signs of the nearness of his second coming. But it does not have to be that way. A careful "interpreting" of the signs of the times will enable us to know what time (*kairos*) it is. Only those who take the effort to discern and "interpret" may claim Christ's assurance: "Blessed are your eyes, for they see" (Matt 13:16).

Thousand Years

Few topics have been as dominant in end-time expectations as the thousand-year period of Rev 20, usually referred to as the millennium. Much more than in Europe, American Christians have long been deeply interested, and often even obsessed, by the millennium. Earnest R. Sandeen (1931–1983), in the 1970s and early 1980s a professor of history at Macalester College in St. Paul (Minnesota), once famously declared that "America in the early nineteenth century was drunk on the millennium."[46]

45. Schwarz, *Eschatology*, 384.

46. Sandeen, *Roots of Fundamentalism*, 44.

The view of Augustine, that the "reign" of the church between the two advents covered the period of the millennium, had been dominant for many centuries (so-called amillennialism), but Protestants from the eighteenth century onward have been mostly divided between *postmillennialists* and *premillennialists*. Postmillennialists believe that Christ will return *at the end* of the millennium. They believe the thousand years of Rev 20 symbolize a period in which conditions on earth will steadily improve before Christ will come. But among those who were particularly interested in apocalyptic prophecy various versions of *premillennialism* became popular. According to this explanation, Christ's coming would *introduce* the thousand years! William Miller and his movement were part of a broader revivalist wave that swept through the United States and also had some influence in Europe. His views about the return of Christ and the other "last things" were prime examples of premillennialism.

It is in many ways surprising that one single—and in some respects rather confusing—chapter of the Bible has given rise to so many theories and speculative ideas about the time of the end. The millennium (the common Latin-derived name for the thousand years of Rev 20) continues to play an important role in Adventist eschatology. At the beginning of the thousand years, it is believed, the believers of all ages will be resurrected and the followers of Christ, who are alive at the moment of Christ's return, will be changed and receive immortality. These two categories will accompany Christ to heaven and "reign" with him during this thousand-year period (v. 4). This "reigning" appears to refer to their involvement with God's final judgment (see also 1 Cor 6:2–3).

During the millennium the earth is uninhabited. The unbelievers who saw Christ coming have died instantly and, with all the "wicked" who have died through the ages, they remain dead until the end of the thousand years. With all believers in heaven and all unbelievers dead, Satan is "bound" and must wait before he can have one final try at overthrowing God's government. This is when the old world is replaced by a new world that descends from heaven with all God's people, and when the unbelievers of all times are resurrected. The terrible clash that ensues ends in the "second death" (vv. 6, 14) of all God's adversaries, including the devil himself.

Adventists have always interpreted the second death as total annihilation and have insisted that the Bible does not support an eternally burning hell, where the ungodly will suffer throughout eternity. The mention of eternal fire in the context of their punishment is seen as eternal in its consequences, rather than as in duration.

Questions Remain

Does this short summary of what happens at the beginning, during, and end of the millennium leave you with many questions? One of the issues that I keep wondering about is why this second resurrection is necessary. If God is determined to destroy the wicked, why resurrect them first? And why in the world would God allow Satan to organize one last vicious hate campaign? Why allow God's people to undergo one last murderous satanic attack?

I know the traditional answers that have been given: it must become clear, once and for all, what will be the end result of rebellion against God. God is at last fully justified throughout the universe and recognized for what he is: love—even in his punishments. It is apparently important for the redeemed to witness the ultimate destruction of those who have done evil and have willfully opposed God's love and grace. This will guarantee that there will never again be an experiment of rebellion against God. But is this course of events at the close of the thousand years the only divine option to make this clear?

I have come to the conclusion that I will not allow these and similar questions to dominate my thinking. We must keep in mind that Rev 20—like the rest of the book of Revelation—is full of symbolic representations. We do not get a straightforward, point-by-point, strictly chronological account of what will happen. Human language is totally inadequate to give us a full picture that our limited, mortal, human minds can comprehend.

What we can grasp is clear and complete enough. God is just. Going against him comes at a terrible cost. On the other hand, loyalty towards him brings an eternal reward of perfect love and eternal peace. Beyond the chaos of our present world and the thousand-year interim of a devastated planet looms a glorious new world. Paradise lost will soon be transformed into paradise restored. All our remaining questions are insignificant in the light of the glorious promise that everything is going to be eternally okay.

Eternal Bliss

The images that people paint of eternal bliss—on canvas, and in prose or poetry—will always, at least to some extent, reflect the present world in which they live. When the prophet Isaiah was inspired to write about the new heavens and the new earth, he used the kinds of images he had in his creative arsenal and his audience could understand (chapters 65–66). John the Revelator, when writing about the new heaven and the new earth, used some of the same images, but added others that were more reflective of his own days. This is what happens when inspired writers try to put into words what God revealed to them. They search for words and metaphors that will do justice to what God has told them or shown them, and that is even more challenging when uninspired people try to imagine the future reality. Not surprisingly, therefore, medieval paintings of the new earth differ significantly from the illustrations by artists of the twentieth century.

Even if we build our imaginations on the good things we know in this present life, we can become even more excited about the things that will be no longer be there, as "the old order of things has passed away." God "will wipe every tear" from our eyes. "There will be no more death or mourning or crying or pain" (Rev 21:4). That means no more funerals or cremations, no more bodies that slowly waste away, no more HIV, no more cancer, no more heart attacks or renal failures—not even a slight headache or a few days with the flu, or a return of COVID-19. And the inhabitants of this perfect world will not have to put up with people who are dishonest or mean, who are unfaithful or egocentric.

Symbols with Meaning

How much of what we read in such parts of Scripture as Rev 21 and 22 should we take as literal? How much of it is symbolic? It would require more space than we have in this chapter to provide a full answer; a few remarks will, hopefully, be helpful. The entire book of Revelation has a highly symbolic content, and this does most certainly also apply to the last two chapters.

Let us take a specific example. Throughout the Apocalypse the term *Babylon* is used symbolically. It is a comprehensive label for all powers—religious and political—that oppose God and the true worship of him. In the prophecies of the last Bible book the name *Babylon* does not refer to a literal city but is used as a powerful symbol for the enemies of God. Now, what about its counterpart, the "New Jerusalem"? Opinions differ and many people prefer the traditional view of the New Jerusalem as a literal city. However, it would be consistent to conclude that the term *New Jerusalem* does not denote a literal city but is a fitting symbol for all those who will eternally be with God. This is confirmed by what we read at the very beginning of Rev 21. A well-known symbol for God's people is that of a woman, the bride of Christ. John merges these two symbols—the holy city and the bride—when he says that he saw the city descending from heaven as a bride who is going to meet her groom! If we understand the portrayal of the New Jerusalem symbolically, we can make more sense of the description of this heavenly city. It is an immense cube, with thick walls and a dozen gates. Of course, in John's days people would think of walls and gates when picturing a city, just as we would now think of skyscrapers, highways, and other important pieces of infrastructure. The fact that the gates of this city will no longer need to be closed means that all dangers have ceased to exist. God's people enjoy their Creator's eternal protection. The fact that the city is a cube immediately reminds us of the holiest compartment of the Old Testament tabernacle and of the Jerusalem temple, which also was a perfect cube (1 Kgs 6:20). There God was present among his people in a very special way. No wonder, then, that the idea of a cube emerges when a city is described where God will be more directly present among his people than he has ever been.

So, yes, much of the language is symbolic. But symbols are not "just" symbols. They point to something very real. They are needed because human limitations make it impossible to speak about God's eternal reality in a more direct and propositional manner. In spite of all the questions and uncertainties that remain, the Bible provides us with a clear enough picture to get excited about the very real future that God has in store for humanity. The main points may be summarized as follows:

1. Eternal life, in heaven and on the new earth, will be characterized by a total eradication of sin. Total love now governs all relationships.
2. Death and decay will forever be things of the past. All traces of sin will be removed from the environment; all consequences of sin are reversed, and God's reign is realized without any imperfections or distortions.

3. As a result, eternal life will be characterized by a total absence of all things that cause pain and fear. The new world will be so close to its source of light that everything bathes in this glory and all dark shadows have forever receded into oblivion.
4. Through all eternity God's creatures will enjoy perfect relationships. We need not worry whether, or how, our present social arrangements, such as marriage and family, will be continued. God ensures eternal bliss of an absolute kind. To know that should be enough.
5. One of the great differences with our present life is that in eternity we can relate to God in an immediate way. The "veil" between God and us has been lifted. At last, Christ is the center of all things.[47]

"I Make All Things New"

God must have had a purpose in not providing us with a more detailed description of the destiny of humankind, of this planet and of the universe. Apparently, he does not want us to spend all our time and energy in thinking about what will be. It seems almost easier to list some of the things that will no longer be part and parcel of the eternal future that God has prepared for his children than to describe the things that will be there. God "will wipe every tear" from the eyes of the saints. "There will be no more death or mourning or crying or pain" (Rev 21:4). There are many "rooms" (John 14:2), but there will be no place for "the cowardly, the unbelieving, the vile, the murderers, the sexually immoral, those who practice magic arts, the idolaters and all liars" (Rev 21:8). The night will no longer exist, since all darkness is eclipsed by the ultimate source of light: God (Rev 22:5). The ancient fear of the dangers of deep waters will forever be banished from the hearts of God's children. Therefore, in the new world that is to be their home, there is no more sea! (Rev 21:1).

God's promise, "I am making everything new" (Rev 21:5), is of great significance. But note that God does not say that he is going to make all kinds of new things. There is a major degree of discontinuity between this temporal existence and the future eternal life. If that were not so, it would not be something to look forward to. It would just be more of the same, forever and ever. On the other hand, if there were no continuity, God's promise that we can "inherit" eternal life would lose all meaning. In this

47. Berkhof, *Christelijk Geloof*, 556–64.

promise that all things will be made new, the Greek text uses the word *kainos* rather than *neos*, which is another Greek word for new. *Neos* has the root meaning of new, in the sense of the next one. The new things that God promised are not new in the *neos* sense, but new in the *kainos* sense: they are radically renewed, new in quality, with an eternal warranty.[48] Thus, the word *new* refers to discontinuity as well as continuity.

Directly connected with this is one of the most frequently asked questions about the hereafter: shall we recognize our loved ones? We will be changed radically when we are raised "imperishable" (1 Cor 15:52). First John 3:2 emphasizes the discontinuity between what we are now and what we will be: "What we will be has not yet been made known. But we know that when he appears, we shall be like him, for we shall see him as he is." When Jesus appeared to some individuals and some groups of people in the few weeks between his resurrection and his ascension, he was recognized by these people, in spite of the changes in him that were clearly noticeable. We look in vain in the Bible for any clear affirmation that we will recognize our loved ones in heaven, but the fact that Jesus was recognized in his new "spiritual" body—albeit not always straightaway—may lead us to think that our new "spiritual" bodies will also allow for recognition. Perhaps Paul's statement in 1 Cor 13:12—"Then we shall see face to face. Now I know in part; then I shall know fully, even as I am fully known"—indicates that we shall know each other more profoundly than we do now.

The underlying question is whether our identity can and will survive death. Richard Rice argues that the person who is resurrected will be a previously existing person rather than a new human being.[49] This happens in a preliminary way when I see someone after I have not seen this person for a very long time. The person has changed, but I recognize him not only by aspects of his physical appearance but also by specific personality traits.

When I fall asleep and awake eight hours later, most of my mental activity has been suspended, but I am the same person I was when I dozed off. And it is also important to note that even during this life our identity does not depend on physical continuity, as most cells of our body are regularly renewed. In the hereafter we will return to a new life and live in a new world that radically differs from our present life and

48. Kittel and Friedrich, *Theological Dictionary*, s.vv. "kainos" and "neos."

49. Rice, *Reign of God*, 155–56.

present circumstances, but at the same time is a radical restoration of what we leave behind us when we die. "Heaven" does come. Our ultimate destination is a reality. While we are still here in the present this gives significance to our day-to-day activities.[50] In that limited sense, "heaven" can even now be ours while we continue to faithfully serve God here and enjoy our relationship with him.

Is there nothing more we can say about the new creation than that all the bad things will have disappeared and that it will exceed even the most exquisite things we can imagine today? It seemed that way to the apostle Paul, but that did not cause him any dismay. He expressed his confidence in these few words: "No eye has seen, no ear has heard, and no mind has conceived what God has prepared for those who love him" (1 Cor 2:9–10). And he wrote to the Christians in Rome, "I don't think there's any comparison between the present hard times and the coming good times. The created world itself can hardly wait for what is coming next. Everything in creation is being more or less held back. God reins it in until both creation and all the creatures are ready and can be released at the same moment into the glorious times ahead." And he adds, "Meanwhile, the joyful anticipation deepens" (Rom 8:18–19 MSG).

50. Rice, *Reign of God*, 346.

Chapter 10

The People of God

A KEY PASSAGE IN most, if not all, books and essays on the doctrine of the church is Matt 16:13–20.[1] At a given moment Jesus asked his disciples, "Who do people say the Son of Man is?" After receiving various answers, Jesus repeated the question in a more personal way, and asked, "Who do you say I am?" Peter then answered, "You are the Messiah, the Son of the living God." Jesus responded to Peter's confession with these remarkable words: "Blessed are you, Simon son of Jonah, for this was not revealed to you by flesh and blood, but by my Father in heaven. And I tell you that you are Peter, and on this rock I will build my church, and the gates of Hades will not overcome it. I will give you the keys of the kingdom of heaven; whatever you bind on earth will be bound in heaven, and whatever you loose on earth will be loosed in heaven" (vv. 17–19).

According to Roman Catholic doctrine, this statement by Jesus clearly points to Peter as the first leader of the church and as the "rock" on which the church would be built. Protestants disagree and believe that Peter's confession of Jesus as "the Messiah, the Son of the living God" is the rock on which the church of Christ was to be built. And what Jesus added about the keys of the kingdom and the authority to "bind" and to "loose" did not only apply to Peter, but, according to Matt 18:18, to all disciples.

1. I have written about this topic in greater detail in *The Body of Christ*.

The decisive element in this passage is Jesus's affirmation that he wanted to build a church and that this project would be successful. This must be our point of departure when we look at the doctrine of the church. The church is not a human enterprise, a religious alliance of like-minded individuals, or a club of pious men and women who have decided to join in common spiritual activities. It is a divine initiative—a gift to all who want to be connected with the Lord of the church. Dietrich Bonhoeffer (1906–1945) stated that the church is not just a community of worshippers but is "Christ himself who has taken form among people."[2] In a general audience on May 10, 2006, Pope Benedict XVI expressed the same thought: "The Church is not an association that people have made, but a gift of God, which precedes us, a gift through which we find life."[3]

What Does *Church* Mean?

The term *church*, or its equivalent in other European languages, is employed in a range of different meanings, depending on the context. It is used to indicate all believers in Jesus Christ in all ages, but also for a local community of Christians, who meet in a particular place. The word can also point to the institutional church and to a denomination or tradition. And in everyday language it may simply mean a building for religious use. In several European languages the word for "church" betrays a common Greek root—for instance: *kerk* (Dutch), *Kirche* (German), *kyrka* (Swedish), *kirke* (Danish, Norwegian), *kirkja* (Icelandic). These words are derived from *kuriakē*, which means "the Lord's."[4] Another Greek word—*ekklesia*—is visible in the term for "church" in other European languages—for example, *ecclesia* (Latin), *iglesia* (Spanish), *chiesa* (Italian), *église* (French).

The Greek word *ekklesia* is not only frequently used in the New Testament but is also found in the Septuagint to define Israel as a community. It is composed of two parts: *ek* (out of) and *kalein* (to call).[5] The word is the defining marker for people who are called from the world, called for a task and called to form a community. In the Greek world *ekklesia* was originally a political term for the assembly of the people.

2. Bonhoeffer, *Letters and Papers*, 133.
3. Benedict XIV, "Having a Vision."
4. Etymonline, "Church."
5. Coenen, "Church, Synagogue," 296–307.

But it did not come into the Christian New Testament vocabulary through an adaptation of its Hellenistic meaning, but from the biblical language of the Septuagint.[6]

In the New Testament, "church" always refers to *people*, and never to a building. Church buildings belong to a later era. The earliest Christian communities gathered in the homes of fellow believers (Rom 16:5; 1 Cor 16:19). In many Bible passages the *ekklesia* is the universal church as, for instance, in Paul's letter to the believers in Ephesus. He describes the church as Christ's "body, the fullness of him who fills everything in every way" (1:22). The universality of the church is also emphasized in the beautiful words of Eph 3:20–21: "To him who is able to do immeasurably more than all we ask or imagine, according to his power that is at work within us, to him be glory in the church and in Christ Jesus throughout all generations, for ever and ever!" When Paul refers in 1 Cor 10:32 to "the church of God," it very clearly also has this universal meaning.

However, in many instances the *ekklesia* is the local faith community. In chapters 2 and 3 of the Revelation we find letters that are sent to individual *ekklesiai* in seven cities in Asia Minor. The apostle Paul sends letters to "churches" in Rome, Corinth, Ephesus, Phillippi, Colossae, and Thessaloniki. But he could at times also more specifically use the word for a *gathering* of a group of believers, as, for instance, in 1 Cor 14:18–19.

Biblical Foundations

A large part of the Old Testament is devoted to the history of the *qahal*. In the Hebrew Bible *qahal* is used for the assembled people of Israel, when gathered before God for worship, instruction, or important events.[7] In the Greek Septuagint *qahal* is often translated as *ekklesia*, which subsequently became the New Testament term for "church."

From the earliest strata of salvation history, it is evident that God wanted a relationship with a designated "people." This was the basis for his covenant with Abraham. God promised Abraham that he would be blessed and become a great nation, through which all other nations would be blessed (Gen 12:1–3). Israel was to be God's people, and "all the peoples on earth will see that you are called by the name of the

6. Phan, *Gift of the Church*, 152.

7. Brown, *New International Dictionary* 1:293.

Lord" (Deut 28:9–10). Acts 7:38 refers to the *ekklesia* in the desert. The King James Version translates it as "the church in the desert" and the New King James Version as "the congregation in the wilderness." The New International Version of Lev 16:17 mentions "the whole community of Israel." Isaiah 56:6–7 underlines how Israel's mission included leading "the foreigner" to the Lord. The sacrifices of these people who were not part of Israel were nonetheless acceptable on God's altar, and the temple, the prophet adds, "will be called a house of prayer for all nations" (Isa 56:6–7).

Several images that are used in the Old Testament for God's church return in the New Testament writings—for instance, the marriage union, the father-son relationship, the vineyard, and the symbol of the shepherd and the flock.[8]

The church was founded by Jesus Christ but has roots that go back to the people of Israel. When describing the people who are going to be saved, John the Revelator used the symbolic number of the 144,000 who came "from all the tribes of Israel" (Rev 7:4–8). The continuity between the Old and the New Testament people of God is also strikingly illustrated in the symbolic description of the New Jerusalem, which will be the eternal abode of the saints. The city has a great, high wall with twelve gates. On the gates are written the names of *the twelve tribes of Israel.* The wall of the city has twelve foundation stones, with the names of *the twelve apostles* of the Lamb written on them (Rev 21:11–14).

The twelve apostles were the core group who, at the command of their Lord, started the *missio Dei.*[9] Jesus had called the twelve "that they might be with him, and that he might send them out to preach" (Mark 3:14). Luke says that Jesus designated them as "apostles" (Luke 6:13). Ellen G. White comments, "With the calling of John and Andrew and Simon, of Philip and Nathanael, began the foundation of the Christian church."[10] In preparation of their future work they received thorough training from their Master (Mark 6:7–12; Matt 9:35—10:38). Judas was later replaced by Matthias (Acts 1:15–26). Others, also referred to as "apostles," were added to this core group (Acts 14:14; Gal 1:19; Rom 16:7), with the apostle Paul acquiring a special place among them (see

8. Jacob, *Theology of the Old Testament*, 201–3.

9. This Latin theological term, which can be translated as the "mission of God" or the "sending of God," is often used for the missionary task of the church.

10. White, *Desire of Ages*, 141.

1 Cor 9:1–3). A larger group than just the twelve were with Jesus as his followers. Among them were the seventy-two[11] disciples whose mission experience is described in Luke 10:1–24, and a group of women, some of whom are specifically named: "Mary (called Magdalene) from whom seven demons had come out; Joanna, the wife of Chuza, the manager of Herod's household; Susanna, and many others (Luke 8:1–3; see also Mark 15:40–41).

Jesus made it clear that he wanted his followers to continue his work after his death and gave them what is known as the Great Commission—the raison d'être of the church: "Go and make disciples of all nations, baptizing them in the name of the Father and of the Son and of the Holy Spirit, and teaching them to obey everything I have commanded you" (Matt 28:19–20).

Immediately after the ascension a community of Christ-believers gathered in Jerusalem, with the apostles as the key figures (Acts 1:12–26), while the temple and the synagogues also remained important meeting places for them (Acts 2:45). Believing that Christ would very soon come back again, they "sold property and possession" to help the poor, and they shared what they had with all members of the community (Acts 2:44; 4:32–35).

Once the church got off to a start, it grew exponentially. At Pentecost "about three thousand were added to their number" (Acts 2:41), and "the Lord added to their number daily those who were being saved" (Acts 2:47). It should be noted that, from the beginning, the church was diverse in its composition (Acts 6:6). The execution of Stephen ignited "a great persecution" of the believers in Jerusalem, with the result that "all, except the apostles, were scattered throughout Judea and Samaria" (Acts 8:1). From that point onward the account of the "acts of the apostles" focuses on the missionary endeavors of Philip in Samaria, the emergence of a church in Damascus, Peter's mission in Caesarea, and, from chapter 13 onward, on the missionary journeys of Paul and his associates.

The status of the original apostles, together with Paul, remained unique, but besides other "apostles" soon also "deacons" (Acts 6:1–7)

11. Some manuscripts mention seventy rather than seventy-two disciples. Jesus may have chosen this number to represent the nations of the Jewish tradition (sometimes counted as seventy, but also sometimes as seventy-two), pointing symbolically to the mission to the Gentiles. See also the seventy elders with the prophetic gift of Num 11:24–25, plus Eldad and Medad (Num 11:26). See Keener, *IVP Bible Background Commentary*, 215–16.

were playing an important role. The emergence of elders (presbyters) or bishops (*episkopoi*) is clearly attested in the book of Acts and in the Pauline letters (Acts 11:29–30; 20:17, 28). In the letters of Paul to Timothy and Titus the spiritual and other qualities of these local church leaders are specified (1 Tim 3:2–7; Titus 1:5–9; see also 1 Pet 5:1–3; Jas 5:14–15; Acts 14:23; 15:1–2, 4, 6).

Metaphors and Models

According to the *Cambridge Dictionary* a metaphor is "an expression, often found in literature, that describes a person or object by referring to something that is considered to have similar characteristics to that person or object."[12] The New Testament attempts to catch aspects of the essence of the church in a broad number of metaphors. In his book *Images of the Church in the New Testament* the Catholic theologian Paul S. Minear (1906–2007) enumerates no less than ninety-six different metaphors for the church. It is important not to play any of the metaphors off to some others, but to allow them to give, together, a picture of the church.

One of the most prominent metaphors to characterize the church is that of the body. This powerful image points to unity in diversity; to being a community of members who depend on each other and support each other, with Christ as its head. A body must be alive and grow. Paul expresses this in these words: "Now you are the body of Christ, and each one of you is a part of it" (1 Cor 12:27) and "He [Christ] is the head of the body" (Col 1:18). The ultimate consequence of the body metaphor is speaking of the church as the bride of Christ.[13] It builds on Old Testament images of God's people as the bride of Yahweh, in her loyalty as well as her unfaithfulness (e.g., Hosea; Isa 54:5–7). Significantly, the New Jerusalem is also referred to as the bride of Christ (Rev 21:2, 9–10).

The church is also compared to a temple "built on the foundation of the apostles and prophets, with Christ Jesus himself as the chief cornerstone. In him the whole building is joined together and rises to become a holy temple in the Lord. And in him you too are being built together to become a dwelling in which God lives by his Spirit" (Eph 2:20–22; see also Rev 21:3). And the church is being described as "the people of God" (1 Pet 2:9; see also Exod 19:5–6), who, as "saints," have

12. *Cambridge Dictionary*, s.v. "Metaphor."

13. Richardson, *Introduction*, 257.

been "bought" and "redeemed" by the blood of the Lamb. The leaders of the church in Ephesus are admonished to "be shepherds of the church of God, which he bought with his own blood" (Acts 20:28). Among the many other metaphors are the images of the church as a family of brothers and sisters (Heb 2:11), as a pillar (1 Tim 3:15), or as an army (2 Cor 10:3–5), with appropriate weaponry (Eph 6:10–18).

Another approach to clarify the essence of the church has been to identify a few characteristic models of church life. The name of Avery Dulles (1918–2008), a Catholic convert who became a theologian and was appointed cardinal in 2001, is especially connected with this approach. His book *Models of the Church* is deeply steeped in Catholic tradition, but Protestants will also find many noteworthy elements in this important study. At the beginning of his survey of different models, he mentions this important caveat: "Images are useful up to a point, and beyond that point they can become deceptive." For instance, when the church is called the "flock of Christ," we are reminded that the believers must follow their Master, "but it does not follow that the members of the church grow wool."[14] Dulles points to five "models" for understanding the essence of the church: an institution, a mystical community, a sacrament, a herald, and a servant. The last two models are most appealing to Protestants. The herald model focuses on the mission of the church, but it does not always sufficiently stress the incarnational nature of the church and the moral action that must accompany its words.[15] The servant model is inspired by the one who came to serve us (Mark 10:45), but is perhaps the most difficult one to put into practice.

The "Marks" of the Church

In the Nicene Creed four attributes are listed that characterize the Christian church: unity, holiness, catholicity, and apostolicity. These are usually referred to as the *notae* (Latin) or "marks" of the universal church, but in the historic creeds and confessions (and in more recent theological statements) they are also applied to the local congregations of Christians. In a document of the World Council of Churches it is stated, "The Church is called to be one, holy, catholic and apostolic in each place and in all

14. Dulles, *Models of the Church*, 15.

15. Bruinsma, *Body of Christ*, 174.

places."[16] Provided the term *catholic* is understood in its original sense, Adventists are in full accord with this view of the church.

Unity is not an automatism, but a goal the church must work and pray for, in the footsteps of the Lord, who prayed for its unity (John 17). As we saw, several New Testament metaphors emphasize the church's unity. One of them is the image of the vine and the branches, which refers to Christ's intense desire of unity between himself and his followers (John 15:1–17). In all human diversity the church has the challenge to be one body, "whether Jews or Gentiles, slave or free—and we were all given the one Spirit to drink" (1 Cor 12:12–13). Reaching this unity is a steady process towards a lofty goal: "Make every effort to keep the unity of the Spirit through the bond of peace. There is one body and one Spirit, just as you were called to one hope when you were called; one Lord, one faith, one baptism; one God and Father of all, who is over all and through all and in all" (Eph 4:4–6).

Although the church members are far from perfect, the church may call itself *holy*, as long as this demonstrates its awareness of being set apart. Holiness is not primarily a matter of moral distinction, but rather of being assigned to a particular purpose. It, first of all, has to do with the church's mission. God's people constitute "a holy nation" that has been assigned "to declare the praises of him who called you out of darkness into his wonderful light" (1 Pet 2:9). However, this holiness certainly also includes ethical awareness and sanctification.

The *catholicity* mark is not exclusively linked to the Roman Church. The term is the English rendering of the Greek word *katholikos*, which means "according to the whole" or "universal."[17] It underscores the multiracial, multicultural, and multiethnic reality of the church, comprising all social layers of society (Eph 2:14–16), and present in the entire world (Rev 14:6; Matt 28:19).

The fourth mark, *apostolic*, emphasizes the historic roots of the church. It does not necessarily point to apostolic succession (that is, to an uninterrupted line of apostolic authority), but it stresses the bond with the apostolic origin and mission of the church, and the foundation the apostles laid and on which later generations, until today, have been able to build.

16. World Council of Churches, *Church*, paras. 23, 29.

17. Wikipedia, "*Catholic* (Term)," para. 1.

Ecclesiology Through the Centuries

Before we move on to the ecclesiological self-understanding of the Seventh-day Adventist Church, it is important to say a few words about the development of the doctrine of the church throughout church history.[18] Ecclesiology (the doctrine of the church) did not figure very prominently in doctrinal discussions in early Adventism. This mirrored what happened in the history of Christianity in general: in the early centuries the developing church had other theological priorities.

Documents from the first two centuries, from the apostolic fathers[19] and the apologists,[20] provide us with only a sketchy picture of the earliest developments of church organization, with the appointment of deacons and elders (*presbyteroi*), who were soon referred to as bishops (*episkopoi*). Having one bishop in a local church became a common arrangement, with bishops in some prominent cities—Rome in particular—emerging as more important than others.

The rise of heretical movements made it necessary to establish criteria by which the true church could be known. Among these heretical, schismatic movements Montanism[21] (middle second century), Novatianism[22] (middle third century), and Donatism[23] (beginning fourth century) were the most important. A returning issue were the conditions for readmission of people who had turned away from the church and subsequently wanted to return. Another question that needed a solution was the validity of sacraments that were administered by apostate priests.

18. For a useful survey of the history of the doctrine of the church, see Berkhof, *History of Christian Doctrines*, 227–41; also Bruinsma, *Body of Christ*, 123–42.

19. The apostolic fathers were Christian theologians who lived in the first and second centuries AD. They are believed to have personally known some of the twelve apostles or to have been significantly influenced by them.

20. The apologists were a group of early Christian writers (ca. AD 120–ca. 220) who defended their beliefs against contemporary critics and recommended their faith to outsiders. In addition to Origen and Tertullian, the apologists include Justin Martyr, Clement of Alexandria, and the author of the Epistle to Diognetus.

21. Montanism was an early Christian movement around Montanus. He was active with his ecstatic preaching in ca. AD 156 in Asia Minor, together with two prophetesses, Priscilla and Maximilla.

22. Novatianism was an early Christian sect, named after Novatian (ca. 200–ca. 258), that refused the readmission to communion of those who had lapsed in their faith during the persecutions under Emperor Decius in AD 250.

23. Donatism was a heretic schism that claimed that the validity of the sacraments depends on the moral character of the minister; also that sinners cannot be members of the church, nor can they be tolerated by the true church, if their sins are publicly known.

An important voice in the ecclesiological debate was that of Cyprian (bishop of Carthage from 248 to 258). One particular statement of his would prove to be extremely influential: "He can no longer have God for his Father, who has not the Church for his mother. . . . Outside the Church there is no salvation (*extra ecclesiam nulla salus*)."[24] While some of the church fathers stressed the need for purity in the church, Augustine (bishop of the North African city of Hippo, 395–430) believed that the church will always be a mix of sinners, who are at various stages in their spiritual growth. He viewed the visible church as the institution where salvation was mediated through the sacraments, especially through baptism and the Eucharist. In the medieval period, the church became increasingly institutionalized, with growing emphasis on papal authority, canon law, and sacramental hierarchy. The church was seen as the *mater et magistra* (mother and teacher) of all Christians.

The doctrine of the church underwent significant developments during the Reformation era.[25] Martin Luther defined the church primarily as the place where the word of God is preached correctly, and where the sacraments are administered rightly. John Calvin built on this, but he added a more detailed ecclesiological structure with more emphasis on church discipline. He defended a more visible and ordered church, governed by a plurality of elders, and rooted in divine election. In many European countries the dominant Protestant churches developed into state churches, with membership based on infant baptism.

Anabaptism (also known as the "Radical" Reformation) radically diverged from Lutheran and Calvinistic ecclesiology. The Anabaptists rejected infant baptism. For them the true church was a community based on believer's baptism, mutual accountability, and a strict ethic of discipleship.

Overall, Protestants continued to emphasize the primacy of Scripture and spiritual fellowship, while Roman Catholics emphasized sacramental continuity and institutional authority. The First Vatican Council (1871) declared the pope infallible when speaking *ex cathedra* about official doctrine. The Second Vatican Council (1962–1965) made progress in the recognition of other denominations as part of the Church of Christ. The council emphasized the status of the church as the *People of God*, God's household or family.

24. Cyprian, *Unity*, 99. See also McGrath, *Historical Theology*, 72–74.

25. For a good overview see Jankiewicz, "Sixteenth Century Protestant Reformation," 191–217.

Adventist Ecclesiology

Seventh-day Adventists borrowed many aspects of their views concerning the doctrine of the church from the Magisterial Reformers and from the Anabaptist tradition.[26] Adventist historical theologian Darius Jankiewicz comments, "The early [Adventist] pioneers tended to be eclectic and pragmatic, drawing from the variety of Christian traditions," while ensuring that these elements were grounded in Scripture.[27] In many ways their views reflected the basics of the ecclesiology of Lutheranism, and especially of Calvinism, but they were also strongly influenced by the Anabaptist concept of the church as a community of "believers," who voluntarily join the church when they are baptized upon the confession of their faith.

Though initially opposed to any form of organization, the Sabbatarian Adventists soon concluded that some organizational arrangement at the local level was inevitable, and after a short time they also saw that a broader organizational structure was needed if the new movement was to be effective in its mission. With regard to the status and role of the gospel ministry and the governance of the local church, Calvinistic influences dominated, but in the early development of umbrella organizations (conferences and a General Conference), the Methodist model was mainly followed. In spite of its constant heavy criticism of Roman Catholicism, over time a multilayered denominational governance model was adopted that in its hierarchical nature in several respects resembles that of the Catholic Church.

The Seventh-day Adventist Church does not believe that its members are the only Christians who will be saved. But the Adventist attitude towards other Christians has contradictory elements, which are not easily reconciled. On the one hand, for over a century the Adventist church has included this remarkably ecumenical statement in its policy book: "We recognize those agencies that lift up Christ before men as a part of the divine plan for the evangelization of the world, and *we hold in high esteem Christian men and women in other communions who are engaged in winning souls to*

26. George R. Knight wrote a very accessible history of the development of the Adventist Church structure: *Organizing for Mission and Growth*. See also Timm, "Seventh-day Adventist Ecclesiology," 219–42.

27. Jankiewicz, "Sixteenth Century Protestant Reformation," 217.

Christ."[28] In an official statement published by the General Conference of Seventh-day Adventists in 1997, this same sentiment is expressed: "Seventh-day Adventists regard all men and women as equal in the sight of God. We reject bigotry against any person, regardless of race, nationality, or religious creed. Further, *we gladly acknowledge that sincere Christians may be found in other denominations, including Roman Catholicism*, and we work in concert with all agencies and bodies that seek to relieve human suffering and to uplift Christ before the world."[29]

Although the Adventist Church has been reluctant to become a member of ecumenical bodies—except in a few countries where Adventists have decided to join a national council of churches or a similar organization—the church has held consultations with a number of other denominations,[30] and leaders have been known to attend important ecumenical gatherings as observers. From early on, Adventist authors have been inspired by books of other Christian authors. Ellen White (while extremely critical of the Roman Catholic Church and other Christian bodies in her book *The Great Controversy*) leaned in her writing heavily on other Christian authors. She also went repeatedly on record to admonish pastors and church members to show appreciation and respect for the adherents of other churches, including Roman Catholics.[31]

There is, however, another side to the picture. In the Adventist prophetic interpretation other denominations were mostly viewed as apostate. "Babylon" became the catchword for Roman Catholicism and "apostate" Protestantism, and its progressive "fall" was predicted to spell great trouble for the "remnant" which kept God's commandments and treasured "the spirit of prophecy." The Adventist believers self-identified as this loyal end-time remnant and have often manifested a significant measure of hostility towards other Christians.

Adventists have traditionally regarded their church as the "true" church, which has the "truth" for these last days of earth's history. In line with this conviction is the last part of the baptismal vow to which prospective members are expected to reply in the affirmative: "Do you accept and believe that the Seventh-day Adventist Church is the remnant church of Bible prophecy and that people of every nation, race, and language are

28. General Conference, *Working Policy*, O 100; italics added. For the origin of this statement, see Höschele, "From Mission Comity."

29. Dabrowski, *Statements, Guidelines*, 90–91; italics added.

30. Höschele, *Adventist Interchurch Relations*, 341–97.

31. For examples see Bruinsma, *Adventists and Catholics*, 150–55.

invited and accepted into its fellowship? Do you desire to be a member of this local congregation of the world Church?"[32] This statement includes "every nation, race and language" but, regrettably, omits a reference to "every gender." Besides this painful omission, it also does not make any attempt to define the relationship between the "remnant church" and Christendom at large. Can only Adventist believers belong to God's remnant church?[33] And what about the concept of the invisible church of all ages, the membership of which is only known to God?

Claiming to "have the truth" is not only rather arrogant, but perhaps even blasphemous. No human being can claim to possess the full truth about God—about who he is and what he does. Not all denominations may be equally observant with regard to biblical principles and instructions. Some do better than others, but none can claim to have "the truth." The very fact that the Adventist Church also defines itself as a "denomination" (from the Latin *nominare*: to name) indicates that it recognizes itself as a particular segment of Christendom. In other words, God's church is larger than the Adventist denomination, or any other denomination for that matter. This, however, does not mean that the Adventist Church is just one voice among a plethora of other Christian voices and has no special calling. Adventism holds many theological convictions in common with other Christians, but it enriches the Christian testimony by its emphasis on a number of "special truths," which we have discussed in previous chapters—the Sabbath, events connected with the second coming of Christ, the holistic view of man with its implications for man's state in death, and the strong emphasis on a range of stewardship responsibilities.

The expression *Three Angels' Messages* (referring to Rev 14:6–12) remains a familiar term in Adventist discourse. It is, however, increasingly evident that many church members possess only a limited or superficial understanding of its meaning. This calls for a renewed and contextually relevant interpretation that resonates with contemporary believers and engages both mind and conscience.

Such an interpretation may be structured around three core elements:

32. General Conference, *Seventh-day Adventist Church Manual*, 52.

33. For various interpretations of the remnant concept in current Adventism, see Hasel, "Remnant," 159–80.

a. The first angel's message reaffirms the centrality of divine worship, emphasizing God as Creator, Sustainer, and Sovereign over all reality—a foundational truth with profound implications for the entire doctrinal and ethical tradition of Adventism. It shifts the emphasis from peripheral matters to what really counts.

b. The second message underlines a prophetic critique of prevailing cultural and moral decline, protesting against the growing disregard for biblical principles and ethical norms in both societal and religious contexts.

c. The third message presents a decisive call to full accountability, urging all of us to make an existential choice regarding allegiance, lifestyle, and ultimate loyalty, as we engage our heart, mind, and entire being in discipleship.

The Church as Community

In 2002 Richard Rice, whose book *The Reign of God* has been cited several times in previous chapters, published another important book: *Believing, Behaving, Belonging: Finding New Love for the Church.* It points to a dramatic shift in the trajectory of new members into faith communities in the Western world. Even until a few decades ago people who considered joining a new congregation or another denomination went through a phase of studying the particular beliefs of that community and *then* began to wonder whether this church could provide them with a new spiritual home. In other words: *believing came before belonging.* Rice argues that nowadays the process has been mostly reversed: *belonging now tends to precede believing.* People who are searching for a new spiritual roof over their heads wonder whether the community they have come into contact with is indeed a place where they can truly belong—where they feel accepted and find the space to be themselves—before unduly worrying about doctrinal fine print. It means that the aspect of the church as a community is more important than ever, and this it has a tremendous impact on strategies for church growth.

There is a range of different communities: *geographic* communities, such as our neighborhood, suburb, village, or town; but also cultural, biological, and virtual communities. In this present context we are concerned with *faith* communities. Based on various dictionary definitions, a faith community may be described as a group of people who share the same particular set of religious beliefs, and are joined together by particular forms of worship, usually gathering in a specific place of worship. It could be said that this is also the definition of church, but the concept of *community* stresses a particularly important aspect of being church; it relates to a process of showing deep respect and of true listening, in order to discover the needs of people in and around the faith community.

The apostolic church in Jerusalem, as described in Acts 2:42–47, was a genuine community, in which the emphasis was not primarily on establishing a well-oiled organization, or on defining doctrines in ever greater detail, but on *people*. In a true community the key factor for church growth is faith that is *lived* and that will thereby attract and inspire others. This community aspect has implications for the entire denominational structure, but first of all for the local church. Dietrich Bonhoeffer strongly emphasized the visible and tangible aspect of the community of believers: "Christian community means community through and in Jesus Christ. . . . Whether it be a brief, single encounter or the daily fellowship of years, Christian community is only this. We belong to one another only through and in Jesus Christ."[34] Communal prayer, confession, and table fellowship are the concrete expressions of this community.

The experience of community is intensely relational and incarnational, says Jean Vanier, the founder of the L'Arche communities, who grounded his theology in the experience of living with people with disabilities. He remarked, "Community is a place of pain, of the death of ego, of difficulty in relationships. But it is also a place of joy, of growth, of celebration and of peace."[35] For John Howard Yoder, a well-known Mennonite theologian, the essence of the church is not in its rituals but in how, as a community, Christians are concretely living out the gospel: "The church's social ethic is enacted in the small, participatory practices through which Christians live their life together in faithfulness to Jesus."[36]

The Table of the Lord

Eating together is a communal activity par excellence, and nothing is a more deeply communal experience for Christian believers than participating in the Lord's Supper. In the Catholic, Orthodox, and Anglican

34. Bonhoeffer, *Life Together*, 21.

35. Vanier, *Community and Growth*, 32.

36. Yoder, *Body Politics*, 22.

traditions the Eucharist is celebrated on a much more frequent basis than the communion service is held in most Protestant traditions. Early Adventists decided to follow the Methodist practice of celebrating the Lord's Supper once every quarter. This was seen as maintaining a good balance between frequency and solemnity. The Adventist theology of the communion service mostly resembles that of the Swiss reformer Huldrych Zwingli (1484–1531), rather than the views of Luther or Calvin. The elements of bread and wine (in Adventist churches typically unfermented grape juice) are not transformed into any other substance but are *symbols* representing Christ's body and blood. When Jesus instituted the Communion service and said, "This is my body" and "This is my blood," the word *is* clearly meant "represents." We may thus conclude with Adventist theologian Raoul Dederen (1925–2016), "Christ's body and blood are no more present today in the elements of bread and wine than they were when the Lord instituted the ordinance."[37]

Adventists have usually preferred to stay away from the terms *Eucharist* and *sacrament* as sounding too Catholic. They refer to the communion as an *ordinance*. It was instituted by Jesus at the end of the Passover meal, just before his death, as a practice to be regularly observed by his followers (Matt 26:26–30; Mark 14:22–26; Luke 22:17–22; 1 Cor 11:23–26). It was to serve as a remembrance of Jesus's sacrificial death, but also in anticipation of his return in glory. "For whenever you eat this bread and drink this cup, you proclaim the Lord's death until he comes" (1 Cor 11:26).

Since Jesus allowed even the disciple who would betray him to participate in the Last Supper, Adventists practice an "open" communion service. Paul recommends a self-examination before participation in the communion service (1 Cor 11:27–28), but people should be encouraged to take part as a vivid reminder that Jesus did indeed also gave his life to redeem *them*. Often people have been too fearful to participate, afraid that they might eat and drink in "an unworthy manner" that would "result in judgment" (vv. 28–32).

Adventists and a few other Christian communities have connected the rite of foot washing with the communion service. The Gospel of John is the only Gospel to refer to the example Christ gave, and to cite Jesus's promise that a blessing rests upon following it (John 13:1–17). In all probability early Adventists inherited the practice of foot washing, as

37. Dederen, "Church," 558.

a preparation for the Lord's Supper, from the Christian Connection, a group with Anabaptist roots to which some Adventist pioneers had belonged.[38] Many in the Adventist Church still consider this practice as an integral part of the communion service that has continued meaning.[39] Whether it should be considered obligatory that all who want to participate in the Lord's Supper first also take part in the foot washing is another matter. The fact that the Synoptics and Paul do not even mention it does not seem to point in that direction.

Becoming a Church Member

Baptism is the rite by which a person becomes a member of the church of Christ. A ritual that involves the administration of water is not unique to Christendom. Other religions, as for instance Hinduism and Judaism, have also practiced ritual washings. The New Testament baptism for the remission of sins that was practiced by John the Baptist, and which developed into the Christian baptism in the name of the Father, the Son, and the Spirit, has clear antecedents in Jewish ritual washings.[40]

In the New Testament men and women who joined the church were baptized by immersion. Baptismal rites have varied through the ages and still do. It has sometimes been by triple immersion. The one baptizing could be inside or outside the baptismal pool. Often the baptism of infants or older persons is by sprinkling or by pouring a small quantity of water over the person's head, while in Orthodox Christianity infants are baptized by triple immersion. Seventh-day Adventists and many other Protestant traditions since Reformation times have baptized people by immersion upon the confession of their faith.[41]

The Greek verb *baptizoo*, which is most commonly used in the New Testament when describing the act of baptizing, does not have the meaning of "sprinkling" or "pouring" but of "dipping in."[42] All New Testament evidence points to immersion, after a person's conscious choice, as the original mode of baptism. Archeologists also have found

38. Bruinsma, "Origin of Foot Washing."
39. Bruinsma, "Foot Washing."
40. Dockey, "Baptism," 55–58.
41. Cross, *Oxford Dictionary*, 125–29.
42. Beasley-Murray, "Baptism."

evidence for the practice of baptism by immersion in the ruins of the oldest church buildings.

It appears that infant baptism began to emerge already in the third century.[43] Origen (ca. 185–ca. 254) was most likely the first church father to advocate infant baptism. Through the influence of Augustine (354–430) infant baptism soon spread around Christendom. It was linked to the belief in original sin, while, as time went by (especially in the days of Calvin) infant baptism was viewed as a counterpart of Old Testament circumcision, as an outward sign of being included in the covenant.

The biblical evidence points to the following main aspects of baptism:

1. John the Baptist practiced baptism by immersion, as is evidenced by the fact that he baptized at a location where "there was plenty of water" (John 3:23).
2. Jesus gave the people an example by going to John the Baptist to be baptized (Matt 3:13–17). After his baptism Jesus "came up out of the water" (v. 16).
3. The Ethiopian eunuch was baptized by immersion: "He went down into the water and Philip baptized him" (Acts 8:38).
4. The words of Jesus to Nicodemus emphasized the importance of baptism: "Very truly I tell you, no one can enter the kingdom of God unless they are born of water and the Spirit" (John 3:5).
5. Baptism must be preceded by faith (Acts 8:13; 10:33) and by repentance (Acts 2:38).
6. Christian baptism is in the name of the triune God (Matt 28:19).
7. Baptism is a sign of sharing in the death and resurrection of Jesus Christ by symbolically dying to one's former life and beginning a new life through the grace of God (Rom 6:1–7).
8. Baptism marks the entrance into the Christian community: "We are all baptized by one Spirit so as to form one body" (1 Cor 12:13).

Adventists have long defended their position that being baptized in an Adventist setting also implies becoming a member of the Adventist denomination. Their standpoint is not unique; in many Christian traditions baptism is tied to membership in a local congregation or a specific

43. Brown, *Baptism Through the Centuries*, 23–30.

denomination, but perhaps Adventists are more explicit and structured about it. When someone asks for baptism but refuses to accept this as an entrance into the Adventist Church, the persons will usually be advised to ask for baptism elsewhere. The Scriptures do point to the intimate connection between baptism and becoming a member of the body of Christ, but that cannot automatically lead to the assumption that the "body" must be understood as a specific Christian tradition. Various commentators on 1 Cor 12:13 stress the context of this verse and argue that new believers become part of a body that in all its diversity is a unity. Everett Ferguson (b. 1933), who before his retirement taught Biblical Studies at the Abilene Christian University in Texas, concludes, "Baptism places one in the church. . . . This again is God's doing, to incorporate a person in the body of Christ. Baptism is not just an individual transaction. It is not just an act of personal salvation. It is a community or social act. One is now made a part of God's people. The Spirit places the person in the one body. Having the one Spirit is the means of sharing in the one body."[44]

The Adventist Church does, under certain circumstances, accept people into church membership upon their "confession of faith" but, unless there are exceptional situations, these persons must have been baptized earlier by what the church considers a biblical mode of baptism. Officially, new members must, at the time of their baptism, or when they are admitted upon the profession of their faith, know and accept the twenty-eight fundamental beliefs of the church. Theory and actual practice are at considerable distance. Most baptismal candidates only have a limited knowledge of the content of these so-called fundamental beliefs, even when they respond with a clear "yes" to all baptismal questions. Often, the duration and intensity of the catechetical instructions (especially in the context of short public evangelistic campaigns) do not allow for a thorough study of all Adventist doctrines. And for many, the Adventist doctrinal system is simply too complex to fully comprehend. Most of those asking for baptism do get baptized, without too much scrutiny of what they know about the church's teachings. Problems do arise, however, when baptismal candidates indicate that they do not agree with some of the twenty-eight beliefs. In such cases baptism may be refused. This is an issue that needs urgent attention from the denomination's theologians and leaders. It makes sense to expect from new members of a denomination

44. Ferguson, *Church of Christ*, 191–92.

that they are comfortable with its main tenets, but the question remains into what detail their beliefs must be prescribed.

The Ministries of the Church

Reference was already made to the eclectic way in which the Seventh-day Adventist Church developed its organization. It is, however, important to return to an underlying principle that Adventists share with Protestants in general—namely, that Christ is the head of his church, and that no other authority shares in his unique position: "For there is one God, and one mediator between God and mankind, the man Christ Jesus" (1 Tim 2:5). Coupled with this fundamental truth, there is another foundational principle—namely, that all members of the church as Christ's body have the same status. This notion is usually referred to as the priesthood of all believers. First Peter 2:9 expresses this in the following words (italics added in the following verses): "But you are a chosen people, *a royal priesthood*, a holy nation, God's special possession." John the Revelator echoed the same sentiment, when he said that the believers in Asia Minor, whom he addressed in this passage, have been made "to be a kingdom and *priests*" (Rev 1:6), a thought that is repeated in 5:10: "You have made them to be a kingdom and *priests* to serve our God."

The Roman Catholic theologian Richard R. Gaillardetz (1958–2023) made the following incisive comment: "The substance of this common priesthood is the life of discipleship, following Christ in such a way that one's entire life becomes an offering to God. This suggests that ordinary believers engage in priestly ministry whenever they seek to cooperate with God's grace in transforming their lives and the world around them in accord with the ethos of God's reign in the teaching and ministry of Jesus."[45]

The basic premise of the priesthood of *all* believers is that there is no qualitative difference between clergy and "ordinary" members. Some of the members may have a special calling—to be pastors, elders, deacons, or to fulfill some other specific role—but all have the same status before God.

45. Gaillardetz, *Ecclesiology*, 189.

This is an important principle to always keep in mind when discussing the role of the clergy and the issues surrounding ordination.[46] A majority of Adventist theologians have concluded that there is no theological reason to object to the ordination of female pastors.[47] However, for two reasons the dilemma whether or not to ordain female clergy should, in fact, be a nonissue. The principle of the priesthood of all believers does not allow for any discrimination between women and men. They are, regardless of their gender, priests in God's kingdom. Moreover, this is also crystal clear in the words of Paul to the Galatians: in Christ "there is neither Jew nor Gentile, neither slave nor free, nor is there male or female, for you are all one in Christ Jesus" (3:28). This principle is embedded in number fourteen of the fundamental beliefs: "In Christ we are a new creation; distinctions of race, culture, learning, and nationality, and differences between high and low, rich and poor, *male and female*" are totally unscriptural.[48]

The second reason is that the ordination of clergy, male or female, is not a biblically mandated rite. Bertil Wiklander, an Old Testament scholar and long-time church administrator, concludes in his profound study of ordination, "No biblical text commands or illustrates ordination as it is practiced in the Seventh-day Adventist Church today, and this applies whether or not one reads the [biblical] text literally. No *male* disciple, servant-minister, or apostle was ordained, and the imposition of hands for ordination was not conducted for any of the church offices existing in the church today, such as gospel ministers, the local church elder, or the deacon-deaconess."[49]

The Mission of the Church

Our discussion about the mission of the church must begin with a fundamental question: Should the church's mission focus be horizontal or vertical? In other words, should the church be only concerned with spiritual matters or also with social projects and the well being of society? The answer is it is definitely not a matter of either-or, but

46. For a survey of the discussion in recent decades of the acceptance of female clergy in the Adventist Church, see Valentine, *Struggle for Gender Equality*.

47. General Conference, *Theology of Ordination Study Committee*.

48. General Conference, "What Do Adventists Believe?," no. 14; italics added.

49. Wiklander, *Ordination Reconsidered*, 291.

of both-and. Christians—also Seventh-day Adventist Christians—need to stand for compassion and justice in the world. Followers of Christ cannot ignore issues such as refugee care, human rights, war and peace, fair trade, a just distribution of wealth between rich and poor, climate change, energy transition, et cetera. The choice is not between distributing the water of life and drilling wells in the Sahel. Both aspects are vital parts of the church's mission,

In the late nineteenth and early twentieth centuries, the United States and Canada were the scene of a powerful movement in Protestant Christianity: the Social Gospel movement, which emphasized the importance of applying Christian ethics to the many social problems in the world. Walter Rauschenbusch (1861–1918), one of the key leaders of this movement, was very clear about the core message of this movement: "The Kingdom of God is not a matter of getting individuals to heaven, but of transforming the life on earth into the harmony of heaven. It is not a rescue operation for a few, but the salvation of the human world in all its relationships."[50]

Many conservative Christians criticized the Social Gospel movement for being too liberal, since it seemed to focus more on social reform than on personal salvation and spiritual matters. They accused it of downplaying such essential doctrines as sin, repentance, and the need for Christ's atonement, replacing them with a this-worldly activism that resembled secular progressive movements. Until recent decades many evangelicals were reluctant to get involved in organizations and projects of developmental work and humanitarian assistance, believing that this would draw their attention away from their "soul-saving" work of preaching the gospel. It took Seventh-day Adventists also considerable time before starting such initiatives as SAWS (Seventh-day Adventist Welfare Service; 1956) and its successor ADRA (Adventist Development and Relief Agency; 1984).

The criticism directed at the Social Gospel movement was to some extent justified. There must be a balance between the horizontal and the vertical aspects of the missional activities of the church. As it follows the example of Christ, the church must make sure it has a clear message for today's world, but it must also remember that Christ "went around doing good" (Acts 10:38).

50. Rauschenbusch, *Theology*, 65.

The church is not only a *herald* of good tidings (Isa 52:7) but must also stand in the biblical *prophetic* tradition. For many people, the word *prophet* has "predictor of the future" as its primary meaning. Yet, foretelling the future is not the first and most important assignment of a prophet. A prophet is a person who speaks on behalf of someone else (Exod 7:1). In biblical times, prophets were men and women who, before anything else, announced God's displeasure when Israel did not follow divine directives, or when other nations had aroused God's displeasure. They criticized nations, peoples, and events at God's bidding, and urged sweeping reforms.

Christians have a prophetic role in society. They must be future-oriented and should place great value on the biblical picture of the future. Their vision of the future is a mixture of pessimism and optimism, of despair and hope. They see many things in the world that they disapprove of. They observe all kinds of negative developments, but they believe that in the end things will work out. The kingdom of God will finally become a reality. This world with all its violence, injustice, and immorality will eventually be replaced by a new world of peace, justice, and goodness. One belief Adventists have in common with almost all Christians is that Jesus Christ will return to this earth and that this will bring the final revolution for good.

But there is much more than this *future*-oriented aspect. Adventist Christians especially have a prophetic role regarding the *present*. It is important for them that, based on careful reflection, they praise the good they see and commend the positive developments they observe. Fortunately, not everything in society is deteriorating. There still is also much good in the world, and in many areas improvements can be seen. Adventists lose credibility if they consistently place themselves in the category of doomsayers. But while they should be happy and thankful for good developments, they must also dare to clearly name what is wrong in our society and reject trends and opinions, if there are valid reasons for doing so. They must find ways to take part in the public debate about matters of principle and ethics. Their intention must not be to impose their will on others. As a matter of fact, in most cases this will not work anyway. Participating in a debate—also in the public debate in society—presupposes a willingness to listen carefully to others and, if necessary, to adjust or radically change one's own opinion.

Adventist Christians can only fully take part in a debate (and thereby command respect) if they understand the issues and have thoroughly studied the arguments of the other participants. Unfortunately, not infrequently Adventists experience how others make a caricature of their views, but it is only honest to admit that Adventists also sometimes ridicule others or misrepresent their ideas. In addition, it is also important that Adventist Christians are able to speak the language of our time and that, when defending and explaining their views, they do not use the kind of jargon that may be understood in their own circles, but only raises question marks elsewhere.

Being a prophetic voice and actively working for peace and social justice, and being vigorously involved in the defense of religious liberty and other human rights, is as much part of the mission of the church, as is preaching the biblical message. This is as true at the macro-level of the church as a worldwide institution as it is for each individual believer in his personal environment.

Sharing the Good News

Jesus Christ promised his followers that the gospel will be proclaimed "to all nations" before "the end" will come (Matt 24:14). It is the privilege of his followers to be involved with this magnificent project. But the question might be asked how far has the church progressed in accomplishing its task. Around the year 1900 about 30 percent of the people in the world self-identified as Christians. A century later the population of the world had vastly increased, but the percentage of Christians has remained virtually the same. A few decades into the twenty-first century, mission experts report that the percentage of Christians in the world has slightly increased—from around 30 to just over 31 percent.[51] However, the world population keeps growing, so that the number of non-Christian people in the world, in actual fact, keeps going up. Each day some 385,000 people are born into this world—all of whom must be "reached" with the gospel.

Seventh-day Adventists have traditionally assumed that it is their God-given duty to bring (their version of) the gospel message to the entire world. They point to impressive statistics to show that significant progress has been made. In 1970 there was one Adventist in this world for every eighteen hundred people. In 2020, just fifty years later, the

51. Pew Research Center, "Future of World Religions."

ratio of Adventists to non-Adventists had improved to about 1:350.[52] Yet, the absolute number of people that has not heard the Adventist message is increasing and the challenges of evangelizing the big cities of the world and the regions where non-Christian religions dominate are enormous.

Are Adventists correct in thinking that the end will not come until they have succeeded in acquainting the entire world population with the "three angels' messages"? Are they the only ones in the world who are serious about obedience to the gospel mandate? Looking back on the evangelistic methods Adventist have traditionally used, it is clear that to a very large extent they have built on the work of others. Not only could they gratefully profit from the work of the Bible societies, but the vast majority of their "converts" already learned about the gospel in other denominations.

As Adventists we share the gospel commission with all other Christians. We can cooperate with them, learn from them, enter in critical dialogue with them and supplement their teachings with the special emphases that are part of our heritage. This approach demands a rethinking of our own self-understanding. It will bring a great benefit to our own faith community, as well as to Christianity at large, if we are willing to do this.

"Finishing the Work"

Adventists insist that "the work" must and can be "finished." But the question looms ever larger: Will this assignment of bringing the message of Christ to "all the world" ever be accomplished? The answer is, yes, it will. Somehow, and at God's time. That is all we can say. We must allow God to surprise us. In the meantime, it is our responsibility to do all we can to share our faith with others in ways that are relevant to them. It means that we must translate the gospel message in ways that remain true to the essence of God's word but that can be understood, and will be appreciated, by the secular, postmodern men and women of today.

For many Seventh-day Adventists proclaiming the gospel message equals giving doctrinal instruction. And, certainly, doctrines are not unimportant. As mentioned earlier, they help us to provide structure to our faith and to our witness, just as grammar gives structure to our

52. General Conference, *Ratios of Seventh-day Adventists.*

communication through language. The famous American theologian Richard Niebuhr (1894–1962) underlined, in a frequently quoted statement, that the gospel proclamation has often lacked the substance that it should have: "A God without wrath brought men without sin into a kingdom without judgement, through the ministry of a Christ without a cross."[53] As Adventist Christians we must, however, not just focus on the doctrinal *correctness* of what we bring to the Christian table, but, more than ever, on its *relevance*. *Postmodern* people want to know—more than the *modern* generations before them—what the Christian message can *do* for them. What can the words of Christ mean during the week for our daily life of work and recreation? How do "fundamental beliefs" translate into a life of meaning and true happiness? How do doctrinal truths nurture the relationship with the One who is Life and Truth? When Jesus spoke about the truth, he told his disciples that the truth would make them free (John 8:31). In other words, the truth must do something for us. It must be relevant and relate to all aspects of who, and what, we are. This realization adds a vital dimension to our already immense missionary task.

While we do this, let us ever remember that we are not dealing with something we can refer to as *our* project. It is *God's* project. The words of George E. Ladd, who was a prominent teacher at Fuller Theological Seminary (1911–1982), seem particularly apt for the present generation of Adventists in the Western world: "Christ has not yet returned; therefore, the task is not yet done. When it is done, Christ will come. . . . So long as Christ does not return, our work is undone. Let us get busy and complete our mission."[54]

When all is said and done the question remains: *Does the Christian church have a future?*

The task of Christian missions has never seemed as daunting, never so impossible. It is an *impossible* dream. But God loves that word *impossible*. "With men this is impossible, but with God all things are possible" (Matt 19:26).

53. Niebuhr, *Kingdom of God*, 193.

54. Ladd, *Gospel of the Kingdom*, 137.

Epilogue

This book is about authentic Adventist theology. I hope it has delivered what I set out to do, as I explained in the introductory chapter. But one concluding remark seems appropriate. Even though I am a committed member of the Seventh-day Adventist Church, and have served in various professional roles in my denomination, I trust it has become clear that I do not believe that God's church fully overlaps with Seventh-day Adventism. I hope, on the other hand, that my arguments have been convincing why the Adventist community remains an important voice in the Christian choir and has a major role in the proclamation of the gospel in the world.

But not all is well in the Adventist Church. It suffers from an increasing polarization and in many parts of the world conservative (or even fundamentalist) forces become ever stronger. This gives the question, *Does the Seventh-day Adventist Church have a future?* an ever-greater urgency.

To the Adventist readers I emphatically say, *Remember: you and I are the Seventh-day Adventist Church.* The church has a future only if you and I protect our heritage but are also open to change; if we are positive towards the diversity in our faith community and allow space to each other. The Adventist Church will only constitute a vital part of the living body of Christ if we succeed in overcoming our provincialism and are able to authentically communicate the gospel to the people around us—which means, above all, if we are able to listen to the real concerns of our fellow man and to speak the kind of language that people of our time understand.

As Seventh-day Adventists we can be a healthy faith community if we are relevant, clear, and spiritual in the expression and experience of our faith; if we are generous with what God has given us; and if we show that we are God's hands and feet in our twenty-first century world.

As long as we are in this world the Christian church (including the Adventist denomination) will remain imperfect, with two different—opposite, yet complementary—characteristics. It offers the privilege of belonging to a community of saints while also serving as a school for sinners. What the institutional form of the Adventist Church will be like twenty or thirty years from now, no one can tell. Neither do we know whether the current exodus of young people from the church will be reversed, and large numbers of people (also in the Western world) will continue to seek comfort and spiritual support in the Adventist community. But we do know that God loves each of us individually and that he loves the Adventist corner of his church, despite all its shortcomings. I hope and pray that as a community we will succeed in more effectively reflecting that divine love in what we preach and practice.

Bibliography

Aamodt, Terrie Dopp, et al. *Ellen Harmon White: American Prophet*. Oxford: Oxford University Press, 2014.

Almendrala, Anna. "*The Year of Living Biblically*: Interview with Author A. J. Jacobs." Sojourners, April 14, 2008. https://sojo.net/articles/year-living-biblically-interview-author-aj-jacobs?utm_.

Anderson, Eric, ed. *Reclaiming the Prophet: An Honest Defense of Ellen White's Gift*. Boise: Pacific, 2025.

Andreasen, Niels-Erik A. "Death: Origin, Nature, and Final Eradication." In *Handbook of Seventh-day Adventist Theology*, edited by Raoul Dederen, 314–46. Commentary Reference Series 12. Hagerstown, MD: Review and Herald, 2000.

Aquinas, Thomas. *The Summa Theologica*. Translated by the Fathers of the English Dominican Province. New York: Benziger Bros., 1947.

Arnold, Clinton E. *The Colossian Syncretism: The Interface Between Christianity and Folk Belief at Colossae*. Grand Rapids: Baker, 1996.

Augsburger, Daniel. "The Sabbath and the Lord's Day During the Middle Ages." In *The Sabbath in Scripture and History*, edited by Kenneth A. Strand, 190–214. Washington, DC: Review and Herald, 1982.

Aulén, Gustaf. *Christus Victor: An Historical Study of the Three Main Types of the Idea of the Atonement*. London: SPCK, 1970.

Baab, Lynne M. *Sabbath Keeping: Finding Freedom in the Rhythms of Rest*. Downers Grove, IL: InterVarsity, 2005.

Bacchiocchi, Samuel. *From Sabbath to Sunday: A Historical Investigation of the Rise of Sunday Observance in Early Christianity*. Rome: Pontifical Gregorian University Press, 1977.

———. *Immortality or Resurrection*. Berrien Springs, MI: Biblical Perspectives, 1997.

Ball, Bryan. *The Seventh Day Men*. Oxford: Clarendon Press, 1994.

Barret, C. K. *The Gospel According to St. John*. London: SPCK, 1967.

Barth, Karl. *The Doctrine of Reconciliation*. Vol. 4, pt. 2, of *Church Dogmatics*, edited by G. W. Bromiley and T. F. Torrance, translated by G. W. Bromiley. Edinburgh: T&T Clark, 1958.

———. *The Doctrine of the Word of God*. Vol. 1, pt. 2, of *Church Dogmatics*, edited by G. W. Bromiley and T. F. Torrance, translated by G. T. Thomson and Harold Knight. Edinburgh: T&T Clark, 1956.

Bartsch, Hans Werner, ed. *Kerygma and Myth*. New York: Harper & Row, 1961.

Baumann, Michael. *Pilgrim Theology: Taking the Path of Theological Discovery*. Grand Rapids: Zondervan, 1992.

Beasley-Murray, G. R. "Baptism." In *The New International Dictionary of New Testament Theology*, edited by Colin Brown, 1:145–50. Translated by Lothar Coenen et al. Exeter, UK: Paternoster, 1975.

Benedict XVI, Pope. "Having a 'Vision from on High.'" General Audience, May 10, 2006. https://www.vatican.va/content/benedict-xvi/en/audiences/2006/documents/hf_ben-xvi_aud_20060510.html.

Berkhof, H. *Christelijk Geloof*. Nijkerk, The Netherlands: Callenbach, 1973.

Berkhof, Louis. *The History of Christian Doctrines*. Edinburgh: Banner of Truth Trust, 1937.

Berkouwer, Gerrit Cornelis. *Faith and Sanctification*. Translated by John Vriend. Studies in Dogmatics. Grand Rapids: Eerdmans, 1952.

———. *Holy Scripture*. Edited and translated by Jack B. Rogers. Studies in Dogmatics. Grand Rapids: Eerdmans, 1975.

———. *The Person of Christ*. Translated by John Vriend. Studies in Dogmatics. Grand Rapids: Eerdmans, 1954.

———. *The Return of Christ*. Edited by Malin J. Van Elderen and translated by James Van Oosterom. Studies in Dogmatics. Grand Rapids: Eerdmans, 1972.

Bible Hub. "5034. Tachos." https://biblehub.com/greek/5034.htm.

———. "5035. Tachu." https://biblehub.com/greek/5035.htm.

Biblical Research Institute. "Is Michael Another Name for Jesus?" https://www.adventistbiblicalresearch.org/materials/is-michael-another-name-for-jesus/.

Blazen, Ivan T. "Salvation." In *Handbook of Seventh-day Adventist Theology*, edited by Raoul Dederen, 271–313. Commentary Reference Series 12. Hagerstown, MD: Review and Herald, 2000.

Bloesch, Donald. *God the Almighty: Power, Wisdom, Holiness, Love*. Downers Grove, IL: InterVarsity, 1995.

Boa, Kenneth, and William Kruidenier. *Romans*. Holman New Testament Commentary. Nashville: Broadman and Holman, 2000.

Bonda, Jan. *The One Purpose of God*. Grand Rapids: Eerdmans, 1998.

Bonhoeffer, Dietrich. *The Cost of Discipleship*. Translated by Reginald H. Fuller. New York: Macmillan, 1963.

———. *Letters and Papers from Prison*. Translated by Reginald H. Fuller. New York: Macmillan, 1971.

———. *Life Together*. Translated by John W. Doberstein. New York: Harper & Row, 1954.

Brams, Steven J. "The Creation and Its Aftermath." In *Readings in Genesis: Beginnings*, edited by Beth Kissileff, 7–23. London: T&T Clark, 2016.

Brown, Colin, ed. *The New International Dictionary of New Testament Theology*. Translated by Lothar Coenen et al. 3 vols. Exeter, UK: Paternoster, 1975.

Brown, Henry F. *Baptism Through the Centuries*. Mountain View, CA: Pacific, 1965.

Bruce, F. F. *The Book of Acts*. The New London Commentary on the New Testament. London: Marshall, Morgan & Scott, 1954.

———. *The New Testament Documents: Are They Reliable?* Westmont, IL: InterVarsity, 1988.

Bruinsma, Reinder. *Adventists and Catholics: The History of a Turbulent Relationship.* New York: Lang, 2024.

———. *The Body of Christ: A Biblical Understanding of the Church.* Hagerstown, MD: Review and Herald, 2009.

———. *The Day God Created.* Grantham, UK: Stanborough, 1992.

———. *Facing Doubt: A Book for Adventist Believers "on the Margins."* London: Flankó, 2016.

———. *Faith—Step by Step: Finding God and Yourself.* Grantham, UK: Stanborough, 2006.

———. "Foot Washing and Other Adventist Rituals." *Adventist Today*, February 12, 2020. https://atoday.org/adventist-traditions-and-rituals/.

———. "Grace vs. Works: A Plea Against Keeping Them in Balance." *Adventist Today*, April 3, 2025. https://atoday.org/grace-vs-works-a-plea-against-keeping-them-in-balance/?utm.

———. *He Comes: Why, When and How Jesus Will Return.* Grantham, UK: Stanborough, 2021.

———. *I Have a Future: Christ's Resurrection and Mine.* Grantham, UK: Stanborough, 2019.

———. *In All Humility: Saying No to Last Generation Theology.* Westlake Village, CA: Oak & Acorn, 2018.

———. "Is the Adventist Hermeneutical Approach to Daniel and Revelation Changing?" *Spes Christiana* 31 (2020) 5–24.

———. *It's Time to Stop Rehearsing What We Believe and Start Looking at What Difference It Makes.* Grantham, UK: Stanborough, 1998.

———. *Keywords of the Christian Faith.* Hagerstown, MD: Review and Herald, 2008.

———. *Matters of Life and Death: An Adventist Pastor Looks at Abortion, Cloning, Physician Assisted Suicide, Capital Punishment.* Nampa, ID: Pacific, 2000.

———. "Origin of Foot Washing Among Seventh-day Adventists—Is There a Link with Anabaptism?" Lecture, Adventism and Anabaptism Symposium, Friedensau Adventist University, Möckern, Germany, April 15–18, 2024.

———. *Our Awesome God.* Nampa, ID: Pacific, 1999.

———. *Present Truth Revisited: An Adventist Perspective on Postmodernism.* Self-published, 2014. Kindle.

———. *Seventh-day Adventism and Fundamentalism: The Beach Lectures for 2000.* Occasional papers no. 4. Bracknell, UK: Centre for the Study of Religious and Cultural Diversity, 2006.

———. "Who Controls Our Theological Narrative?" *Adventist Today*, January 15, 2025. https://atoday.org/who-controls-our-theological-narrative/.

Buettner, Dan. "The Secrets of Long Life." Photographs by David McLain. *National Geographic* (November 2005) 2–27. https://www.bluezones.com/wp-content/uploads/2015/01/Nat_Geo_LongevityF.pdf.

Bull, Malcolm, and Keith Lockart. *Seeking a Sanctuary: Seventh-day Adventism and the American Dream.* Rev. ed. Bloomington: Indiana University Press, 2006.

Burke, Edmund. *Thoughts on the Cause of the Present Discontents.* London: Dodsley, 1770.

Burt, Merlin D. "History of Seventh-day Adventist Views on the Trinity." *Journal of the Adventist Theological Society* 17 (2006) 125–39.

Calvin, John. *Commentary on the First Book of Moses called Genesis*. Vol. 1. Translated by John King. Edinburgh: Calvin Translation Society, 1847. Repr., Grand Rapids: Baker, 1996.

———. *Institutes of the Christian Religion*. Translated by Henry Beveridge. Peabody: Hendrickson, 2008.

Cambridge Dictionary. "Metaphor." https://dictionary.cambridge.org/us/dictionary/english/metaphor.

Campbell, Michael W. "Christian Connexion or Connection." Encyclopedia of Seventh-day Adventists, November 7, 2023. https://encyclopedia.adventist.org/article?id=994E.

Carson, D. A., ed. *From Sabbath to Lord's Day: A Biblical, Historical and Theological Investigation*. Grand Rapids: Zondervan, 1982.

Chaj, Fernando. *Preparation for the Final Crisis*. Nampa, ID: Pacific, 1966.

Chase, Nan K. "Ancient Wisdom." *Hemispheres* (July 1997) 118.

Clark, Jerome L. "The Crusade Against Alcohol." In *The World of Ellen White*, edited by Gary Land, 131–41. Hagerstown, MD: Review and Herald, 1987.

Coenen, Lothar. "Church, Synagogue." In *The New International Dictionary of New Testament Theology*, edited by Colin Brown, 1:291–307. Translated by Lothar Coenen et al. Exeter, UK: Paternoster, 1975.

Cohen, Shaye J. D. *From the Maccabees to the Mishnah*. Louisville: Westminster John Knox, 2006.

Colón, May-Ellen Netten. "Sabbath-Keeping Practices and Factors Related to These Practices Among Seventh-day Adventists in 51 Countries." PhD diss., Andrews University, 2003. https://digitalcommons.andrews.edu/dissertations/295/.

Cottrell, Raymond F. "The Untold Story of the Bible Commentary." *Spectrum* 16 (1985) 35–51.

Cross, F. L., ed. *The Oxford Dictionary of the Christian Church*. London: Oxford University Press, 1958.

Cullmann, Oscar. *The Christology of the New Testament*. Philadelphia: Westminster, 1963.

———. *Immortality of the Soul or Resurrection of the Dead? The Witness of the New Testament*. In *Immortality and Resurrection: Death in the Western World; Two Conflicting Currents of Thought*, edited by Krister Stendahl, 9–53. New York: McMillan, 1963.

Cyprian. *The Unity of the Catholic Church*. Translated by Roy J. Deferrari. In *St. Cyprian Treatises*, 91–124. The Fathers of the Church: A New Translation 36. Washington, DC: Catholic University of America Press, 1958. https://ia801301.us.archive.org/2/items/TheUnityOfTheChurchByStCyprianOfCarthage/Cyprian_The_Unity_Of_The_Church.pdf.

Dabrowski, Rajmund, ed. *Statements, Guidelines and Other Documents*. Silver Spring, MD: Communication Department of the General Conference of Seventh-day Adventists, 2005.

Daily, Steve. *Ellen G. White: A Psychobiography*. Conneaut Lake, PA: Page, 2020.

Dancy, Jonathan. *Introduction to Contemporary Epistemology*. Oxford: Blackwell, 1985.

Davidson, Richard M. "Biblical Interpretation." In *Handbook of Seventh-day Adventist Theology*, edited by Raoul Dederen, 58–104. Commentary Reference Series 12. Hagerstown, MD: Review and Herald, 2000.

Dederen, Raoul. "Christ: His Person and Work." In *Handbook of Seventh-day Adventist Theology*, edited by Raoul Dederen, 160–204. Commentary Reference Series 12. Hagerstown, MD: Review and Herald, 2000.

———. "The Church." In *Handbook of Seventh-day Adventist Theology*, edited by Raoul Dederen, 538–81. Commentary Reference Series 12. Hagerstown, MD: Review and Herald, 2000.

De La Torre, Miguel A. *Reading the Bible from the Margins*. Maryknoll, NY: Orbis, 2002.

Dockey, D. S. "Baptism." In *Dictionary of Jesus and the Gospels*, edited by Joel B. Green et al., 55–58. Downers Grove, IL: InterVarsity, 1992.

Doukhan, Jacques B. *Secrets of Revelation: The Apocalypse Through Hebrew Eyes*. Hagerstown, MD: Review and Herald, 2002.

Dulles, Avery. *Models of the Church*. New York: Doubleday, 1974.

Dybdahl, Jon. *Exodus*. Nampa, ID: Pacific, 1994.

Edwards, James R. *The Gospel According to Mark*. The Pillar NT Commentary. Grand Rapids: Eerdmans, 2001.

Emerson, Ralph Waldo. *Nature*. Boston: Munroe, 1836. https://en.wikisource.org/wiki/Nature_%281836%29?utm.

Etymonline. "Origin and History of *Church*." https://www.etymonline.com/word/church?utm_source=.

Faber, Frederick William. "There's a Wideness in God's Mercy." Hymnary, 1862. https://hymnary.org/text/theres_a_wideness_in_gods_mercy.

Fackre, Gabriel, et al. *What About Those Who Have Never Heard?* Downers Grove, IL: InterVarsity, 1995.

Ferguson, Everett. *The Church of Christ: A Biblical Ecclesiology of Today*. Grand Rapids: Eerdmans, 1996.

Festinger, Leon. *A Theory of Cognitive Dissonance*. Redwood City, CA: Stanford University Press, 1957.

Flew, R. Newton. *The Idea of Perfection in Christian Theology*. Eugene, OR: Wipf & Stock, 2005.

Fowler, John M. "Sin." In *Handbook of Seventh-day Adventist Theology*, edited by Raoul Dederen, 233–70. Commentary Reference Series 12. Hagerstown, MD: Review and Herald, 2000.

Froom, Leroy E. *The Conditionalist Faith of Our Fathers*. 2 vols. Washington, DC: Review and Herald, 1965, 1966.

Gaillardetz, Richard R. *Ecclesiology for a Global Church: A People Called and Sent*. Maryknoll, NY: Orbis, 2008.

Gane, Roy E. *Old Testament Laws for Christians. Original Context and Enduring Application*. Grand Rapids: Baker Academic, 2017.

General Conference of Seventh-day Adventists. *Bible Study: Presuppositions, Principles and Methods*. Office of Archives, Statistics, and Research, 1986. https://www.adventistarchives.org/rio-statement-on-bible-study-annual-council-1986.pdf.

———. "Commitment to Health and Healing." October 14, 2009. https://gc.adventist.org/official-statements/commitment-to-health-and-healing/?utm_.

———. *Ratios of Seventh-day Adventists to World Population (1863–2024)*. Office of Archives, Statistics, and Research, July 24, 2025. https://documents.adventistarchives.org/Statistics/Other/RatiosofSDAtoWorldPop1863-2024.pdf.

———. *Seventh-day Adventist Church Manual*. 20th ed. Silver Spring, MD: Secretariat of the Seventh-day Adventist Church, 2022.

———. *Theology of Ordination: Study Committee Report*. Silver Spring, MD: General Conference of Seventh-day Adventists, 2014. https://www.adventistarchives.org/final-tosc-report.pdf.

———. "What Do Adventists Believe?" Seventh-day Adventist Church. https://adventist.org/beliefs#official-beliefs.\.

———. *Working Policy*. 2024–2025 ed. Silver Spring, MD: Secretariat of the Seventh-day Adventist Church, 2024.

Goldstein, Clifford. *Baptizing the Devil: Evolution and the Seduction of Christianity*. Nampa, ID: Pacific, 2017.

González, Justo L. *A Brief History of Sunday: From the New Testament to the New Creation*. Grand Rapids: Eerdmans, 2017.

Graybill, Ronald D. "The Development of Adventist Thinking on Clean and Unclean Meats." Shelf Document, Ellen G. White Estate. Washington, DC: 1981.

———. "Enthusiasm in Early Adventist Worship." *Ministry* (October 1991), 10–12.

———. *Visions and Revisions: A Textual History of Ellen G. White's Writings*. Westlake Village, CA: Oak & Acorn, 2019.

Green, Joel B., et al. *Dictionary of Jesus and the Gospels*. Downers Grove, IL: InterVarsity, 1992.

Grenz, Stanley J., and John R. Franke. *Beyond Foundationalism: Shaping Theology in a Postmodern Context*. Louisville: Westminster John Knox, 2001.

Grondin, Jean. *Introduction to Philosophical Hermeneutics*. New Haven: Yale University Press, 1994.

Gulley, Norman R. *God as Trinity*. Vol. 2 of *Systematic Theology*. Berrien Springs, MI: Andrews University Press, 2011.

Guy, Fritz. *Thinking Theologically: Adventist Christianity and the Interpretation of Faith*. Berrien Springs, MI: Andrews University Press, 1999.

Habermas, Gary H. *Ancient Evidence for the Life of Jesus*. Nashville: Nelson, 1984.

Hagner, Donald A. *Encountering the Book of Hebrews*. Grand Rapids: Baker Academic, 2002.

Halík, Tomáš. *The Afternoon of Christianity*. South Bend: University of Notre Dame Press, 2024.

Hanciles, Jehu J. *Migration and the Making of Global Christianity*. Grand Rapids: Eerdmans, 2011.

Hart, David Bentley. *That All Shall Be Saved: Heaven, Hell, and Universal Salvation*. New Haven: Yale University Press 2019.

Hasel, Frank M. "The Remnant in Contemporary Adventist Theology." In *Towards a Theology of the Remnant*, edited by Ángel Manuel Rodríguez, 159–80. Silver Spring, MD: Biblical Research Institute, 2009.

Hasel, Gerhard F. "The Sabbath in the Pentateuch." In *The Sabbath in Scripture and History*, edited by Kenneth A. Strand, 15–43. Washington, DC: Review and Herald, 1982.

———. *Speaking in Tongues: Biblical Speaking in Tongues and Contemporary Glossolalia*. Berrien Springs, MI: Adventist Theological Society, 1991.

Hook, Milton. *Desmond Ford: Reformist Theologian, Gospel Revivalist*. Riverside, CA: *Adventist Today* Foundation, 2008.

Horn, Siegfried H., ed. *Seventh-day Adventist Bible Dictionary*. Washington, DC: Review and Herald, 1960.

Horton, Michael. *The Christian Faith: A Systematic Theology for Pilgrims on the Way*. Grand Rapids: Zondervan, 2011.

Höschele, Stefan. *Adventist Interchurch Relations*. Göttingen, Ger.: V&R Unipress, 2022.

———. "From Mission Comity to Interdenominational Relations: The Development of Adventist Statements on Relationships with Other Christian Churches." In *Exploring the Frontiers of Faith: Festschrift in Honour of Dr. Jan Paulsen*, edited by Børge Schantz and Reinder Bruinsma, 389–404. Lüneburg, Ger.: Advent, 2009.

Jacob, Edmond. *Theology of the Old Testament*. London: Hodder and Stoughton, 1958.

Jacobs, A. J. *The Year of Living Biblically: One Man's Humble Quest to Follow the Bible as Literally as Possible*. New York: Simon & Schuster, 2007.

Jagersma, H. *Verklaring van de Hebreeuwse Bijbel: Genesis 1:1—25:11*. Nijkerk, The Netherlands: Callenbach, 1995.

Jankiewicz, Darius. "The Sixteenth Century Protestant Reformation and Adventist Ecclesiology." In *Message, Mission and Unity of the Church*, edited by Ángel Manuel Rodríguez, 191–217. Silver Spring, MD: Biblical Research Institute, 2013.

Jews for Judaism. "How Many Messianic Jews Are There?" https://jewsforjudaism.org/knowledge/articles/many-messianic-jews/?utm_.

Johnston, Robert M. "The Rabbinic Sabbath." In *The Sabbath in Scripture and History*, edited by Kenneth A. Strand, 70–91. Washington, DC: Review and Herald, 1982.

Keener, Craig S. *The IVP Bible Background Commentary: New Testament*. Downers Grove, IL: IVP Academic, 1993.

Kidder, S. Joseph, and Katelyn Campbell Weakley. "Baptismal Vows." Encyclopedia of Seventh-day Adventists, September 6, 2021. https://encyclopedia.adventist.org/article?id=EHYU.

Kittel, Gerhard, and Gerhard Friedrich, eds. *Theological Dictionary of the New Testament*. Translated by Geoffrey W. Bromiley. 10 vols. Grand Rapids: Eerdmans, 1964–1976.

Kline, Meredith G. *Treaty of the Great King: The Covenant Structure of Deuteronomy*. Grand Rapids: Eerdmans, 1963.

Knight, George R. *Ellen White's Afterlife*. Boise: Pacific, 2019.

———. *Ellen White's World: A Fascinating Look at the Times in Which She Lived*. Hagerstown, MD: Review and Herald, 1998.

———. *End-Time Events and the Last Generation*. Nampa, ID: Pacific, 2018.

———. *Exploring Galatians and Ephesians*. Hagerstown, MD: Review and Herald, 2005.

———. *Exploring Hebrews: A Devotional Commentary*. Hagerstown, MD: Review and Herald, 2003.

———. *Joseph Bates: The Real Founder of Seventh-day Adventism*. Hagerstown, MD: Review and Herald, 2004.

———. *Matthew: The Gospel of the Kingdom*. Nampa, ID: Pacific, 1994.

———. *Millennial Fever and the End of the World*. Boise: Pacific, 1993.

———. *Organizing for Mission and Growth*. Hagerstown, MD: Review and Herald, 2006.

———. *Sin and Salvation: God's Work for and in Us*. Hagerstown, MD: Review and Herald, 2008.

———. *A User-Friendly Guide to the 1888 Message*. Hagerstown, MD: Review and Herald, 1998.

Knitter, Paul F. *No Other Name? A Critical Survey of Christian Attitudes Toward the World Religions*. Maryknoll, NY: Orbis, 1990.

Korpman, Matthew J. "A Brief History of the Apocrypha." *Spectrum* 48 (2018) 56–65.

Kubo, Sakae. *God Meets Man: A Theology of the Sabbath and Second Advent*. Nashville: Southern, 1978.

Kuitert, Harry M. *I Have My Doubts: How to Become a Christian Without Being a Fundamentalist*. London: SCM, 1993.

Ladd, George E. *Crucial Questions About the Kingdom of God*. Grand Rapids: Eerdmans, 1952.

———. *The Gospel of the Kingdom: Scriptural Studies in the Kingdom of God*. Grand Rapids: Eerdmans, 1959.

Lapide, Pinchas. *The Resurrection of Jesus: A Jewish Perspective*. Translated by Wilhelm C. Linss. Minneapolis: Augsburg Fortress, 1982.

LaRondelle, H. K. *Perfection and Perfectionism: A Dogmatic-Ethical Study of Biblical Perfection and Phenomenal Perfectionism*. Kampen, The Netherlands: Kok, 1971.

Levterov, N. "The Development of the Seventh-day Adventist Understanding of Ellen G. White's Prophetic Gift, 1844–1889." PhD diss., Andrews University, 2011.

Lewis, C. S. *Mere Christianity*. New York: HarperCollins, 1980.

Liddell, Henry George, and Robert Scott, comps. *A Greek-English Lexicon*. Revised by Henry Stuart Jones with Roderick McKenzie. Oxford: Clarendon Press, 1940.

Loma Linda University. "Findings for Longevity." https://adventisthealthstudy.org/studies/AHS-1/findings-longevity?utm.

Lubac, Henri de. *The Discovery of God*. Edinburgh: T&T Clark, 1996.

Luther, Martin. *De servo arbitrio (On the Bondage of the Will)*. In *D. Martin Luthers Werke: Kritische Gesamtausgabe*, 18:551–787. Weimar, Ger.: Hermann Böhlau, 1909.

Maarsingh, B. *Numbers: A Practical Commentary*. Grand Rapids: Eerdmans, 1987.

Macquarrie, John. "The Keystone of the Christian Faith." In *If Christ Be Not Risen: Essays in Resurrection and Survival*, edited by Elizabeth Russell and John Greenhalgh, 9–24. New York: HarperCollins, 1988.

———. *The Scope of Demythologizing: Bultmann and His Critics*. New York: Harper & Row, 1960.

Mascall, Eric. "Did Jesus Really Rise from the Dead?" In *If Christ Be Not Risen: Essays in Resurrection and Survival*, edited by Elizabeth Russell and John Greenhalgh, 56–66. New York: HarperCollins, 1988.

McAdams, Donald R. *Ellen White & the Historians*. Westlake Village, CA: Oak & Acorn, 2022.

McGrath, Alistair. *Christelijke Theologie*. Translated by H. Ferguson-Postma. Kampen, The Netherlands: Kok, 1997.

———. *Historical Theology: An Introduction to the History of Christian Thought*. Malden: Blackwell, 1998.

McIver, Robert K. "The Historical-Critical Method: The Adventist Debate." *Ministry* (March 1996) 14–18. https://www.ministrymagazine.org/archive/1996/03/the-historical-critical-method.

McKenzie, Steven. *How to Read the Bible*. Oxford: Oxford University Press, 2005.

McKeown, Jonah. "Where Is Mass Attendance the Highest?" EWTN News, January 29, 2023. https://www.catholicnewsagency.com/news/253488/where-is-mass-attendance-highest-one-country-is-the-clear-leader.

Mead, Frank S. *Handbook of Denominations in the United States*. Revised by Samuel S. Hill. 10th ed. Nashville: Abingdon, 1995.

Meesters, J. H. *Op Zoek naar de Oorsprong van de Sabbat*. Assen, The Netherlands: Van Gorcum, 1964.

Merriam-Webster. "Theodicy." http://www.merriam-webster.com/dictionary/theodicy.

Merriam-Webster Collegiate Dictionary. 11th ed. Springfield, MA: Merriam-Webster, 2003.

Minear, Paul S. *Images of the Church in the New Testament*. London: Lutterworth, 1961.

Moltmann, Jürgen. *Der Gekreuzigte Gott*. Gütersloh, Ger.: Gütersloher, 2002.

Moore, Marvin. *The Case for the Investigative Judgment: The Biblical Foundation*. Nampa, ID: Pacific, 2010.

Moskala, Jiří. "Clean and Unclean (Leviticus 11)." Encyclopedia of Seventh-day Adventists, November 27, 2021. https://encyclopedia.adventist.org/article?id=GFRG&highlight=unclean.

———. *The Laws of Clean and Unclean Animals in Leviticus 11: Their Nature, Theology, and Rationale (An Intertextual Study)*. Adventist Theological Dissertation Series 4. Berrien Springs, MI: Adventist Theological Society, 2000.

Moskala, Jiří, and John Peckham, eds. *God's Character and the Last Generation*. Boise: Pacific, 2018.

Moule, C. F. D. *The Gospel According to St. Mark*. The Cambridge Greek Testament Commentary. Cambridge, UK: Cambridge University Press, 1966.

Müller, Eike. "Cleansing the Common: A Narrative-Intertextual Study of Mark 7:1–23." PhD diss., Andrews University, 2015.

Murphey, Nancey. *Beyond Liberalism and Fundamentalism: How Modern and Postmodern Philosophy Set the Theological Agenda*. Harrisburg: Trinity Press International, 1996.

Netland, Harold A. *Dissonant Voices: Religious Pluralism and the Question of Truth*. Grand Rapids: Eerdmans, 1989.

Newbigin, Lesslie. *The Gospel in a Pluralist Society*. Grand Rapids: Eerdmans, 1989.

Nicene Creed. Christian Classics Ethereal Library. https://www.ccel.org/creeds/nicene.creed.html.

Nichol, Francis D., et al., eds. *Seventh-day Adventist Bible Commentary*. 7 vols. Washington, DC: Review and Herald, 1953–1957.

Niebuhr, Richard. *The Kingdom of God in America*. Middletown: Wesleyan University Press, 1988.

Numbers, Ronald L. *The Creationists: The Evolution of Scientific Creationism*. New York: Knopf, 1992.

———. *Prophetess of Health: A Study of Ellen G. White*. New York: Harper & Row, 1976.

Odom, Robert Leo. *The Lord's Day on a Round World*. Nashville: Southern, 1970.

OSV News. "Gallup: Just 3 in 10 US Adults Regularly Attend Religious Services." Franciscan Media, April 1, 2024. https://www.franciscanmedia.org/news-commentary/gallup-just-3-in-10-us-adults-regularly-attend-religious-services/?utm_term=&utm_.

Ottati, Douglas F. *Theology for Liberal Protestants*. Grand Rapids: Eerdmans, 2013.
Otto, Rudolph. *The Idea of the Holy*. Oxford: Oxford University Press, 1950.
Oxford English Dictionary. "Angel." https://www.oed.com/dictionary/angel_n?tl=true.
———. Edited by Edmund Weiner et al. 2nd ed. Oxford: Clarendon Press, 1989.
———. Edited by Michael Proffitt et al. 3rd ed. Oxford: Oxford University Press, 2000–.
Ozolins, Aivars. "Doctrinal Dissonance and Adventist Leadership: Recapturing Spiritual Wholeness Through Crisis." Paper presented at the ASRS/SBL Annual Meeting, Boston, MA, November 2008. https://web.archive.org/web/20150503032913/https://lasierra.edu/fileadmin/documents/religion/asrs/ASRS-Papers-2008-05-Aivars-Ozolins-Doctrinal-Dissonance.pdf.
Paas, Stefan. *Vrede op Aarde: Over Heil en Redding in deze Tijd*. Zoetermeer, The Netherlands: KokBoekencentrum, 2023.
Papaioannou, Kim. *The Geography of Hell in the Teaching of Jesus*. Eugene, OR: Pickwick, 2013.
Paulien, Jon K. "The Hermeneutic of Biblical Apocalyptic." In *Understanding Scripture*, edited by George W. Reid, 245–70. Silver Spring, MD: Biblical Research Institute, 2006.
———. *Seven Keys: Unlocking the Secrets of Revelation*. Nampa, ID: Pacific, 2000.
Peckham, John C. *Divine Attributes: Knowing the Covenantal God of Scripture*. Grand Rapids: Baker Academic, 2021.
———. *The Doctrine of God: Introducing the Big Questions*. Edinburgh: T&T Clark, 2020.
Pew Research Center. "The Future of World Religions: Population Growth Projections, 2010–2050." April 2, 2015. https://www.pewresearch.org/religion/2015/04/02/religious-projections-2010-2050/?utm_.
———. "Religious Practice and Belief." May 29, 2018. https://www.pewresearch.org/religion/2018/05/29/religious-practice-and-belief/.
Phan, Peter C., ed. *The Gift of the Church: A Textbook on Ecclesiology*. Collegeville, MN: Liturgical, 2000.
Pinnock, Clark H. *A Wideness in God's Mercy: The Finality of Jesus Christ in a World of Religions*. Grand Rapids: Zondervan, 1992.
Plantinga, Alvin. *Warranted Christian Belief*. New York: Oxford University Press, 2000.
Quine, W. V., and J. S. Ulian. *The Web of Belief*. New York: McGraw-Hill, 1976.
Ratzinger, Joseph. *Jesus of Nazareth: From the Baptism in the Jordan to the Transfiguration*. New York: Doubleday, 2007.
Rauschenbusch, Walter. *A Theology for the Social Gospel*. New York: Macmillan, 1917.
Reid, George W. *A Sound of Trumpets: Americans, Adventists and Health Reform*. Washington, DC: Review and Herald, 1982.
Rice, George E. "Spiritual Gifts." In *Handbook of Seventh-day Adventist Theology*, edited by Raoul Dederen, 610–50. Commentary Reference Series 12. Hagerstown, MD: Review and Herald, 2000.
Rice, Richard. *Believing, Behaving, Belonging: Finding New Love for the Church*. Roseville: Association of Adventist Forums, 2002.
———. *Future of Open Theism: From Antecedents to Opportunities*. Downers Grove, IL: IVP Academic, 2020.
———. *The Reign of God: An Introduction to Christian Theology from a Seventh-day Adventist Perspective*. Berrien Springs, MI: Andrews University Press, 1997.

———. *Suffering and the Search for Meaning: Contemporary Responses to the Problem of Pain*. Downers Grove, IL: IVP Academic, 2014.

Richards, W. Larry. *1 Corinthians*. Abundant Bible Amplifier. Nampa, ID: Pacific, 1997.

———. *2 Corinthians*. Abundant Bible Amplifier. Nampa, ID: Pacific, 1998.

Richardson, Alan. *An Introduction to the Theology of the New Testament*. London: SCM, 1961.

Richardson, William E. *Speaking in Tongues: Is It Still the Gift of the Spirit?* Hagerstown, MD: Review and Herald, 1994.

Robinson, D. E. *The Story of Our Health Message*. Nashville: Southern, 1965.

Rodin, R. Scott. *Stewards in the Kingdom: A Theology of Life in All Its Fullness*. Downers Grove, IL: InterVarsity, 2000.

Rodríguez, Ángel Manuel, ed. *Andrews Bible Commentary*. International ed. Berrien Springs, MI: Andrews University Press, 2024.

———. "The Gift of Tongues in 1 Corinthians 14." Biblical Research Institute. https://www.adventistbiblicalresearch.org/materials/the-gift-of-tongues-in-1-corinthians-14/.

———. "Sabbath." *Adventist World* (June 2007) 34.

———, ed. *Towards a Theology of the Remnant*. Silver Spring, MD: Biblical Research Institute, 2009.

Rorabaugh, W. J. *The Alcoholic Republic: An American Tradition*. New York: Oxford University Press, 1979.

Rordorf, Willy. *Sunday: The History of the Day of Rest and Worship in the Earliest Centuries of the Christian Church*. London: SCM, 1968.

Sandeen, Earnest R. *The Roots of Fundamentalism: British and American Millenarianism, 1800–1930*. Chicago: University of Chicago Press, 2008.

Sanders, John. *No Other Name: An Investigation into the Destiny of the Unevangelized*. Grand Rapids: Eerdmans, 1992.

Sanford, A. *A Choosing People: The History of Seventh Day Baptists*. Nashville: Broadman, 2012.

Schippers, R. "Goal." In *The New International Dictionary of New Testament Theology*, edited by Colin Brown, 2:59–65. Translated by Lothar Coenen et al. Exeter, UK: Paternoster, 1975.

Schwarz, Hans. *Eschatology*. Grand Rapids: Eerdmans, 2000.

Schwarz, Richard W., and Floyd Greenleaf. *Light Bearers: A History of the Seventh-day Adventist Church*. Nampa, ID: Pacific, 2000.

Schweitzer, Albert. *The Quest of the Historical Jesus: A Critical Study of Its Progress from Reimarus to Wrede*. Translated by W. Montgomery. London: Black, 1910.

Shakespeare, William. *Hamlet*. Edited by Barbara Mowat et al. Washington, DC: Folger Shakespeare Library, n.d. https://www.folger.edu/explore/shakespeares-works/hamlet/read/.

Smith, David L. *A Handbook of Contemporary Theology*. Wheaton, IL: Victor, 1992.

Smith, Uriah. *Thoughts on Daniel and the Revelation*. Nashville: Southern, 1944.

Specht, Walter F. "The Sabbath in the New Testament." In *The Sabbath in Scripture and History*, edited by Kenneth A. Strand, 92–113. Washington, DC: Review and Herald, 1982.

Stefanovic, Ranko. *Revelation of Jesus Christ: Commentary on the Book of Revelation*. Berrien Springs, MI: Andrews University Press, 2002.

Stefanovic, Zdravko. *Daniel—Wisdom to the Wise*. Nampa, ID: Pacific Press, 2007.

Strand, Kenneth A. "The Lord's Day in the Second Century." In *The Sabbath in Scripture and History*, edited by Kenneth A Strand, 346–51. Washington, DC: Review and Herald, 1982.

———, ed. *The Sabbath in Scripture and History*. Washington, DC: Review and Herald, 1982.

Tacitus. *The Annals of Imperial Rome*. Translated by Michael Grant. London: Penguin, 1996.

Tasker, David R. "Proverbs." In *Psalms, Proverbs, Ecclesiastes, Song of Songs*, by David Tasker et al., 701–925. Seventh-day Adventist International Bible Commentary 6. Nampa, ID: Pacific, 2022.

Taves, Ann. *Fits, Trances & Visions: Experiencing Religion and Explaining Experience from Wesley to James*. Princeton: Princeton University Press, 1999.

Thiselton, Anthony C. *The Holy Spirit—In Biblical Teaching, Through the Centuries, and Today*. Grand Rapids: Eerdmans, 2013.

Thuesen, Peter J. *Predestination: The American Career of a Contentious Doctrine*. Oxford: Oxford University Press, 2011.

Tiessen, Terrance L. *Who Can Be Saved? Reassessing Salvation in Christ and World Religions*. Downers Grove, IL: InterVarsity, 2004.

Timm, Alberto R. "The Seventh-day Adventist Doctrine of the Sanctuary (1844–2007)." In *For You Have Strengthened Me: Biblical and Theological Studies in Honor of Gerhard Pfandl in Celebration of His Sixty-Fifth Birthday*, edited by Martin Pröbstle et al., 331–59. St. Peter am Hart, Austria: Seminar Schloss Bogenhofen, 2007.

———. "Seventh-day Adventist Ecclesiology, 1844–2012: A Brief Historical Overview." In *Message, Mission and Unity of the Church*, edited by Ángel Manuel Rodríguez, 219–42. Silver Spring, MD: Biblical Research Institute, 2013.

Tonstad, Sigve. *The Lost Meaning of the Seventh Day*. Berrien Springs, MI: Andrews University Press, 2009.

———. *Revelation*. Paideia Commentaries on the New Testament. Grand Rapids: Baker Academic, 2019.

———. *Saving God's Reputation: The Theological Function of Pistis Iesou in the Cosmic Narratives of Revelation*. Library of New Testament Studies. London: T&T Clark, 2007.

Trim, David. *Seventh-day Adventist Global Data Picture: Report on Global Research, 2011–13*. Presented at the Annual Council of the General Conference of Seventh-day Adventists, Silver Spring, MD, October 2013. https://www.adventistarchives.org/ac-research-report,-2013-revised.pdf.

Turner, Laurence A. *Genesis*. Sheffield, UK: Sheffield Academic Press, 2000.

Valentine, Gilbert M. *The Prophet and the Presidents*. Nampa, ID: Pacific, 2011.

———. *The Struggle for Gender Equality: The Ordination of Women in the Seventh-day Adventist Church*. Silver Spring, MD: General Conference Office of Archives, Statistics, and Research, 2019.

———. *The Struggle for the Prophetic Heritage*. Muak Lek, Thailand: Institute, 2006.

Van der Kooi, Cornelis, and Gijsbert van den Brink. *Christian Dogmatics: An Introduction*. Translated by Reinder Bruinsma with James D. Bratt. Grand Rapids: Eerdmans, 2017.

Vanier, Jean. *Community and Growth*. New York: Paulist, 1989.

Veloso, Mario. "The Law of God." In *Handbook of Seventh-day Adventist Theology*, edited by Raoul Dederen, 457–92. Commentary Reference Series 12. Hagerstown, MD: Review and Herald, 2000.

Verrecchia, Jean-Claude. *God of No Fixed Address: From Altars to Sanctuaries, Temples to Houses*. Eugene, OR: Wipf & Stock, 2015.

Vick, Edward W. H. *Is Salvation Really Free?* Washington, DC: Review and Herald, 1983.

———. *Let Me Assure You*. Mountain View, CA: Pacific, 1968.

———. *Speaking Well of God*. Nashville: Southern, 1979.

Vyhmeister, Werner K. "The Sabbath in Egypt and Ethiopia." In *The Sabbath in Scripture and History*, edited by Kenneth A. Strand, 169–89. Washington, DC: Review and Herald, 1982.

Weber, T. P. "Fundamentalism." In *Dictionary of Christianity in America*, edited by Daniel G. Reid et al., 461–65. Downers Grove, IL: InterVarsity, 1990.

Weiss, Herold. *A Day of Gladness: The Sabbath Among Jews and Christians in Antiquity*. Columbia: University of South Carolina Press, 2003.

Wesley, John. "A Plain Account of Christian Perfection." In *Thoughts, Addresses, Prayers, and Letters*, edited by Thomas Jackson, 366–446. Vol. 11 of *The Works of John Wesley*. London: Wesleyan Methodist Book Room, 1872.

Westermann, Claus. *Genesis 1–11: A Commentary*. Translated by John J. Scullion. Minneapolis: Augsburg Fortress, 1984.

Wheeler, Gerald. *Beyond Death's Door: The Hope of Reunion*. Hagerstown, MD: Review and Herald, 2009.

Whidden, Woodrow. *Ellen White on the Humanity of Christ*. Hagerstown, MD: Review and Herald, 1997.

———. "Humanity of Christ." In *The Ellen G. White Encyclopedia*, edited by Denis Fortin and Jerry Moon, 692–96. Hagerstown, MD: Review and Herald, 2013.

Whidden, Woodrow, et al. *The Trinity*. Hagerstown, MD: Review and Herald, 2002.

White, Arthur L. "Charismatic Experiences in Early Seventh-day Adventist History." *Review and Herald*, 1972–1973. Repr., Ellen G. White Estate. https://whiteestate.org/legacy/issues-charism-alw-html/.

White, Ellen G. *Acts of the Apostles*. Nampa, ID: Pacific, 1911.

———. *Christ's Object Lessons*. Washington, DC: Review and Herald, 1900.

———. *Counsels on Diet and Foods*. Washington, DC: Review and Herald, 1938.

———. *The Desire of Ages*. Nampa, ID: Pacific, 1898.

———. *Early Writings*. Washington, DC: Review and Herald, 1882.

———. *Evangelism*. Washington, DC: Review and Herald, 1946.

———. *The Great Controversy*. Mountain View, CA: Pacific, 1911.

———. *Manuscript Releases*. Vol. 14. Silver Spring, MD: Ellen G. White Estate, 1990.

———. *The Ministry of Healing*. Mountain View, CA: Pacific, 1905.

———. *Selected Messages*. 3 Vols. Washington, DC: Review and Herald, 1958–1980.

———. "The Signal of Advance." *Review and Herald* (January 20, 1903) 8–9.

———. *Spirit of Prophecy*. Vol. 4. Battle Creek, MI: Review and Herald, 1884.

———. *Spiritual Gifts*. Vol. 4a. Battle Creek, MI: Seventh-day Adventist, 1864.

———. *Testimonies for the Church*. Vol. 1. Mountain View, CA: Pacific, 1948.

———. "Search the Scriptures." *The Youth's Instructor* (October 13, 1898). https://m.egwwritings.org/en/book/469.3134#3134.

White, James. "Signs of the Times." *Signs of the Times* 6 (January 8, 1880) 2–3. https://adventistdigitallibrary.org/islandora/object/adl%3A356487/%3Fview_only%3Dtrue.

Wikipedia. "*Catholic* (Term)." Last edited January 16, 2026. https://en.wikipedia.org/wiki/Catholic_(term).

———. "Chalcedonian Definition." Last edited January 26, 2026. https://en.wikipedia.org/wiki/Chalcedonian_Definition#.

———. "Credo ut intelligam." Last edited July 11, 2025. https://en.wikipedia.org/wiki/Credo_ut_intelligam.

Wiklander, Bertil. *Ordination Reconsidered: The Biblical Vision of Men and Women as Servants of God*. Binfield, UK: Newbold Academic, 2015.

Wolterstorff, Nicholas. "The Grace That Shaped My Life." In *Philosophers Who Believe*, edited by Kelly James Clark, 259–75. Downers Grove, IL: InterVarsity, 1993.

Wood, W. Jay. *Epistemology: Becoming Intellectually Virtuous*. Downers Grove, IL: IVP Academic, 1998.

World Council of Churches. *The Church: Towards a Common Vision*. Faith and Order Paper 214. Geneva, Switz.: WCC, 2013. https://www.oikoumene.org/sites/default/files/Document/The_Church_Towards_a_common_vision.pdf.

The World Counts. "How Many Babies Are Born Each Day?" https://www.theworldcounts.com/stories/how-many-babies-are-born-each-day.

World Health Organization. "Constitution." https://www.who.int/about/governance/constitution.

Wright, N. T. *The Resurrection of the Son of God*. Minneapolis: Fortress, 2003.

———. *Surprised by Hope*. London: SPCK, 2013.

Yancey, Philip. *What's So Amazing About Grace?* Grand Rapids: Zondervan, 1997.

Yoder, John Howard. *Body Politics: Five Practices of the Christian Community Before the Watching World*. Scottdale, PA: Herald, 1992.

Young, Norman H. "Jesus—Divinity Revealed in Humanity." In *The Essential Jesus: The Man, the Message, the Mission*, edited by Bryan W. Ball and William G. Johnsson, 103–123. Boise: Pacific, 2002.

Young, W. Paul. *The Shack*. Newbury Park, CA: Windblown Media, 2006.

Subject and Author Index

Scripture Index

1 Chronicles

2 Chronicles

Nehemiah

Job

Psalms

Proverbs

Ecclesiastes

Song of Songs

Isaiah

Jeremiah

Ezekiel

Daniel

Hosea

Joel

Amos

Micah

Mark *(continued)*

Luke

John

Acts

Romans

1 Corinthians

2 Corinthians

Galatians

Ephesians

Philippians

Colossians

1 Thessalonians

2 Thessalonians

1 John

2 John

3 John

Revelation

www.ingramcontent.com/pod-product-compliance
Lightning Source LLC
LaVergne TN
LVHW020535100826
845148LV00010B/1474